BILLY GRAHAM

HIS LIFE AND INFLUENCE

DAVID AIKMAN

CHRISTIAN LARGE PRINT
A part of Gale, Cengage Learning

GALE
CENGAGE Learning™

Detroit • New York • San Francisco • New Haven, Conn • Waterville, Maine • London

LP
B
Graham B

LIBRARY OF CONGRESS CATALOGING-IN-PUBLICATION DATA

Aikman, David, 1944–
    Billy Graham : his life and influence / by David Aikman.
        p. cm. — (Christian large print originals)
    Originally published: Nashville, Tenn. : Thomas Nelson, c2007.
        ISBN-13: 978-1-59415-325-9 (softcover)
        ISBN-10: 1-59415-325-6 (softcover)
        1. Graham, Billy, 1918– 2. Evangelists—United States—Biography.
I. Title. II. Series.
BV3785.G69A35 2010
269'.2092—dc22   2010012602

Published in 2010 by arrangement with Thomas Nelson, Inc.

Printed in the United States of America
    1 2 3 4 5   14 13 12 11 10
ED155

CONTENTS

11/10

FOREWORD

For the last fifty years, evangelist Billy Graham has made such a gigantic mark on the religious life of both the U.S. and the world that he has transformed the age in which he has lived. He has turned evangelical Protestantism into *the* normative form of the Christian faith as practiced by Protestants. He has reached out in an extraordinary way to Roman Catholics, and in many ways been embraced by them as a "brother." Christians of more liberal theological persuasion might gripe under their breath about "those Fundamentalists," but they have never been able to challenge the dominance of evangelicals. Globally, Billy Graham has accomplished something similar. He has injected a self-confidence into many national Christian movements that helped propel them, in some cases, into positions of national power. Finally, internationally, Graham was at least a partial catalyst for some of the most important events of our era: the collapse of Communism in the Soviet Union and Eastern Europe and the peaceful transition from apartheid to black African majority rule in South Africa.

Many biographies have been written about Graham, some of them thorough and well documented. There is also, of course, Billy Graham's own autobiographical story, *Just as I Am* (HarperOne, 2007). Like all biographies, however, even Graham's own account is incomplete, mainly because it is a personal narrative and doesn't focus on explaining things in a historical context. Other biographies are detailed, but by now are significantly outdated.

I first came across David Aikman's biography of Billy Graham as an audiobook when it appeared in 2007. I was immediately dazzled by it. Not only did it tell in gripping terms the fascinating narrative of how God improbably raised up a North Carolina teenage farm boy into the greatest evangelist the world has ever seen; it poignantly captured his proximity to power, the mistakes he made, and his major impact on the world as a whole. David Aikman described in fascinating detail Billy's painful parting of the ways with America's leading Fundamentalists in the 1950s, his complex, and sometimes tormented coping with the American civil rights movement of the 1950s and 1960s, and his fascinating, but not always smooth, relationships with eleven of America's presidents. In recounting the different stages — and sometimes lurches — of Graham's life, I found that David Aikman fascinatingly, but always succinctly, sketched in just enough of the historical and political background to bring the entire story vividly to life.

The same is true of those parts of the book that deal with Billy Graham's travels overseas. David Aikman was for twenty three years a correspondent of *Time* magazine, and for much of that time was a foreign correspondent and assigned to *Time* bureaus all over the world. He became very familiar with the international settings of many of Graham's most important foreign journeys and knew personally some of the personalities with whom Graham met. His insights into the collapse of Communism, the rise of Christianity in China, and the peculiar nature of North Korean Communism are worth reading for their own sake.

Billy Graham, of course, was first and foremost an American original. But in many ways he also belonged to the entire world, a world which to this day has been profoundly affected by his life. Billy Graham's enduring passion to preach the Gospel of Jesus Christ to anyone and everyone who would listen, is one of the most fascinating stories of the past century. I've read many Billy Graham biographies, but this one is by far my favorite.

Joel Rosenberg
February 2010
Fairfax, VA

ONE:
A LIFE OF INFLUENCE

The nation's pastor. Billy Graham would be a shoo-in for the job, if such a job existed. After all, he has held that position unofficially for decades already. Of course, Americans, who first settled this land precisely because they were fleeing government-run churches, would never agree to an official religious post along the lines of Britain's archbishop of Canterbury or Iran's ayatollah. But Billy Graham has been doing the job without need for the title for at least a quarter century, on hand for the major milestones of American life: the presidential inaugurations every four years, the scandals that have led occasionally to resignation or impeachment, the inevitable deaths of presidents, and the shocking and senseless national tragedies. He has been the great consoler, the eloquent unifier in hard-to-define adversity, the articulator of the troubling questions that tragedy invari-

11

ably raises.

Slowly and somewhat unsteadily, Billy Graham took the national limelight once again after the September 11, 2001, terror attacks. At the September 14 memorial service broadcast live on national television from Washington National Cathedral, Graham articulated the burning question on everybody's mind more than any other: Why? "But how do we understand something like this?" he asked. "Why does God allow evil like this to take place?" As probably no other American could have done with as much credibility, Billy Graham assayed an answer. Acknowledging that many people doubtless were questioning God or were angry with God, he said, "I want to assure you that God understands these feelings that you may have. We've seen so much on our television and . . . on our radio — stories that bring tears to our eyes and make us all feel a sense of anger. But God can be trusted, even when life seems at its darkest."

Graham's presence has seemed to be so comforting that no American state funeral or memorial service would seem complete without him. Even into his late eighties, when his activities have necessarily been scaled back, he has remained one of the most consistently admired of all Americans, as reflected in polls such as those by George Gallup Jr. In 2006, Billy Graham ranked among Gallup's list of the top 10 most-admired men in the world for a record fiftieth time.[1] In a Barna Group poll in 2007, he was among the top 10 public figures with the highest favorability ratings, and the only religious figure in the top 10.[2] What accounts for this consistent and long-standing favorable view? Could it be that Americans feel that in Graham is reflected their best self, perhaps even that Graham represents everything that is decent about America? Some may resent the religious right — even criticizing Graham's outspoken eldest son, Franklin — and some may be suspicious of faith in the White House or anywhere else in the political arena. But Billy Graham himself? He seems to have attained a Mount Rushmore–like status, standing loftily above the fray of the major controversies of public life: a figure who symbolizes an acceptable, unthreatening religiosity.

That's not to say, though, that Billy Graham's life and career have been without their controversies, nor that he has no detractors or people who have differed with him or his approach in a variety of arenas.

13

The pages that follow will consider those controversies and the criticisms, weighing them against the enormous breadth of the worldwide impact he has had, to reach — it is hoped — a balanced and honest assessment of this man who started out as a humble preacher from rural America but went on to represent more than any other individual the face of Protestant Christianity, to Americans and ultimately to the whole world. *Newsweek* magazine, putting him in the context of the entire history of Christianity, called him "one of the most formidable figures in the 2,000-year story of Christian evangelism."[3]

For some evangelical Christians, though, the very fact that Graham is viewed as nonthreatening and is accepted by a majority of Americans is itself a problem. In their view, as Graham's life journey took him from the sometimes unappealing world of Protestant fundamentalism, and later from what came to be called "neo-evangelicalism" (wags might in turn describe this as "fundamentalism lite"), he stopped being a bona fide evangelical altogether and crossed over into some sort of spiritual universalism. Evangelists, it has been understood from apostolic times, are not supposed to make peace with the world at all. Rather, they are to "turn it upside down." Was Graham faithful throughout his life to this injunction? This is a topic that we will explore in greater detail in the following pages.

But whether Graham watered down the fiery evangelical faith of his early years or compromised with the spirit of the age, he has, simply put, been a colossus overshadowing our national life for more than half a century. He bestrode America at first like a train conductor, anxious to ensure that everyone was properly ticketed for the journey. Later, he became more the wise family uncle, counseling and consoling the nation in time of trouble. Former CBS news anchor Dan Rather put it this way: "He stands with a handful of American religious leaders from the Great Awakening forward who helped define the country. And he did that in a particularly tumultuous time in our history, the last half of the twentieth century."[4]

And yet — and this is surely an arena where many Americans may be quite unaware of the extent of his impact — Graham now belongs to the world. The experience of two American Protestant ministers who were in southern Sudan for a few weeks in the summer of 2002 tellingly illustrates how closely the rest of the world associates

Graham with the preaching of the gospel. They told me that a suspicious Sudanese official had approached them at an airport demanding to know what they were in his country to do. "We're evangelists," one replied. "You mean like Billy Graham?" the official asked. For this Sudanese bureaucrat, a Muslim — as for thousands, perhaps millions, of people in foreign lands — Graham is quite simply equated with Christianity and is regarded as the prototype evangelist. In Beijing, China, a large photograph of Billy Graham was the sole decorative element on the living room wall of the prominent evangelical Protestant house church leader, the late Yuan Xiangchen, also known by his English name Allen Yuan. Yuan held unregistered, and hence illegal, weekly meetings of believers in his apartment and was one of two Christian leaders from these "house churches" who met Graham when the evangelist visited China for the first time in 1988. For Yuan, the crucial element of the vast expanse of Graham's entire life ministry was the American evangelist's trademark invitation to listeners to "make a decision" for Christ.

Indeed, Graham has preached the gospel in person to more people than any other man or woman in history: 210 million people in 185 nations and territories around the globe by the end of his sixty-one-year active career in 2005. When he preached in Seoul, South Korea in 1973, it was, at the time, the largest audience in history to hear a preacher live: 1.12 million people. In many ways, though, the greater mark of his global impact was what he set in motion behind the scenes: the conferences for largely unknown and itinerant evangelists, the training sessions for young men and women rising in ministry, the unceasing encouragement of Christian evangelism in all its varied forms.

Even more significant still is that Graham's evangelical style of Protestantism has become *the* style of Protestantism for most of the entire world. In the late 1940s, it was generally only the fundamentalist church groups that laid any stress on "conversion," much less being "born again," as necessary to being a Protestant Christian. By the first years of the twenty-first century, however, the only Protestant groups who eschewed such emphasis and even terminology were mainline denominations whose leadership was pronouncedly liberal.

When Graham first emerged on the American stage in the late 1940s, it was far from clear what direction global Protestantism was headed. The World Council of Churches, based in Geneva, was emerging as a force favoring a version of reform Christianity that was, if not Christian syncretism, at least nonconfrontational and conciliatory toward other faiths. Richard Ostling, who covered religion for the Associated Press news service and who reported about Graham for several decades while at *Time* magazine, said: "When Graham started out, a fairly soft, accommodating type of theology or religion characterized a lot of Protestant churches in this country. Graham came on the scene with a very strong, Bible-based message, an old-fashioned gospel of repentance — 'come to Jesus, change your life, get right with God' — and it really had an electric effect."[5] Of course, some argue that an accommodating Christianity was a good thing, especially in light of the shrill debates among religions that began to blight world affairs in the 1980s and 1990s. But Graham, through the appealing nature of his personality and the palpable power of his crusades in the 1950s and 1960s, overwhelmed the World Council of Churches and mainstream Protestantism's easy-going ecumenicalism with the "hot gospel," that is, a presentation of Christianity that demanded acceptance or

18

rejection from those who heard it.

Graham's religious influence, moreover, was not limited to Protestantism. Though he emerged from the shadow of a fundamentalism deeply antagonistic toward the Catholic Church and Catholic doctrines of Christianity, by the late 1950s, he had started to invite Catholic churches to cooperate with his crusades and was refusing to repeat the usual Protestant strictures against the genuineness of the Christian faith nurtured in the Roman Catholic tradition. Graham's Christian ecumenicism culminated in a well-reported meeting with Pope John Paul II in 1981, at which the pope said to him, "We are brothers." The more significant part of the meeting was that it was Graham and not the pope who told reporters about this exchange. It might have been broadly acceptable for the pope, within the context of an evolving, post-Vatican II Catholicism, to have been quoted saying that. That it was, in fact, Graham who told the story was for many Protestants powerfully revealing.

Also by the late 1950s, Graham's fame and perceived influence, as well as his close ties with the occupants of the Oval Office, resulted in his assuming another role as a bridge builder. With surprising regularity for an ordinary citizen who held no formal title and had scant political background or experience, Billy Graham was tapped by US presidents to carry messages to the leaders of many of the countries where he was holding his crusades. His innate patriotism was stimulated by such roles, and he fulfilled them faithfully and with as much discretion and decorum as the role required. Many foreign countries by the late 1950s had come to view Graham as embodying the religious (i.e. Protestant Christian) essence of America, and by the 1990s, when his foreign travels took him to genuinely volatile countries, such as North Korea, his long-time association with American presidents over many decades lent him an authority that neither his achievements as an evangelist nor his fame on its own could otherwise have secured.

Graham's initiatives into Eastern Europe and the Soviet Union at the height of the Cold War were not universally admired. Even the White House, to which Graham always deferred whether under Nixon or Reagan, only somewhat grudgingly tolerated his moves. His North Korean trips in 1992 and 1994 caused some ripples internationally, but they also provided him with the opportunity of accomplishing the hitherto unthinkable: explaining the gospel to entrenched atheist Kim Il Sung, North Korea's "Great Leader." By then, Graham had already moved far away from the anti-communist rhetorician of the 1950s into a mellow proponent of global nuclear stand-down and the virtues of a Christianity de-linked entirely from global politics. "I think of myself as a world citizen," Graham once said. "I've traveled over this world a great deal, and I feel that I am part of a great mosaic of the human race that God has created."[6]

Did the Graham of this new, significantly apolitical Christianity accomplish as much globally, or even theologically, as the Graham of the first decade of his national prominence? It depends. To those who believe that evangelism should be totally disconnected from national politics and world affairs, the answer would be yes. But for those who assume that every American evangelist is dependent on and responsible to the international role that happens to befall the United States at any historical juncture, their view would be no.

Certainly over the six decades of his public life, Graham's views on various controversial social issues have evolved. Though never a racist, and in fact a propo-

21

nent of racially integrated crusades within the United States from early on in his public career, Graham also assiduously avoided publicly taking political positions that might arouse opposition from any segment of American society. It is true that not until the mid-1950s did he publicly take the unequivocal position that segregation in any form was wrong. In 1957, at his Madison Square Garden crusade in New York City, he invited Dr. Martin Luther King Jr. to sit with him on the platform, a controversial move that alienated many of his white supporters in the South. But he studiously avoided taking any position on the larger issue of racism in America that could be construed as political. Graham has critics who remain upset to this day about his unwillingness to identify publicly with King's civil rights movement. One of them, Rev. Jesse Jackson, holds the view that Graham would have been even more powerful if he had used his evangelistic rallies in the struggle to achieve racial equality. Yet African American and Jewish organizations have honored Graham with awards recognizing his contributions to racial harmony.

Even Graham's cherished reach into the White House throughout many US presidencies landed him in trouble more than once. Most recently, the disclosure of taped Oval Office conversations in which Graham agrees with Richard Nixon's blatantly prejudiced remarks about American Jews made headlines. Graham was quick to apologize publicly when the tapes were released, and the leaders of America's Jewish community were just as quick to publicly forgive him. They did not, it seems, regard this single instance of a racially prejudiced comment as representative of Graham's views about American Jews or feel that it negated all of his public statements over many decades on behalf of Jewish causes and in support, for example, of the State of Israel.

This reluctance to stand up to Nixon's own prejudices, however, points to what may be one of the manifest weaknesses of the great evangelist's overall character, that is, Billy Graham's desire throughout his life to be liked. It would be quite wrong to say that Graham manipulated his message to appeal to certain groups: in effect, that he watered down the Christian gospel or trimmed it of hard sayings. It would not be incorrect, however, to say that Graham went out of his way to avoid offending people. Ordinarily, this is regarded as a virtue, but on certain occasions, it might also be considered a failing. Graham defended his uncritical approach to the Watergate-era Nixon on the grounds that his relationship to the president was more pastoral than prophetic. A valid point: prophets speak uncomfortable truths to people in power. They often do not get invited back to palaces a second time.

The keeping of presidential confidences, though, goes part and parcel with the job, and in this Graham has been exemplary. Not once has he compromised this by being loose-lipped about his role as confidant or spiritual advisor to those in power. No more is known of his private conversations with President Eisenhower than of his private remarks to North Korean tyrant Kim Il Sung. But his obvious enjoyment of proximity to power — no other American has stayed in the White House Lincoln Bedroom more often than Graham — leaves him open to the criticism that it diluted his potential moral influence on national power in the White House. Simply put, Graham liked to be invited back. Was this a weakness? Some might say so.

The last administration through which he was still conducting public crusades was, appropriately enough, that of the president with whom Graham played a personal role in his rediscovery of faith, that of George W. Bush. Yet he had far fewer contacts with the younger Bush during his White House years than with the forty-third president's many predecessors. Graham never visited George W. Bush in the White House, never spent a night there as had been customary with previous presidents, and had little communication even by phone with the president. Graham, already in the twilight of his life, was afflicted by a broken hip, prostate cancer, hydrocephalus, and numerous other ailments. He had spent much more time in the White House of George W. Bush's father, overnighting there when Operation Desert Storm was launched in January 1991 to oust Iraq from Kuwait, and in general providing solid pastoral support for a family he had come to know well over the years. Yet Graham's influence on George W. Bush, who epitomized a politician-turned-Christian-in-adulthood more explicitly than any other president in modern times, will remain the stuff of study and speculation for historians. Graham spoke to many presidents about his view of faith, of salvation, of heaven and hell, but of them all, only George W. Bush represented the legacy of Graham's life's preaching in the political realm.

Billy Graham's life will continue to challenge biographers and historians alike for decades, perhaps even longer. His ministry flourished during a unique period in the American experience, when the nation was coming to terms, like a gangly teenager, with its unexpected new strength in the world and was grappling with the most serious racial and social upheavals since the Civil War. Graham preached urgently to a nation faced with the uncertainty of the Cold War struggle with the Soviet Union. Ultimately, his message and his preaching transcended the demands of geopolitics and found a new, far deeper level than that of transitory — albeit important — strategic needs.

As Graham approached his own appointment with eternity, the America that he led into a knowledge of the Christian gospel had changed completely from the one in which he had grown up and from which he emerged into national and later international prominence. Though Americans who call themselves Christians still comprise roughly three-quarters of the population, the variety of Christianity they believe in is now altogether different from what Graham had known as a child and from which he himself had preached. A bare 22 percent in

2001 said they believed in absolute moral truth, and that figure itself had plunged from a more robust 38 percent of respondents just a scant year earlier, according to polling by the respected chronicler of Americans' beliefs, George Barna.[7] As it has for its entire history, America was changing in ways that could scarcely have been foreseen at its founding. In 2000 and 2004, the religious right, i.e. Christian conservatives, helped ensure both a Republican presidency and Republican Senate and House of Representatives. With 24 percent of the population describing themselves as "evangelical," America was indeed, by many external indicators, showing its colors as a "Christian" nation. Yet in many ways, the very definition of "Christian" was changing, constantly being updated.

Billy Graham has often commented on the singularly universal response when he preached the gospel and quoted the Bible. "All over the world people have a difference in the way they react and respond, but not to the gospel. When the gospel of Jesus Christ is proclaimed, I just cannot see any difference. Anywhere in the world, whether it's Africa, or Asia, or Europe or a university group or a primitive tribe," he said.[8] For as long as Graham was able to evangelize in public settings, he was surely right. People did indeed respond to his preaching with singularly dramatic effect: more than three million people recorded "decisions" to follow Jesus in Graham's more than half a century of evangelism. (After the September 11 terror attacks, the Billy Graham Evangelistic Association stopped using the word *crusades* to refer to these massive evangelistic meetings because of the odium that word aroused in the Islamic world.) But by the early twenty-first century, the world no longer resembled what it had been in the late 1940s, when Graham strode into the public limelight for the first time. No one, we can be sure, is likely to replicate Graham's achievement — his life — within the lifetime of even the youngest among us.

This book is not intended as a chronological biography of Billy Graham's life, though it does contain new biographical material about him that previously was not available. By far the most complete Billy Graham biography to date is William Martin's *A Prophet with Honor: The Billy Graham Story,* to which I wish with complete openness to acknowledge my debt in writing this book. Martin's book, however, was published in 1992, and thus could not have included material from the last decade and a half of

Billy Graham's career. The present book will deal in detail with some important episodes of Graham's life, episodes that I think illustrate significant features both of current affairs in the twentieth and twenty-first centuries and of global Christianity. *Billy Graham: His Life and Influence* thus is an attempt — no doubt the first of many — to evaluate the life of one of the foremost American personalities of the past century.

TWO:
A CHILD OF THE 1920s

At the time of Billy Graham's birth, the twentieth century was less than two decades old, but already it was taking on a whole new coloration. The entire span of Graham's nine-decade life was to be lived out against the backdrop of changes in the United States more rapid and longer-lasting than any period since the Civil War. He entered the world on November 7, 1918, in a wood frame farmhouse on Park Road in a neighborhood on the outskirts of Charlotte, North Carolina, that was still a rural farming community. Probably no one on that day recalled that exactly one year earlier the October Revolution had swept across Russia, igniting the dominant political struggle of the twentieth century, that is, the struggle between totalitarian communism and democracy. Surely no one imagined that this infant would not only live to see the near-complete collapse of the Marxism-Leninism that would endure for almost the entire rest of the century, but that he would try to coax the megalomaniac leader of one of Communism's last holdouts — North Korea's Kim Il Sung — to open up his hermit kingdom to positive outside influences.

Billy Graham was born during the administration of a Democratic president — Woodrow Wilson — who was a pious Christian driven to extend American democratic ideals beyond American shores (in Wilson's words, "to make the world safe for democracy"). Wilson believed firmly that he was called by the Almighty to govern ("If I didn't feel I was the personal instrument of God, I couldn't carry on," he said) and to spread his ideas of democratic and Christian influence overseas. In the last years of his life, Billy Graham saw the reelection of a Republican embodiment of Christian piety in the administration of George W. Bush, a man who had been deeply influenced at the age of thirty-nine by his own encounter with Graham. Republican Bush, like the Democratic Wilson, longed to push the ideals of American democracy as far overseas as they would travel, albeit with a different perspective from Wilson on the means. To grasp fully the magnitude of the impact Billy Graham has had on this country, and subsequently on the world, it is necessary to understand just what a different world it all was nearly a century ago.

Little more than a month after Frank Graham and Morrow Coffey Graham welcomed the birth of their firstborn, William Frank Graham Jr. — quickly abbreviated to Billy Frank — President Woodrow Wilson was standing on the bridge of the USS *George Washington* bound for Europe, the first sitting US president to leave the New World. He was on a mission to try to bring order to a Europe whose empires had broken up and whose peoples were starting to agitate for self-rule in the tumultuous wake of World War I. In persuading Europe to order its affairs along the lines of the political system deemed by Wilson — and by many Americans — to be the only workable one, the American leader achieved only limited success. And he had no success at all in persuading Americans to engage their energies with the new international order he had sketched out in Europe: the League of Nations. It was an organizational body whose supranational authority seemed altogether at odds with the firmly held American tradition of robust independence from the world.

Americans had grown tired of the stress and burdens of the wartime years and longed to return to "normal" life and let their hair down. In the election of November 1920, they voted overwhelmingly for a Republican president, the genial Warren G. Harding, who promised a return to normalcy. "Normalcy" to farming families like the Grahams meant a restoration of pre-1914 levels of agricultural prices, which had been seriously depressed by the post–World War I recession. But "normalcy" was certainly not the word that ever after characterized the decade of the 1920s; rather, the period came to be known as the "Roaring Twenties" or the "Jazz Age." This decisive decade transformed the United States more dramatically than any previous ten-year period, including that of the Civil War. It was also the most dramatically transformative of any subsequent decade until the 1960s. The changes encompassed all aspects of life: from global relations to technological advances to personal values. Prior to the 1920s, Americans, even if they were not truly isolated from the rest of the world, behaved in many ways as if they would rather be so isolated.

At the start of the 1920s, America was a nation whose values were still largely rural, but the new decade suddenly brought the United States face-to-face with a new and challenging notion: modernity. Even more challenging, an entire generation of Americans seemed to be in revolt against received wisdom and accepted social conventions. It was the age of the "flapper," the term for young women who dressed and acted unconventionally and who epitomized an almost brazen attitude toward the values embraced by their parents.[1] It was also the era when the appeals of a socialist way of life were for the first time proclaimed on the North American continent. The year 1920 was the year of the Red Scare, which opened with the US Justice Department reacting to bomb explosions late the previous year by rounding up on New Year's Day some six thousand suspected Communist radicals. Terrorism, albeit in embryonic form, was afoot. In the same election that brought Warren Harding into the White House, the Socialist Party candidate Eugene Debs received nearly a million votes. Never mind that he was at the time serving a ten-year sentence in the Atlanta penitentiary for sedition.

The Charlotte into which Billy Frank was born was largely a city characterized by Protestant Christian fundamentalism. To understand exactly what that means, it is important to understand that the term *fun-*

damentalism has a narrow definition and should not be applied indiscriminately to all varieties of Protestantism that believe in the supernatural and consider the Bible to be inerrant. (Even less should "fundamentalists" be used to refer to followers of the Islamic faith who embrace a radical interpretation of the Koran and of Islamic law, the *sharia*. Such people should, more accurately, be called "Islamists.") The term *fundamentalism,* when used in reference to Protestant Christians, comes from *The Fundamentals: A Testimony to the Truth,* twelve paperback volumes published between 1910 and 1915 by sixty-four conservative Christian scholars who wanted to turn back the tide of theological liberalism and modernism that, beginning in the 1890s, had been flowing into the sermons preached from the pulpits of American churches and into seminaries and university departments. In the fundamentalists' view, there are "five fundamentals" of the Christian faith within the Protestant tradition: the "inerrancy" of the Bible, the virgin birth and deity of Jesus Christ, the doctrine of substitutionary atonement through God's grace and human faith, the physical resurrection of Jesus Christ, and the authenticity of Christ's miracles.

About the time that Billy Frank started school, modernity in the form of Darwinism intersected noisily with Protestant Christian fundamentalism; the occasion was the Scopes Trial in Dayton, Tennessee. The state was one of about fifteen that had responded to vigorous lobbying by fundamentalist politician William Jennings Bryan, by introducing legislation banning the teaching of Darwinian evolution in public schools. Bryan believed that teaching evolution, even in the strict context of biology, would seriously undermine the morals of students exposed to this theory. The American Civil Liberties Union (ACLU), champion of individual rights but also an opponent of Christian efforts to influence the culture, wanted to test the anti-evolution law newly passed in Tennessee. In July 1925, *Tennessee v. John Scopes* pitted defense lawyer Clarence Darrow, representing Scopes, a local biology teacher, against prosecution witness William Jennings Bryan in a contest in which Bryan came off looking ignorant and foolish on the witness stand. The story was dramatized in a play called *Inherit the Wind,* and retold in a famous movie of the same name.

One of the more lasting impacts of the trial was that it became a metaphor for what many educated Americans assumed to be an inherent conflict between science and religion. As a result of the trial and the attendant ridicule, fundamentalists largely retreated from interaction with mainstream American culture and thought for most of the rest of the twentieth century. It was not until the 1950s, mainly under Billy Graham's influence, that Americans learned a person could be a committed Protestant Christian — one who sounded like a fundamentalist, using language such as "born-again," "washed in the blood," and "God's Word" — without being, well, a "fundamentalist," that is, someone who was more or less a dumb hick.

One writer who contributed to the perception during the Scopes Trial that modernity, urbanity, and civilization itself were at war with the insufferable nincompoops represented by the fundamentalists was H. L. Mencken (1880–1956), a reporter and columnist for *The Baltimore Sun* and later founder of *The American Mercury,* a literary and satirical periodical. A fellow newspaperman, columnist Walter Lippman, described Mencken as "the most powerful personal influence on this whole generation of educated people."[2] Mencken's acidulous comments on the pet affectations of America's rising middle class — which he mockingly called the "booboisie" — were perfectly suited to an age in which the height of sophistication seemed to be to throw all religious faith out the window. "Heave an egg out of a Pullman [train] and you will hit a fundamentalist almost everywhere in the United States," Mencken wrote with characteristic derision. Mencken's antipathy for Puritanism and fundamentalism was based primarily on a libertarian view of the world, a hedonist's delight in the pleasures of twentieth-century life (he considered the dry martini "the only American invention as perfect as a sonnet"), and his sardonic musings on American popular culture were wholly in tune with what the nation's educated elites regarded as enlightened and progressive.

Referring no doubt to Europe as well as the United States, the poet Archibald Mac-Leish said that the 1920s was the most creative period of artistic creation since the Renaissance. In art, Picasso, Matisse, and Kandinsky were thrilling gallery-goers from Boston to Berlin, and in music, Stravinsky, Schoenberg, and Hindemith seemed to be pushing the Western symphonic tradition in a wholly new direction.[3] American literature was forever enriched by 1920s writers such as F. Scott Fitzgerald, Ernest Hemingway, Sinclair Lewis, John Dos Passos, T. S. Eliot, and William Faulkner.

America was also moving in completely new directions socially. The ratification in January 1919 of the Eighteenth Amendment set the nation on one of its strangest journeys, that of Prohibition, which lasted until December 1933, when the constitutional clause was repealed by the Twenty-First Amendment. Prohibition, of course, in some respects marked the high tide of fundamentalist influence on American culture, for the antibooze crusaders were largely from fundamentalist churches. But the cessation of the legal sale of alcohol throughout the nation had — as well-intentioned social reforms often have — unintended and serious side effects: it fostered the rise of organized crime as it had never existed before. Criminals like Al Capone, with his astonishingly comprehensive gangland rule of Chicago during the 1920s, made the Windy City for much of the twentieth century widely synonymous with organized crime. For a while, the huge public attention to his criminal exploits and the *Time* cover stories made Al Capone seem to be as much a part of the American cultural establishment as genuine heroes such as Charles Lindbergh, who stunned America and Europe with his solo trans-Atlantic flight to France in 1927.

The decade's other constitutional amendment was to have much more far-reaching consequences than the Eighteenth. That was the Nineteenth, ratified in August 1920, which gave women the right to vote. Curiously, this momentous development did not result in immediate, profound changes. It would be more than a decade before Arkansas Democrat Hattie Caraway made history in 1932 as the first woman elected senator. And the real impact on the status of women in American society was not to be felt for nearly a half century, until the 1970s.

On the religious front, the man making headlines was Billy Sunday (1862–1935), also the target of much cruel, though often funny, satire by Mencken. Sunday was squarely in the tradition of revivalist preachers who had begun to emerge in the nineteenth century and who preached a Christianity in which the choice of salvation in many ways seemed little more than a business decision. Indeed, the first of such famous preachers, Charles Finney (1792–1875), prominent in the first quarter of the nineteenth century, believed that the success or failure of a revival was almost entirely dependent on selecting the correct methodology. He preached that "[t]here is nothing in religion beyond the ordinary powers of nature. [A revival] consists entirely in the right exercise of the powers of nature . . . It is a purely philosophical result of the right use of the constituted means — as much so as any other effect produced by the application of means."[4]

Another aspect of revivalism in the late nineteenth- and early twentieth-centuries was that of Protestant piety as the cornerstone of American patriotism and can-do business entrepreneurialism. By the 1920s, with business thinking dominating the minds of almost everyone who was not reading Mencken, it was little surprise that someone would write a novel portraying Jesus Christ as a supremely competent business executive. Bruce Barton, an advertising executive so successful that he has been described as one of the best admen of the twentieth century, came out in 1925 with *The Man Nobody Knows*. It was a big hit and sold thousands of copies. But the twentieth-century titan who bestrode the scene of American Protestantism many decades before Billy Graham was the aforementioned preacher, Billy Sunday.

A former professional baseball player who

was converted listening to a street evangelist outside a bar in Chicago, Sunday held evangelistic rallies that saw no contradiction between American patriotism, secular ideals, and the demands of Christianity. Sunday's revivals began at the turn of the century and reached a climax in New York in 1917, when some ninety-eight thousand people responded to his altar calls during the ten weeks of meetings. It was Sunday's spreading of sawdust on the floor to muffle the sound of feet striding forward to respond to his altar calls that led to the coining of the phrase "hitting the sawdust trail."

Sunday preached to far more of his countrymen than any other American preacher before Billy Graham: an estimated 100 million, and that before the era of microphones. At his most popular, Sunday was the subject of adulatory books, the recipient of invitations to the White House, and the holder of the number No. 8 spot in a magazine poll of "the greatest man in America," a rank he shared with business tycoon, philanthropist, and atheist Andrew Carnegie. Sunday differed from Finney in that he did not regard the success of evangelistic rallies as dependent on methodology so much as on recruiting professional organizers and publicists to prepare the venue and the mood of his meetings. In this, he prefigured Billy Graham in attention to detail and pre-meeting publicity.

In January and February 1924, the past and the future of American Protestantism met when Sunday held meetings in Charlotte, meetings to which the five-year-old Billy Frank was taken by his father. Telling the story years later as an adult, Graham recalled that his fidgeting and boisterousness as he sat next to his father at one meeting prompted Frank Graham to hiss, "Be quiet, or he'll call your name from the platform." Graham recalled, "I sat there frightened to death."[5]

The five-year-old who would grow up to inherit Billy Sunday's mantle was the scion of a family whose Carolina roots went back to the Civil War. Ben Coffey, his maternal grandfather, lost a leg and an eye fighting for the Confederacy at Seminary Ridge on the first day of the Battle of Gettysburg in 1863. Crook Graham, his paternal grandfather, also took a hit from a Yankee bullet in a separate Civil War battle. Crook died in 1910, and his twenty-year-old son Frank was left with the responsibility of running the four-hundred-acre rundown family farm outside of Charlotte. Frank had received barely three years of formal schooling, so when he married Morrow Coffey in 1916, she quickly assumed much of the farm's administrative responsibilities.

But Frank worked hard, and the farm began to prosper. By the time Billy Frank was born just two years later, it was one of the largest dairy farms in the area, with seventy-five cows and four hundred regular customers. By the late 1920s, the Grahams were doing well enough to move to a two-story brick house that Frank built just outside Charlotte, complete with running water and electricity. Both were absolute luxuries for their day in rural America. In the 1920s, only 10 percent of American homes had water piped in and only 7 percent had electricity.[6]

In a move suggesting nascent mythologizing of the Billy Graham story, the house, which remained in the Graham family until 1982, was bought by the PTL Corporation, the televangelism empire that later became a symbol for the financial hucksterism and vulgar showmanship of some Christian TV broadcasting, and was moved to the PTL theme park in Fort Mill, South Carolina. When Jim Bakker's PTL ministry went bankrupt in the wake of sexual and financial scandals, the house went into the hands of another corporation, which in turn sold it back to the Billy Graham Evangelistic Association (BGEA). The house, fully restored, is now part of the new Billy Graham Library on the BGEA compound in Charlotte, four miles from its original site. In a twist to the Jim Bakker story that speaks much of Billy Graham's basic decency, when Bakker was given an inordinately long forty-five-year jail sentence for his financial wrongdoings in connection with PTL and was subjected to widespread ridicule, Graham visited him in jail and called him "my friend."

Frank Graham had been converted to Christian belief at age eighteen when he attended a series of revival meetings organized by three Confederate veterans and held in a Methodist chapel known as the Plank Meetinghouse. His wife, Morrow, was a Christian too, but her coming to faith apparently was a much more gradual process, and she could not pinpoint an exact moment in time. At their wedding, they dedicated their union to God, and their daily life was framed by pious activities. Every meal started with the saying of grace, and at the end of the day, around 8 p.m., after the evening meal, there was the "family altar," the term used by some evangelical Protestants for a time of family prayers and Bible reading. "Daddy would just say it was time for prayer," recalled Jean Ford, Billy Frank's youngest sister. "Mama would read the Scripture, and Daddy would pray. It was as much a routine as eating."[7] Morrow insisted also that all the children memorize a Bible verse each day. A Scripture calendar was kept on the wall of the breakfast room and the daily verse given to the children before they went off to school.

The family attended Associate Reformed Presbyterian Church, which held to the Westminster Confession of Faith, a catechism drawn up in England in 1646 under Oliver Cromwell to define the Reformed Protestant view of the Christian faith. By the age of ten, each child was required to know by heart the Westminster Shorter Catechism, a 1647 abbreviation of the Confession that consisted of 107 questions with set answers.[8] Sunday — the Lord's Day — was serious business in the Frank and Morrow Graham household. No work was done except the milking and feeding of the cows. The children — Billy Frank and his siblings, Catherine, Melvin, and Jean, born fourteen years after Billy Frank — were also forbidden to read newspapers or to play games on Sundays.

Any notion, though, that Billy Frank's formative years were colored by a dour and repressive religiosity would be very wide of the mark. Though both parents were quick to resort to physical punishment for minor, childhood transgressions — mother with a hickory switch, father with a leather belt — it is clear that Billy Frank from a very early age exhibited an exuberance, vitality, and good nature that neither parent sought to stifle. He was a gangly knot of undirected energy rushing hither and yon through the family home, overturning egg baskets, knocking plates off the kitchen table, and even, on one occasion, tipping a bureau chest down the stairs. His mother recalled, "He was always tumbling over something. I was relieved when he started school."[9] Billy Frank's hyperactivity worried his parents, so they took him for a consultation with a physician, who reassured them that it was just the way the boy was made. (If it had been today, Billy Frank might well have been prescribed an instant supply of Ritalin.)

As is true of farm life anywhere, life on the Graham's dairy farm demanded constant, daily physical labor. As soon as they were able to help with the chores, the children were expected to be up at the crack of dawn or well before dawn — sometimes as early as 3 a.m. — to milk the cows, which had to be milked again in the evening. After school, there would often be other physical work, such as hauling and pitching hay. Melvin, younger than Billy Frank by six years, did not mind the sometimes hard labor, but it did not come naturally to the imaginative, restless Billy Frank.

Once he was enrolled in grade school a few miles down the road, the boy's exuberance at least had a new target for release: the school bus. Billy Frank would sometimes shut off the external gas valve after getting off the bus at the farm, causing the vehicle to sputter to a halt a few yards after starting off. But neither the school bus driver nor the teachers found it easy to get angry at Billy Frank. He exuded a likability and a desire to like others that was infectious. A classmate recalled, "It was just this lovable feeling that he himself seemed to have for everybody. You couldn't resist him."10

Irresistible or not, Billy Frank did not make much of an impression on his teachers, except, perhaps, as prankster. Once, he took delight in setting the classroom wastebasket alight, yelling, "Fire!" and jumping out the first-floor window. On another occasion, he filled the pockets of the basketball coach's jacket with old chicken bones and crumbled biscuits.[11] Melvin recalled that

Billy Frank was barely an average student in school,[12] and a former fifth-grade teacher recalled being astonished at seeing the mature Billy Graham, by then the established evangelist, on television many years later. "I simply couldn't believe it," he remembered. "His whole personality was so completely changed . . . I couldn't get over it. I kept thinking, 'Is *that* actually Billy Frank Graham? *What in the world happened to him?*' "[13] Of course, a lot of things had happened to Billy Frank by then, but it is clear that as a young farm boy he was no scholar. He failed French, had trouble memorizing poetry, and in high school had to take one exam over in order not to fail the entire eleventh grade.

But Billy Frank was already excelling in one area not easily quantifiable by teachers: that of the imagination. On the farm, he delighted in the animals he moved among, especially a goat for whom he felt a particular affection. In a rural setting with no close neighbors, the Graham children had to amuse themselves, and they did so with glee, chasing one another through the fields, role-playing the heroes Billy Frank was beginning to read about: Tarzan, whom he discovered at about age ten, or the characters in Zane Grey's novels. In fact, reading seemed to have captivated Billy Frank well before his adolescence, and his siblings recall his curling up for hours in haylofts or on the family room floor, devouring whatever he could: tales of Marco Polo, missionaries in distant lands, and, interestingly, an abridged edition of the eighteenth-century Edward Gibbon epic history classic, *The Decline and Fall of the Roman Empire.* By age fifteen, Billy Frank had read close to one hundred volumes, almost entirely nonfiction except for Zane Grey and the Tarzan series by Edgar Rice Burroughs. In grade school, he even gave an oral report on one of Zane Grey's stories, *The Red-Headed Outfielder and Other Baseball Stories,*[14] an indication of an emerging athletic ambition to be a major-league baseball player. Billy Frank may have imagined himself zooming through the major leagues, but he never developed anything resembling the skill needed to be a serious player. For one thing, he couldn't hit the ball especially well. Though he played first base on his high school team for a season and also played a few innings with a semi-pro team, the apex of that particular ambition may have been shaking Babe Ruth's hand when the superstar, who in the 1920s and 1930s frequently visited North Carolina in the off-seasons to hunt and play golf, came through Charlotte.

Baseball, however, was not the major discovery of Billy Frank's adolescence: girls were. He was tall and lanky, and very skinny, but his fine profile and his piercing blue eyes, along with his unmistakable congeniality and charm and a tendency to dress snappily even just to go to the movies, meant that he achieved easy popularity with the girls. His sister Catherine recalls that "he was in love with a different girl every day. He really did like the girls. And they liked him."[15] It didn't do him any harm either that, at a time when very few American teenagers had easy access to wheels, he could use his father's blue Plymouth for dates. On such dates Billy Frank could — and did — kiss with gusto, but no biographer has ever suggested that he went any farther than that. Looking back, Graham attributes his restraint to protection by a supernatural force. "I was just held back by a force that I don't understand," he said. "I never touched a girl in the wrong way, and I thank God for it."[16] There is little doubt that the childhood years of family prayer and Bible reading had also instilled strong principles of purity in the gangly adolescent.

Something else was at work in him too,

something that would begin to emerge visibly in his life before his sixteenth birthday in the form of a deeply personal Christian faith. One of the books his mother had given him seemed to stir his imagination in a way he could not really grasp at the time. The book contained a photo of the rose window of the Cathedral of Rheims in France, a thirteenth-century masterpiece with a fanlike explosion of stained glass depicting creation. He studied the picture of that window for many hours on the family farm. "I just know that I kept feeling that something was going to happen to me," he said later. "Something was about to happen to take me out of all that, out of the farm and out of Charlotte."

Something was indeed going to happen. In fact, the wheel of providence was already grinding forward, and it was going to take Billy Frank far, far away from the dairy farm in North Carolina.

THREE:
CONVERSION AND THE FIRST STEPS

The atmosphere of Frank and Morrow Graham's home might today be considered "religious" or "devout," but not necessarily fundamentalist. The family had daily prayers after the evening meal, said grace before each meal, rather sternly observed the Sabbath, and did not drink alcohol. The children were required to memorize a Scripture verse before heading for school each day, and the family was faithful in its church attendance. On the other hand, as mentioned in Chapter Two, Billy Frank was allowed to use his parents' car to take girls on dates, kissed those girls passionately whenever he could, went to movies (which many fundamentalists frown upon), and read plenty of Edgar Rice Burroughs and Zane Grey novels. By the standards of the Depression era, in fact, the family lived rather well. Though they lost all their savings in a bank failure in 1933, the income from the farm's dairy sales was good. Billy Frank's classmates considered the boy relatively affluent.

The year 1933, however, marked a turning point in the family's life. The shock of the savings loss that year was significant, of course, but it was also in that year that Frank Graham suffered a near-fatal accident when a rotary saw smashed a piece of wood into his jaw, "cutting his head almost back to his brain,"[1] Graham describes in his autobiography. For days, his survival was in doubt. Life must have seemed alarmingly fragile to Morrow Graham. The family had for several years attended Charlotte's Associate Reformed Presbyterian Church each Sunday. It was not fundamentalist; indeed it was solidly Presbyterian. But perhaps because of the combined shock of Frank Graham's accident and the bank failure, and in any case encouraged by her sister Lil, Morrow turned decisively to fundamentalism. She began attending Bible classes at the Plymouth Brethren Church, a fundamentalist denomination that had come into existence in the mid-nineteenth century and taught an interpretation of biblical history and prophecy called *dispensationalism*.

Dispensationalists believe that biblical history is divided up into seven "dispensa-

54

tions": Innocence — prior to the fall of Adam in the Bible; Conscience — from Adam to Noah; Governance — from Noah to Abraham; Patriarchal rule — from Abraham to Moses; Mosaic Law — from Moses to Christ; Grace — the current church age; and Millennial Kingdom — soon to come. One important characteristic of dispensationalism is a literal interpretation of the Old Testament prophecies concerning Israel: the Jewish temple will be rebuilt in Jerusalem before the second coming of Christ. Another dispensationalist belief is that the Second Coming itself will be a two-stage event, with Christians already dead and all true-believing Christians living at the time of the Second Coming being raised to heaven first before the return of Jesus Christ to earth. This event is commonly called the "Rapture" and is the theological underpinning of the best-selling English-language nonfiction book of the 1970s, Hal Lindsey's *The Late Great Planet Earth,* and of the more recent *Left Behind* series of novels by Tim LaHaye and Jerry Jenkins, which have consistently topped the best-seller charts, selling at least 65 million copies.

Morrow Graham undoubtedly became more fervent in her personal piety, and may have communicated her newfound interest in the Bible to her children, including her oldest, Billy Frank. Meanwhile, other things were stirring in Charlotte. Following Billy Sunday's visit to Charlotte in 1924, a Christian Men's Club had formed. Few records apparently remain of the club's activities, if any, in the years following, but in 1934, stirred by the business failures and a pervasive sense of discouragement that had fallen on the city, club members decided to reconvene for a day of fasting and prayer. Thirty or so men drove their cars onto a field on Frank Graham's farm — at his invitation, of course — and gathered in a loose circle to seek the Lord. Their wives, meanwhile, were assembled with Morrow Graham in the farmhouse, earnestly praying for Charlotte and its spiritual condition. Billy Frank is famously quoted as saying, in response to a friend who asked what all the cars were doing on his father's property, "Oh, I guess they are just some fanatics who talked Dad into letting them use the place."[2]

By the reckoning of the good-natured but rather careless adolescent finishing off his chores on the farm, the men probably were "fanatics." They prayed out loud intermittently all day, sometimes standing, sometimes kneeling in their shirtsleeves and suspenders. Then, toward the end of the day's prayer and fasting, in another iconic moment in the Billy Graham story, a man named Vernon Patterson stood up and prayed. His supplication has since been quoted many times and regarded as unwittingly prophetic: "Oh Lord, out of this very city, out of Charlotte itself, may you raise up such a one as will go out and preach your gospel to the ends of the earth!"[3]

That day of fasting and prayer on Frank Graham's farm took place in May 1934. Within a few months, an event occurred that would eventually result in an answer to Vernon Patterson's prayer. The Men's Club invited a fundamentalist evangelist, Mordecai Ham (1877–1961), to come to Charlotte from late August to the Sunday after Thanksgiving and hold meetings in a temporary tin-roofed structure large enough for some five thousand seats.

Ham was, by his own description, a "hog-jowl and turnip-green" preacher, a balding man with a pencil-thin moustache and thin-rimmed eyeglasses. He was a fierce, fire-and-brimstone revivalist preacher with something of an Old Testament prophet's zeal for denouncing sin. He certainly got results. Tales of Ham's preaching exploits are rich. In Macon, Georgia, thirteen brothels reportedly had to close down after Ham preached there, the girls having all been convicted of sin at one of his meetings. In another famous incident, during the Prohibition years, a gang of moonshiners hurled rocks at the church where Ham was preaching, and many of Ham's personal effects were stolen. When Ham confronted the gang leader, the man pulled a knife on him. Ham is said to have ordered, "Put up that knife, you coward! Now I am going to ask the Lord to convert you or kill you." The man reportedly died the following day, and three of his associates died shortly afterwards in a sawmill explosion. After that, all of the stolen property was quickly returned.[4]

Some of these stories, apocryphal or not, doubtless preceded Ham's visit to Charlotte. But other, less-savory fulminations accompanied Ham's denunciation of sin. He was anti-Semitic, denouncing "apostate Jews" and brandishing the well-known anti-Semitic document "Protocols of the Elders of Zion," which was subsequently shown to be an outrageous concoction of the Tsarist secret police, who wanted to discredit Russian Jews. Like many preachers called in to denounce a city's spiritual lethargy, Ham was quick to excoriate local churches, and, in the case of his visit to Charlotte, sinful misbehavior at the local high schools. The city's ministerial committee decided not to welcome Ham's visit, and for the first few days Frank and Morrow Graham stayed away too because their minister at Associate Reformed Church firmly disapproved of the visit. Looking back at what was to be a singularly pivotal event in his life, the adult Billy Graham might have been reading too much into his initial disdain for Ham when he declared, years later, "I was against him. Our clergy — the clergy in the city, was divided . . . and I just had no use for evangelists. I thought they were emotional."[5]

This reluctance to get too close to emotional religiosity might have had its roots in the recent death of his grandmother, Lucinda Coffey. The fifteen-year-old Billy Frank had been present with his mother and father at the bedside of the nearly ninety-year-old woman when, on the point of death, she suddenly lifted herself up from the pillow and cried out, "I see heaven! Oh, I can see heaven. Yes, yes, I see Jesus. He has his hands outstretched to me." Then, speaking of her late husband, Grandma Coffey said, "I see Ben. There's Ben." And with that, she fell back onto the pillow and died.[6] Billy Frank had been frozen by the scene. To the normally cheerful adolescent who wasn't particularly interested in religion, much less death, it was probably a terrifying moment. And it may be why Billy Frank himself was initially reluctant to get too close to someone who might bring him within uncomfortable proximity to a similarly emotional experience of eternity.

Destiny, however, intervened. One of Frank Graham's tenant farmers, Albert McMakin, planned to attend Ham's meetings and also wanted to bring along some of the local young people. He approached Billy Frank with an attractive offer. Would the young man like to drive the farm truck to the meeting? Billy Frank, though only fifteen, already had ample experience driving his father's Plymouth, and agreed. That was how he started attending the revival meetings on a nightly basis. Eventually, so did his parents, who drove there in their own car.

Ham's preaching style was to get up close and personal, often fixing his eyes on some hapless attendee in one of the front rows and launching a frontal assault upon sin in a manner that seemed to be personally directed at his visually pinioned victim. Billy Graham recalled years later, "This man would stand up there and point his finger at you and name all the sins you had committed. It made you think your mother had been talking to him."[7] To escape the dreaded finger-pointing, Billy Frank joined the choir, which was seated behind Ham on the platform. Next to him was a boy named Grady Wilson, the son of a plumber who was a member of Vernon Patterson's Christian Men's Club. Grady and his older brother, T. W., were to become members of the inner circle of Billy Graham's evangelistic team for his entire career. But in the fall of 1934 in Charlotte, Grady's primary motive in joining the choir was also to avoid Ham's finger-pointing fulminations (like Billy Frank, he had almost no natural musical talent).

There is no record of exactly how many times Billy Frank, with his parents sitting in a different part of the temporary hall with its sawdust-sprinkled floor, attended Ham's meetings, but it is likely that he showed up at the revival meetings for at least a few weeks. Then, on November 6, 1934, the day before his sixteenth birthday, something clicked. His father and mother were in the hall when, with Grady Wilson accompanying him and as the choir sang, "Almost Persuaded,"[8] Billy Frank stumbled awkwardly down the sawdust trail at Mordecai Ham's urging. "I didn't have any tears. I didn't have any emotion, I didn't hear any thunder, there was no lightning," Graham has often told audiences in recalling this momentous event of his adolescence. "I saw a lady standing next to me and she had tears in her eyes, and I thought there was something wrong with me because I didn't feel all worked up. But right there, I made my decision for Christ. It was as simple as that, and as conclusive."[9]

At home that evening, Billy Frank announced to his parents that he was "a changed boy," but he himself may have not yet been convinced of it. Later that night, he fell to his knees beside his bed and prayed, almost dazed by the uncertainty of what he had done, "Oh, God, I don't understand all of this. I don't know what's happening to me. But as best as I can figure out, I've given myself to you." He thought that he ought at least to demonstrate some change in his lifestyle, though there were hardly any heinous sins to repent of. "I knew something was different," he said. "I began to want to read the Bible and to pray. I got hold of a little hymnbook and began to memorize those hymns. I would say them because I couldn't sing."[10] In one way, though, he did change: he started doing what newly converted Christians tend to do, which was to start talking about his conversion experience to his peers. A few of his high school teachers noticed this, and one seemed particularly exasperated by it. She mocked him as "Preacher Boy" in front of a class and told him he would never amount to anything in life. It stung, but Billy Frank consoled himself with the thought that this was an example of the persecution that Ham had warned attends the life of any Christian. For a while, he stopped going to movies, and he was hesitant to join in the dancing at the junior-senior banquet at the high school. But he continued to cut up with his dad's Plymouth on the country roads and even in downtown Charlotte. And he was as attentive as ever to the girls. When he applied to the Tenth Avenue Presbyterian Church in Charlotte, which his parents had started attending, the young people in the Life Service Band turned down his application to join because he was "just too worldly."

The teenager did, however, mark the inner change he had experienced with an interesting and significant outward alteration. He no longer wanted to be called "Billy Frank"; from now on he was to be simply "Billy Graham." He thought it sounded more mature. Even if little visibly changed in the way Billy Graham conducted himself, the name change hinted at how profoundly Ham's message had struck him. He wanted to do more than just get things right with God and then live out his life in myriad ordinary ways. "I wanted to tell others what had happened to me," he said.[11] Something was tugging at his heart, a sense that his own experience of conversion, or at least the phenomenon of conversion itself, was something that as many people as possible needed to know about.

With her newfound zeal for the fundamentalist brand of Christianity, Morrow Coffey now sometimes opened up the Graham home to several itinerant preachers when they passed through Charlotte. Billy was fascinated by their stories, their style, their zeal for saving souls. One of them was a handsome young man of only twenty-three named Jimmie Johnson, and he became quite a role model as a traveling preacher for the recently converted Billy. Jimmie had a growing reputation as a winner of souls, and he took Billy along with him to some of his preaching venues. One of these was a local jail, where, without warning, he asked Billy to give his testimony. It was the first time that the new convert had spoken publicly about his faith, and the experience convinced him that he did not have what it took to be a preacher. Billy also spent time with Vernon Patterson, whose initiative had gathered the Christian Men's Club to the Graham farm in the spring of 1934.

His last two years of high school were something of a struggle. Not only had he never been a particularly good student, but he had to retake an exam to graduate. He did graduate, though, on time in 1936, and it was Albert McMakin, the same tenant who had suggested that Billy drive the farm truck to Mordecai Ham's meetings, who now suggested a summer job for Billy. McMakin had left the Graham farm and was now a commercial salesman, and he persuaded Billy and the Wilson brothers, Grady and T. W., to work that summer for The Fuller Brush Company in the two Carolinas. Although his father and an uncle predicted that Billy would be a flop, he actually proved to be a natural and by the end of the summer he was the most successful salesman in the two states. His capacity for expressing both passionate enthusiasm for his products combined with genuine sincerity undoubtedly helped him achieve this stunning success.

The brief sales stint taught the young man, who had until then led a rather sheltered life, some valuable lessons and opened his eyes to some realities of life. He was away from home for the first time, stayed in some unsavory boarding houses, and on one occasion recognized a drunken man who was regarded as an upright Christian in Charlotte. The sight reinforced a determination in Billy to put his confidence "in Christ, not man" because "man is weak," his lifelong friend Grady Wilson recalled.[12] Some of Graham's later phenomenal success as an evangelist is prefigured by his experiences as a Fuller brush salesman. Reflecting on the summer, Graham later observed, "Sincerity is the biggest part of selling anything, including the Christian plan of salvation."[13]

When summer ended, it was time to enroll in college. Billy had planned to attend the University of North Carolina, but his mother had been impressed with Bob Jones Sr., a fundamentalist teacher and evangelist, when he visited Charlotte during Billy's senior year of high school. Bob Jones had founded his own college, and Morrow decided that Billy had best go there. Frank Graham, whose scant three years of formal education meant he could barely read, wanted Billy to stay on the farm, but he reluctantly agreed.

Bob Jones College was founded in 1927 "to establish a training center for Christians from around the world that would be distinguished by its academic excellence, refined standards of behavior, and opportunities to appreciate the performing and visual arts," as the school's current Web site states. The institution, now Bob Jones University, was founded in Florida, but moved to Tennessee in 1933 and to its current location, Greenville, South Carolina, in 1947. One of the concerns of Bob Jones Sr. was that many Christian youth went to college and lost their faith because of teachers who either rejected Christianity completely or rejected the biblical worldview in their overall teaching philosophy. Jones believed that students must be instructed in a biblical worldview on all subjects. (Anyone who thinks fundamentalists are all a bunch of uneducated yahoos would be in for a big surprise upon visiting the Bob Jones campus, which boasts one of the finest collections of paintings by Old Masters and other great artists in the western hemisphere.)

In Billy Graham's day, those "refined standards of behavior" were inculcated by a rigid system of demerits for everything from being late for class to "loitering" in the hallway. Records were kept of demerit points, and expulsion was automatic upon accumulation of 150 points. Billy, with his limited alacrity for completing arduous tasks and his congenial dislike of regulations, quickly felt cramped and restricted on the campus. He writes in his autobiography, *Just as I Am,* that he was literally "shocked" by the restrictiveness of life at Bob Jones College. On the wall of his dormitory was the intimidating sign "Griping not tolerated!"[14] Dating was restricted to couples talking to each other for no more than fifteen minutes, boy and girl in separate chairs under a chaperone's watchful gaze. Billy lost sleep, lost weight, and also caught colds and the flu as the damp chill of autumn fell across Tennessee his first semester. When he went home for the Christmas break, a doctor suggested that a warmer climate might help. As it happened, a visiting preacher spoke highly of a Bible school known as the Florida Bible Institute, and the whole family decided to combine a trip to see relatives in Florida with a look at the school in Temple Terrace, twelve miles northeast of Tampa. They drove down in January, and Billy instantly decided it was altogether preferable to Bob Jones College.

Although he dutifully returned to the Tennessee campus for the spring semester, word that he was considering another institution reached Bob Jones Sr., who summoned Billy to his office for a tongue-lashing. The exchange has entered the history books as a prediction that turned out to be laughably far off the mark. "Billy, if you leave and throw your life away at a little country Bible school, the chances are you'll never be heard of," the crusty college founder told him. "At best, all you could amount to would be a poor Baptist preacher somewhere out in the sticks."[15] Billy, biting his nails in anguish — a habit he was prone to for most of his early adult life — took several weeks to make up his mind to go south. But he eventually did, arriving at the Florida Bible Institute in early February 1937.

In the warmth of Florida, even in winter, Billy's health quickly recovered. He was delighted by the small Institute of fewer than seventy-five students; the curriculum was as strictly Bible centered as that of Bob Jones College, but the disciplinary style was considerably less restrictive. The campus, formerly a country club that had failed in the Depression, doubled as a short-term vacation center for visiting preachers, and students — Billy included — came to know several big-name evangelists who passed through. Just as he had done with the itinerant preachers who had enjoyed his mother's hospitality, Billy soaked up everything he could from these veteran evangelists. This close contact with the big names of the day in evangelistic circles further fueled his desire to do something big for God. Another incident during this period may have dramatically emphasized for Billy the eternal stakes of preaching the salvation message. He saw a man hit by a car and was transfixed with horror as the man screamed, "I'm lost, I'm lost, I can see hell, I can see hell!"[16]

Billy's first opportunity to preach in a formal setting came during this time in Florida. The school's academic dean, Rev. John Minder, was also pastor of Tampa Gospel Tabernacle, and he encouraged Billy to preach at a small Baptist church in Bostwick, forty miles south of Jacksonville, in northeast Florida. Prepared with notes for four sermons, Billy was so rattled by this first experience of public speaking to complete strangers that he rushed through all his notes in a single eight-minute sprint. He was mortified by the experience, but Minder had plenty of faith in Billy and arranged other preaching opportunities for him. Billy showed serious dedication to honing his preaching skills, sometimes paddling a canoe up the Hillsborough River adjacent to the campus, where he would practice his sermons loudly to the mangroves and dozing alligators. This dedication to preaching, though, did not extend to pastoral work. Billy did not feel a particular call to be a church pastor, with all of the nurturing and shepherding of a congregation that it required. He continued to feel pulled to do something major and lasting for the cause of the gospel. He just didn't know yet what it was.

A sharp rebuff on the romantic front, though, jolted Billy's thinking. His interest in pretty girls had not been the slightest diminished by his experience under Mordecai Ham's preaching, and in Florida he had quickly settled on an attractive dark-haired fellow student, Emily Cavanaugh, in the spring of 1937, just months after arriving on campus. By the summer, though only eighteen, he had asked her to marry him. Though hesitant at first, Cavanaugh accepted, only to change her mind in the spring of the following year. Billy's brother Melvin reflected frankly, "She wanted to marry a man that was going to amount to something, and didn't think he [Billy] was going to make it."[17] The rejection, and perhaps an intuitive sense of why Emily had turned him down, devastated the young

Billy, causing him to turn his thoughts more seriously than ever to prayer and reflection on what God wanted him to do. He was not sure whether the call to preach was a lifelong vocation or just a short-term inclination. In his prayers, he persistently implored God for an answer. It was an early example of one of Billy Graham's lifelong traits: to agonize over important decisions, to storm heaven seeking direction, and then to be quite firm in any decision arrived at in the course of this process of prayer.

Finally, it came to him very late one spring night as he knelt on the grass of the eighteenth green of the country club golf course: a quiet, internal conviction. "Alright, Lord," he prayed, "if you want me, you've got me. I'll be what you want me to be and I'll go where you want me to go."[18]

And go he did. For the remainder of his time at the Florida Bible Institute, Billy made himself available whenever and wherever there was an occasion for an evangelistic sermon. From filling in as a supply preacher to preaching to local congregations to being a full-fledged revival preacher, Billy was willing to go anywhere and everywhere and preach. Sometimes he got a rough reception. Crowds heckled when he preached sometimes several times a day on the streets of Tampa, and a saloon owner once sent him sprawling to the pavement when Billy would not move away from the man's business. (A historical marker now stands at the site.[19]) But Billy Graham's pattern of high conversion rates was set the first time he extended the invitation to come forward and accept the salvation that was available through faith in Jesus Christ, an invitation he first made to the congregation of a small church in the Gulf Coast town of Venice, Florida. Thirty-two of the fewer than one hundred people in the church responded, a startlingly high percentage that prompted the church's Sunday school superintendent to observe: "There's a young man who is going to be known around the world."[20] Indeed, throughout his career as an evangelist, when Billy Graham preached, astounding numbers of people responded by coming forward.

Nevertheless, being a Presbyterian did not really cut it at the fundamentalist Baptist churches that invited Billy to preach at their revivals. Late in 1938, he was baptized by immersion — a core belief of Baptists — in Silver Lake, near East Palatka Baptist Church, where that summer he had held a series of revival meetings. Early the following year, he was ordained a Southern Baptist clergyman, which qualified him to conduct weddings, funerals, and officiate in other matters restricted to the ordained.

His senior year at Florida Bible Institute, Billy was elected class president and named outstanding evangelist of the class, known for the opportunities he seized to preach the gospel wherever he was invited. He took extraordinary care in preparing his sermons, practicing them at full length the day before, sometimes declaiming to an empty auditorium, sometimes making life uncomfortable for the snakes and alligators along Florida's abundant rivers and creeks. He already had developed the style for which he would be known in the early days of his national fame, a rapid, machine-gun like delivery accompanied by dramatic sweeps of his arms and hands. "The preaching windmill" was how he was described in Florida; "God's machine-gun" came a few years later. It would be many years, however, before he settled into the style of preaching that is instantly recognizable as mature Billy Graham: the cadenced, deep-voiced delivery with an unmistakable North Carolina lilt and the rhetorical questions that he put to his audiences, questions to which he supplied carefully nuanced answers.

Even in these early Florida years, though,

Billy already seemed to know intuitively that one day he would be preaching to vast crowds, and as he grew more confident, so did his well-prepared pre-meeting publicity. Visitors to small churches were encouraged to come and hear "dynamic, youthful evangelist, Billy Graham" or "Billy Graham, one of America's outstanding young evangelists."[21] This was not just empty boasting or bravado. At his June 1940 Florida Bible Institute graduation ceremony, valedictorian Vera Resue, with unwitting prophetic accuracy, told the audience of faculty, students, and parents that in times of darkness in the world, God had hitherto chosen spiritual giants to "shine forth His light in the darkness." Referring to Martin Luther, who started the Reformation, John Wesley (1703–1791), founder of Methodism, and D. L. Moody (1837–1899), who was probably the best-known revival evangelist in late nineteenth-century America, she continued, "The time is ripe for another Luther, Wesley, Moody. There is room for another name in this list."[22]

But if Billy Graham's name was to be on that list, he knew that he needed more formal, university-level education. When his parents had first started thinking about college for Billy, they had briefly considered

Wheaton College, the premier liberal arts college of the entire evangelical world. They had, however, dismissed the idea because of the school's distance from North Carolina and its tuition, which was too expensive for the farming family. But when two businessmen, one of them the brother of Wheaton's president, visited the Florida Bible Institute on a vacation trip and heard Billy preach, they offered to pay the entire cost of his first year at Wheaton.

Billy leaped at the opportunity and enrolled in the fall of 1940. At nearly twenty-two years of age, he was several years older than most of the freshmen, and was already trailing a reputation as a zealous evangelist. Billy majored in anthropology, although at Wheaton the approach to this subject was quite different from the deeply skeptical view of revealed religion and incipient multiculturalism that was then favored in major secular universities around the country. At Wheaton in 1940, all subjects were taught in the context of God's creation of man, as opposed to the evolutionary emergence of human beings from primeval slime.

With his enthusiasm and infectious congeniality, and despite his rapid-fire speech and rural North Carolina accent, Billy made friends quickly. With his poised preaching style, he was soon drafted by the Student Christian Council to go out on evangelistic forays into nearby towns. The importance of Wheaton to Billy Graham's life, though, did not lie in his anthropological studies or his evangelistic preaching, but as the place where he met his future wife.

Ruth Bell was a year ahead of him at Wheaton when they met not long after he arrived on campus. The meeting would change his life and would have a lifelong impact on the man and his work. She was the daughter of Presbyterian medical missionaries in China, where she was born and had lived until the age of seventeen. Not only was the slim, hazel-eyed Ruth one of the most attractive and sought-after girls on campus, but she was also witty, well-educated, and mature beyond her years. In China, she had been eyewitness to abject human misery: corpses in the street, the tiny bodies of the victims of infanticide being eaten by dogs, starving families begging by the roadside, and other indescribable human degradation that drove even some of the missionaries to commit suicide in despair.

She had also heard from her father of the appalling behavior of the Japanese, who had launched a full-scale invasion of China in

1937 and the Rape of Nanking that December, committing some of the most bestial atrocities of the twentieth century. Dr. Nelson Bell had even gone to Washington to alert officials there about the threat that he thought Japan posed to the United States, but his warnings fell on deaf ears. Exposure to the "real world" in the form of these war-time horrors in China in the 1930s no doubt helped form Ruth's steel backbone that was to be of decisive influence in Billy Graham's future career.

Ruth, though younger than Billy by two years, had enrolled at Wheaton three years before his arrival, following in the footsteps of her older sister. She was considered a prize catch not just because of her beauty, which Graham in his autobiography described as "stunning" and like that of a "movie starlet," but also because of her renowned piety (she regularly got up pre-dawn to read her Bible and pray) and her unusual life experiences growing up on the mission field in China. They were introduced by a mutual friend who had repeatedly sung her praises to Billy, encouraging him to pursue her since she had already turned away several other suitors. Billy apparently needed no urging after seeing her the first time, and he wrote to his mother before he had even asked Ruth for a date that he had fallen in love. Ruth, however, had decided at age twelve to stay single so that she could be a missionary to Tibet, where she thought she might be martyred for the gospel. She had always respected and admired the missionaries among whom she had grown up, and, fueled by her deep desire to serve God, she seemed to regard being a missionary to Tibet to be the most challenging and meaningful endeavor she could undertake.

But something about Billy, the depth of his faith, his humility, his fearless preaching, and the vibrancy and fervor of his prayer life, caught her attention. She wrote a prayer in her journal that reveals how highly she thought of him even though she still barely knew him. "If you let me serve you with that man," she prayed, "I'd consider it the greatest privilege in my life."[23] Later, she wrote a poem that revealed even more tellingly Billy's first impression on her. It starts out, "Dear God, I prayed, . . . / I do not need a handsome man / But let him be like You" and ends with, "Then, when he comes, . . . / with quiet eyes aglow, / I'll understand that he's the man / I prayed for, long ago."[24]

It took Billy several weeks to work up the

courage to ask for a date, but she readily agreed to his invitation to a performance by the school's glee clubs of Handel's *Messiah*. After the afternoon concert, they took a cold and snowy walk and then talked over tea. Graham recalls, "I just could not believe that anyone could be so spiritual and so beautiful at one and the same time."[25] He wrote home after this first date to say that he planned to marry Ruth because she reminded him so much of his mother.

Billy proposed to her in late spring the following year, 1941. She accepted by letter a few weeks later, but later that year hesitated and wrote that perhaps they should break the engagement. Though crushed, Billy did not give up, and early in 1942 they resumed the engagement, with a wedding date set far ahead, in 1943, upon his graduation from Wheaton. Meanwhile, without consulting her, Billy decided to accept a position as pastor of a struggling Baptist church in Western Springs, Illinois. He had not particularly wanted to be a pastor, but the salary was good for a newlywed couple. Billy's motivation was surely blameless, but Ruth made it quite clear to him that he had been insensitive not to have included her in the decision-making. The incident was an early hint of the spunk and spirit Ruth would bring to their marriage, which by all accounts was a solid partnership of equals even if by outward appearances they seemed to have assumed traditional husband-wife roles. The couple was married in a Presbyterian church in Montreat, North Carolina, in an August 1943 evening ceremony that included two solos by a Chinese singer.

The marriage itself, however, was a challenge, and it was not just a question of two strong personalities in daily contact with each other. Billy had a profoundly authoritarian view of how husbands related to their wives that he had picked up from his father, whose cut-and-dried approach was that the husband makes all the decisions and the wife simply obeys. During their engagement, when Ruth had expressed doubts about marrying him, Billy had pointed to the biblical teaching of wifely submission to husbandly authority and argued that if she thought that God had brought them together, "then I'll do the leading and you do the following."[26] Billy Graham recalled years later in an interview in *McCall's* magazine, "We had come from different backgrounds, and suddenly we were on our own. It was hard, and not just because of our different temperaments."[27]

Billy was, moreover, so deeply committed

81

to his obligations as an evangelist that early on he often completely overlooked the need to be a tender, caring husband. His biographers recount with some disapproval that when Ruth became seriously ill a few days after their honeymoon, Billy checked her into a hospital so that he could keep a commitment for a routine preaching engagement in another state. Later still, there were to be even greater marital challenges when Graham was out on evangelistic missions for up to six months at a time.

The separations were difficult for both husband and wife, but Ruth was equally as committed to Billy's call to be an evangelist as he was. They both saw her as an important member of the team, and her down-to-earth, no-nonsense approach helped counterbalance the praise heaped on Graham throughout his life. At times, she differed almost sharply from him, as when she refused in 1974 to sign the Lausanne Covenant (recounted in Chapter Five) and when she expressed great reluctance for him to accept an invitation in 1982 to a Soviet Peace Conference in Moscow.

Although the Western Springs pastorate was still very early in his career, it was here that Billy Graham began to exhibit two of his most brilliant traits, traits that would be displayed again and again throughout his career and that are the keys to his unmatched success as an evangelist. He had a knack for picking highly talented and loyal associates and for spotting new ministry opportunities and jumping on them as if they would disappear if he did not. Not long after he arrived at Western Springs, he began the Western Suburban Professional Men's Club, a monthly businessmen's dinner program featuring evangelical speakers that drew as many as five hundred men. He also accepted without hesitation an offer to take over a regular, Sunday evening radio broadcast called *Songs in the Night.* In an early example of his talent for tapping and keeping good people, he recruited Chicago-area gospel singer George Beverly Shea to be his musical talent. Shea was to remain closely linked to Graham's evangelistic work for more than half a century as the principal singer at the Billy Graham crusades.

The fame that came with this radio program led to more invitations to speak, with the result that the Western Springs congregation languished under a pastor who was so frequently absent on Sunday mornings. Robert van Kampen, a local businessman and the Western Springs deacon who had invited Billy to be their pastor, defended

Graham with these prophetic words, "There is only one thing that I can say, and that is that God has laid upon Billy a special gift of evangelism and someday he could be another Billy Sunday or D. L. Moody."[28]

When the Japanese attacked Pearl Harbor in December 1941, precipitating America's entry into World War II, Billy had almost immediately applied to the War Department to be a chaplain, even though he still had a year and a half to go in his studies at Wheaton. The military told him that he should graduate first and then acquire pastoral experience. Upon graduation, his job as a full-time clergyman kept him from being drafted as an ordinary soldier while the rest of the country was training and arming itself for the long fight ahead in Europe and the Pacific.

By 1944, America's cities were filled with soldiers on leave, disconnected from their families and home communities, sometimes fearful of the fights ahead, sometimes simply aimless. A Chicago clergyman, Torrey Johnson, who created the radio program *Songs in the Night* that he later handed over to Billy Graham, now began orchestrating across the Midwest evangelistic gatherings to reach the thousands of young men in uniform. He invited Graham to preach at the inaugural rally on May 27, 1944, to a crowd of three thousand young people, mostly soldiers on leave, in Orchestra Hall in Chicago. It was Billy's first real taste of mass evangelism. Though petrified by the size of the crowd, then his largest ever, which precipitated what he describes as "the worst fit of stage fright of my life,"[29] Graham's exuberant style and passionate declamation resulted in a large number of people responding by "coming forward" when invited to accept salvation through belief in Jesus Christ. The meetings at Orchestra Hall continued through the summer, with Billy doing the preaching. By the end of that year, Graham had resigned from his pastorate at Western Springs; the difficulties of juggling the conflicting demands of the calling of evangelism and that of a settled church pastor had become abundantly clear.

Graham's application to be a military chaplain had, meanwhile, finally been accepted, and he would have gone to Harvard Divinity School for training had he not come down with a serious case of mumps. The physical weakness brought on by the six-week illness made him ineligible for overseas service, and he eventually asked to be relieved of his earlier commitment. At about the same time, while in Florida to recuperate, he was offered a position as a traveling evangelist by Torrey Johnson in a new organization he was forming, Youth for Christ International. Johnson also tapped other talented young evangelists, including Canadian Charles Templeton, whose career would eventually go in a vastly different direction from that of Billy Graham.

Graham spent most of 1945 crisscrossing the country by plane, often with Templeton, racking up more miles with United Airlines than anybody else in the country. Logging 200,000 miles, he spoke at civic meetings and at church-organized rallies in forty-seven states, learning in the process how many congregations had been let down by unscrupulous freelance evangelists in the Elmer Gantry vein. Templeton was generally regarded as the better preacher of the two because of his eloquence and his versatility, but by Templeton's own admission, Graham's preaching regularly resulted in more conversions. The two men liked each other from the moment they met, and their friendship was to have important consequences for Graham's ministry.

The Youth for Christ meetings, meanwhile, bordered on the truly outlandish, with the preachers wearing garishly flashy suits, hand-painted ties, and sometimes illuminated bowties. Biographer Martin writes:

> The rallies themselves were a sort of evangelical vaudeville, with usherettes, youth choirs and quartets and trios and soloists, "smooth melodies from a consecrated saxophone," Bible quizzes, patriotic and spiritual testimonies by famous and semi-famous preachers, athletes, entertainers, military heroes, business and civic leaders, and such specialty acts as magicians, ventriloquists, and a horse named MacArthur who would "kneel at the cross," tap his foot twelve times when asked the number of Christ's apostles and three times when asked how many persons constituted the Trinity . . .[30]

The theatrics, though, belied the deep seriousness behind it all. In mobilizing the evangelists and forming Youth for Christ, Torrey Johnson was not simply motivated by a desire to convert large numbers of people. His mission was, in fact, to change the culture of America by creating what he hoped would be a tide of revival in the early postwar world. Furthermore, he hoped that the live-wire enthusiasm of his young evangelists might also rub off on Europe. Even President Harry S. Truman, faced with an immensely complex world at the end of World War II and grappling with the challenge of leading an America that had grown accustomed to more than thirteen years of President Franklin D. Roosevelt's leadership, seemed to have been struck by Youth for Christ's far-reaching ambitions. "This is what I hoped would happen in America," he was quoted as saying in a *Time* magazine report on Johnson's organization.[31]

In the spring of 1946, Graham and Templeton headed off to Europe for a forty-six-day tour of the British Isles and the continent. It must have been mutual culture shock of mammoth proportions, for the two Americans as well as for the Europeans. Exhausted by wartime shortages and the crushing burden of the long military struggle that had affected everything in life, the British in particular were especially leery of the brash, young American evangelists who seemed so light-hearted and filled with confidence. A few, however, were touched by the sheer innocent, gospel-sharing confidence of the young men. It was "like a breath from heaven in a suffocated time," said British lay evangelist Tom Rees, "men who brought brightness in the midst of all our darkness."[32]

Graham returned in the fall of 1946 with part of the team, notably the musical couple Cliff and Billie Barrows, for what turned into a six-month visit to Britain, during which he preached at 360 meetings in twenty-seven cities. Harsh weather conditions made it even more physically challenging than the spring visit had been. Britain was going through its cruelest winter in decades and its snowiest in a century and a half. Heating in many homes was non-existent, and natural gas for heating was in such short supply that at Oxford University some of the tutorial meetings between undergraduates and dons — as professors are called in Britain — were held at night to avoid taxing the gas supply during peak use during the day. Food shortages were as bad as at any time during the war, with rationing even of potatoes.

These trying conditions notwithstanding, the trip was highly significant because of two very important events. The first event was to characterize Graham's response throughout his life to sharp criticism. When Graham's team arrived in the city of Birmingham, Britain's second largest city at the time, they were met with suspicion and hostility on the part of the local clergy, who thought the Americans were cocky. The clergy banded together and petitioned the city leaders to withdraw permission for Graham and his team to use a municipal auditorium for their evangelistic meetings. Instead of fulminating against the clergy, as people such as Mordecai Ham had done even in Charlotte, Graham found out who the principal opponents were and politely and respectfully met with each of them personally with the request only that he be allowed to explain himself and that they agree to pray with him. He apologized for his own failings as a preacher and said he wanted to serve them and also to learn from them. In almost every case, he won over his critics. One recalled, "This fine, lithe, burning torch of a man made me love him and his Lord."[33] The clergy took back its criticism, and the city council agreed to make the auditorium available.

Of all Graham's strengths, none may have been as helpful throughout his career, to his evangelism and his reputation, as this humble teachability. He has surely made many mistakes, as much as anyone would in the course of a highly public life, in statements rashly made, in decisions to hold evangelistic campaigns where there was inadequate preparation, or sometimes in the failure to plan them. But Billy Graham's personal modesty and humility have again and again protected him from the worst attacks of critics and the even harsher judgment of history. His teachability has been a surprising but heartening attribute for a man in a chosen profession — evangelist — that has had its share of arrogant and dogmatic characters.

That teachability showed up again in a highly unusual and, indeed, unexpected encounter in Wales with a young Welsh evangelist named Stephen Olford that was to be the other milestone event of his second visit to Britain. The episode drew lengthy and detailed descriptions in early Graham biographies and reflected what he clearly felt was a major turning point in his spiritual life. Curiously, though, in his own autobiography, *Just as I Am,* Graham makes a mere one-sentence reference to it in a short paragraph: "My contact with British evangelical leaders during this and subsequent trips, especially with Stephen Olford, deepened my personal spiritual life."[34] Whether recounted in lengthy detail or only in a passing reference, though, the Olford encounter had an enormous impact on Billy Graham and his entire ministry.

Graham had met Olford on his first trip

to Britain in the spring of 1946. The young evangelist (1918–2004) — who was born in the same year as Graham — grew up in the African countries of Zambia and Angola, where his parents were missionaries. It was in Angola that Olford made a personal decision to follow Christ, but it was not until his adult years that he experienced what might be called "an encounter with the Holy Spirit." The Holy Spirit as doctrinally part of the Trinity, a person, God Himself, is foundational to Christian belief, although Christians do not agree about its manifestation. The fastest-growing segment of Christianity today is the Pentecostal or Charismatic movement (estimated now to comprise as many as 400 to 500 million Christians worldwide in denominations as varied as the Catholic Church and the Assemblies of God), which originated in a focused search by ordinary Christian believers to recover the spiritual power released by the Holy Spirit in an event in early church history known as the Day of Pentecost as recounted in Acts 2 of the Bible.

Even before the Pentecostal movement came into existence in the United States around the beginning of the twentieth century, some Christians had individually sought the power associated with Pentecost in their personal prayer times. One of those was the great nineteenth-century evangelist D. L. Moody, who indirectly influenced several generations of evangelists up to Mordecai Ham.[35] In 1871, Moody had an experience in prayer that transformed his preaching, about which he later wrote, "I can only say that God revealed Himself to me, and I had such an experience of His love that I had to ask Him to stay His hand. I went to preaching again. The sermons were not different; I did not present any new truths, and yet hundreds were converted."[36] This, in effect, is exactly what happened to Billy Graham in a small hotel in a drab miners' town in Wales called Pontypridd. Graham was scheduled for two nights of preaching in a nearby church, but he spent the days with Olford. The Welshman said he had been changed completely by a personal experience of the power of the Holy Spirit during a time of prayer some months earlier, and Graham wanted to learn, if he could, about the work of the Holy Spirit.

On the first day of this mini-retreat, Olford talked with Graham about the nature of the "quiet time," that period of the day that Christians devote to prayer, meditation, or study of the Bible. Graham had memorized a lot of Scripture, but Olford said that what he meant by "exposing himself to the Word" was not just memorization; it was a much deeper absorption of the core of the gospel message than what could be acquired merely by ordinary reading. Olford was struck by Graham's willingness to learn. "He was so teachable, so beautifully humble and reflective. He just drank in everything I could give him," he recalled.[37] According to both men, the fruits of Graham's evangelistic preaching in the church that first night were still meager. Olford told me in 2001 that a Welshman stood up and shouted at Billy after the young American's brief, formulaic Youth for Christ sermon, "My goodness, that was a good introduction, and now let's hear the sermon!"[38]

The following day, Olford told Graham how his own Christian life had been transformed by the Holy Spirit. Billy did not quite know what this meant, but he was eager for the same experience. They both dropped to their knees and began to pray, Graham pouring out his heart in loud supplications to totally dedicate his life to God. Apparently coming to a breakthrough point, he said exultantly, "My heart is so flooded with the Holy Spirit." Olford recalled years later, "He howled in prayer, 'O God, I've never handed over my life to you.' " Graham spent a long time repenting of his lack of consecration and asking God to fill him with the Holy Spirit. Then, according to Olford, "He burst out, 'I have it!' He jumped up from that posture and said, 'This is the turning point in my life.' "[39]

It was clearly the turning point of his brief visit to Pontypridd. That night, the small church, which the previous evening had been sparsely filled, was crammed to overflowing. As Olford told Graham biographer Martin, "As Billy rose to speak he was a man absolutely anointed."[40] When Graham gave the invitation to accept personal salvation, "practically the entire audience responded," according to Olford. After the meeting, Olford drove to his parents' home a few miles away and walked into the kitchen beaming. His father, a retired missionary, saw his son's expression and asked what had so moved him. Olford replied, "Dad, something has happened to Billy Graham. The world is going to hear from this man. He is going to make his mark in history." Indeed, he was.[41]

But following quickly after this spiritual triumph, Graham first had to wrestle with some serious challenges to his faith, challenges that were to come through one of his closest friends and Youth for Christ associates, Charles Templeton.

FOUR:
A NATIONAL PHENOMENON

Charles Templeton (1915–2001) was one of the most gifted and talented Canadians not only of his generation but of the twentieth century. Television broadcaster, novelist, best-selling non-fiction author, sports cartoonist and columnist, newspaper editor, in his life he excelled in more professions than most people would even think of attempting. His achievements, moreover, were set against the backdrop of a broken home and, until he went back to school at age thirty-three, only a ninth-grade education. His father abandoned the family when Templeton was a teenager, forcing the youth to earn a living by selling his cartoon sketches of sports figures to a Toronto newspaper. By his late teens, he had been exposed to more of raw adult life than virtually any of his peers and was drinking heavily and partying late.

At nineteen — in 1934,[1] the same year

that Billy Graham walked down the sawdust trail — Templeton underwent a profound Christian conversion. He had come home in the wee hours and, after talking to his mother, who had experienced a Christian reawakening herself a few months earlier, found himself unaccountably depressed. In his *An Anecdotal Memoir,* he recalls that after the talk with his mother, he had knelt down at his bedside and felt an immense weight of guilt upon himself, a sense of uncleanness. Templeton wrote,

Involuntarily, I began to pray, my face upturned, tears streaming. The only words I could find were, "Lord, come down. Come down. Come down . . ." It may have been minutes later or much longer — there was no sense of time — but I found myself with my head in my hands, crunched small on the floor at the center of a vast emptiness. The agonizing was past. It had left me numb, speechless, immobilized, alone, tense with a sense of expectancy. In a moment, a weight began to lift, a weight as heavy as I. It passed through my thighs, my belly, my chest, my arms, my shoulders and lifted off entirely. I could have leaped over a wall. An ineffable warmth began to suffuse every corpuscle. It seemed that a light had turned on in my chest and its refining fire had cleansed me. I hardly dared breathe, fearing that I might end or alter the moment. I heard myself whispering softly, over and over, "Thank you, Lord. Thank you. Thank you. . . ."[2]

By every reckoning, Templeton had indeed experienced a Christian conversion. He spent much of the next decade as an itinerant evangelist in Canada, started a church in Toronto, and even saw two people remarkably healed of physical conditions as a result of his prayers. Although in his memoirs he writes that, at the time he prayed, he had no faith at all that anything would happen, in one case an infant with a deformed neck was healed, and in the other his own aunt was cured of stomach cancer. By 1945, Templeton was becoming well-known in Canada, and he and Billy Graham met for the first time backstage at the Chicago Stadium at one of the Youth for Christ rallies organized by Torrey Johnson. "You guys have a lot in common," Johnson said, clapping both men on the back. The two established an immediate rapport, and Graham once wrote of Templeton that he was "one of the few men I've ever loved in my life. He and I had been so close."

Templeton was three years older than Graham and was considered by most contemporaries in American evangelism to be the more talented of the two because he was a better and more lucid speaker. For his part, Templeton marveled at the success he and Billy were experiencing at the Youth for Christ rallies — though Graham always had a bigger harvest of conversions — but he felt that the fruits being reaped were due more to their high energy levels and their good looks than to anything connected with God. "We were just these dynamic, handsome young guys," he said later of it all, "you know, full of incredible energy, full of vitality and we were totally committed, every one of us. We . . . really thought we were involved in a dramatic resurgence of revivalism over the country."[3]

Templeton accompanied Graham on his first European visit in 1946, forty-six days that included an evening in Paris where they shared frantic, though in the end successful, efforts to fend off the attentions of attractive French prostitutes. They liked and respected each other, Graham admiring Templeton for his poise in public and his eloquent preaching style, and Templeton admiring Graham for his remarkable harvest of conversions. Templeton even noticed a new boldness in Billy's preaching after Graham's meeting with Stephen Olford. "He seemed to be taking on more and more, a largeness and authority in the pulpit, to be going for a certain magnificence of effect," Templeton reflected later. "It became fascinating, really impressive, to watch him."[4] Torrey Johnson said of Templeton, "The only danger with him was that he was so eloquent, you were taken up with the eloquence more than with the substance."[5]

By 1948, however, their careers had started to take distinctly diverging paths. The previous year, against his better judgment, Billy Graham had accepted the unpaid position of president of Northwestern Schools, a Bible college in Minneapolis. He had no experience in academic administration and little interest in it, and he stayed at the school for only two years, until 1949. Templeton, despite never having finished high school, was eager for more education about Christianity. He felt that he was successful in his preaching chiefly because of "animal magnetism" and that neither his practical nor his pastoral experience made up for his fundamental lack of theological education. In spite of his not having even a high school diploma, much less a university degree (which Graham, of course, had earned at Wheaton), he was admitted to Princeton Theological Seminary in the autumn of 1948, largely on the strength of his reputation as a high-profile evangelist in Canada.

In fact, Templeton was already experiencing a severe erosion of his faith, and eventually he would abandon the ministry, and even Christianity itself. Small shoots of doubt were beginning to spring up now. "I had been so frenetically busy that there had been little time to take stock," he wrote. "But in the occasional quiet moments, questions and doubts surfaced. There was a shallowness in what we were doing in Youth for Christ, a tendency to equate success with numbers. There seemed to be little concern with what happened to the youngsters who responded to our appeals. If the after-service dragged on, we tended to get impatient, wanting to wrap things up and get back to the hotel or to a restaurant for our nightly steak and shop talk. Billy, too, was troubled by it, and we talked about it many times. It undoubtedly contributed to his move from Youth for Christ to conduct his own campaigns."[6]

In Montreat, North Carolina, where Billy

and Ruth had set up house, Templeton tried to persuade Graham to join him at Princeton. Billy, who would have been embarrassed to step down from the presidency of a Bible school to enroll in an American graduate school, countered with a proposal to go to Oxford University in England, if they could gain admittance. But Templeton rejected the idea. Just getting into Princeton had been difficult enough, and he did not want to squander that opportunity. (Among the luminaries Templeton literally bumped into on the street in Princeton: a disheveled-looking Albert Einstein.) Graham and Templeton stayed in touch, but each was warily aware that they were headed in different directions.

For Graham, the desire to do something really big for God was growing stronger. At a conference in Michigan, Billy was outside one night with his Florida Bible Institute classmate Roy Gustafson and another speaker admiring the celestial phenomenon of the aurora borealis, or northern lights, when they began to speculate on when the Lord might return. Being dispensationalists, they thought the current turmoil in the world indicated that the "end times" — the period just before the return of Christ — might be at hand. That prompted Graham to say, "I want the Lord to come, but I would sure like to do something great for him before he comes." The men ended their reflections with prayer, but when it was Billy's turn to pray, the only thing the others heard was a muffled groaning from the ground. Despite the dew and the fact that he was wearing a suit, Graham was spread-eagled on the grass, like a medieval monk, pleading with God to use him even more. "Oh, Lord — let me do something," he implored. "Trust me just to do something for you before you come."[7]

Templeton, meanwhile, was being challenged in his faith by the Princeton seminary's skeptical approach to all of the basics of fundamentalism — biblical authority, the miraculous, and the biblical account of creation. Whenever Graham came through New York, Templeton would come up from Princeton, in New Jersey, and the two men continued their friendship. In a conversation in New York's Taft Hotel, Templeton challenged Graham on the issue of creationism. Billy said that there were conservative scholars who accepted the biblical view of creation, and he rejected Darwinism and the notion that the world had somehow spontaneously evolved from nothingness. "I have observed that when I preach only the word of God, when I preach the Bible straight, no question, no doubts, no hesitations, then I have a *power* — I'm telling you, Chuck [Templeton], a power that's *beyond me,*" Graham insisted. "It's something I don't completely understand. But I just know I've found that when I say, *The Bible says!* — God gives me a power, this power, this incredible *power.* So that's why I have made a decision simply not to think about all these other things anymore."

"You really want to know what you've done, Billy?" Templeton protested. "You've committed intellectual suicide — that's what."[8]

The words stung, and Graham chewed his nails in anguish. A few weeks later, in August 1949, at Forest Home, a conference and retreat center in the San Bernardino Mountains of California, the sparring with Templeton reached its climax. Templeton, on vacation from Princeton, had been invited as a conference speaker, as had Graham. Their conversation took up again those issues that were eating into Templeton's overall Christian faith.

"Billy," Templeton nagged Graham, "you're fifty years out of date. People no longer accept the Bible as being inspired the way you do. Your faith is too simple.

Your language is out of date. You're going to have to learn the new jargon if you are going to be successful in your ministry."[9] Graham was upset and perplexed. He lacked the education and knowledge to contradict Templeton, but to have let his friend's objections to the Bible just hang unanswered in the summer air would have undermined his own confidence even more. Furthermore, a major campaign in Los Angeles was just a few weeks away, so there was no time to lose in deciding how to respond to Templeton's views.

One night after dinner at the conference, Graham retired to his cabin to read those Bible passages that spoke of the reliability of God's Word. Then, in an incident that has become part of the lore of Billy Graham's life — there is even an historical marker on the spot today — Graham went outside and took a brief walk on the wooded hillside. "So I went, and I got my Bible, and I went out in the moonlight," he recalled to biographer John Pollock. "And I got to a stump and I put the Bible on the stump, and I knelt down, and I said, 'Oh God, I cannot prove certain things, I cannot answer some of the questions Chuck is raising and some of the other people are raising, but I accept this Book by faith as the Word of

God.' "[10] Looking back, he reflected, "I never wavered from that moment to this. I know that some have said I committed intellectual suicide, but I never felt such *power* — such power as after I made that decision. I felt confident from then on that what I was quoting *was* the word of God. It gave me a lasting, unassailable strength."[11]

As for Templeton, he was already moving in a completely different direction. "I could not live without facing my doubts," he said. He did not criticize Billy Graham for his Forest Home decision, but said later that much of Graham's preaching was "puerile nonsense."[12] After serving as an evangelist for the National Council of Churches, he left religious work altogether in 1956, was eventually divorced from his wife, and returned to Toronto to write a column for the *Toronto Star.* He had by now essentially lost his Christian faith. Later, he turned his hand, with considerable success, to fiction writing, screenplay writing, newspaper writing and editing, and television interviewing for the Canadian Broadcasting Corporation. A second marriage also ended in divorce, and he married a third time. His agnosticism deepened, and his last book, *Farewell to God: My Reasons for Rejecting the Christian Faith,* published in 1996, preceded by only a few years the onset of Alzheimer's.[13] He remained to the end affectionate toward Billy Graham, who visited him in his final illness.

Author and fellow journalist Lee Strobel also visited Templeton in his last days and writes of Templeton's extraordinary nostalgia for those early years when he had shared the same faith as Billy Graham. The visit took place in Toronto in the late 1990s, by which time Templeton had been descending into the merciless grip of Alzheimer's for three years. In view of Templeton's settled agnosticism, Strobel gently probed him for his thoughts, not on faith itself, but on Christianity's central figure, Jesus Christ. The aging former evangelist said he adored Jesus for his sheer moral character, describing him as the most perfect human being who ever lived. Then, in a strangely moving and revealing comment made with tears in his eyes, but with no elaboration at all, Templeton said, "I . . . miss . . . him!"[14] He meant the Jesus he had known as a young and zealous evangelist. But something interesting happened to Templeton just before he died on June 7, 2001, according to columnist Tom Harpur. Templeton's wife, Madeleine, "who describes herself as somewhere between an atheist and a deist," reported that when she had visited him in the hospital the day before he died, Templeton suddenly became very animated and looked intensely at the ceiling of the room. "Look at them, look at them," he said, apparently having a vision of heavenly beings. "They are so beautiful. They're waiting for me. Oh their eyes, their eyes are so beautiful." Then, with great joy, he said, "I'm coming."[15]

Templeton had stared into the abyss of unbelief in 1949, then hurled himself into it a few years later. Graham had looked down into the same abyss, but strengthened by the power of faith in the Bible, he flew over it in one mighty leap. He knew that his entire life and ministry were built on the Bible being dependable, not just as a historical document but as the Word of God, every chapter and verse God-breathed.

Graham's decision at Forest Home had come none too soon. Just six weeks ahead was the evangelistic rally that would not only propel him into the limelight in evangelical Christian circles but would bring him to national attention. Nothing would ever be the same for Graham after the stunning success of the Los Angeles revival of late September 1949.

Sherwood Wirt, later the founding editor

of the BGEA monthly, *Decision* magazine, says that a key to the success of the Los Angeles meetings was an all-night prayer meeting held in the Rainbow Room of the Westminster Hotel in Winona Lake, Indiana, on July 13, 1949, even before Graham was challenged by Templeton at the Lake Forest conference. "The leaders had been meeting all week . . . talking evangelism, and they yearned for more power of the Holy Spirit to be manifested . . . Therefore they scheduled an all-night prayer meeting, hoping to go beyond human methods and efforts to God himself," Wirt wrote. By 3 a.m., the prayer meeting had been going for five hours. Cliff Barrows, part of Graham's team since the first half of the 1940s, recalls that night: "We were on our faces before the Lord. Some of us were under the piano praying. The Spirit of God moved in our hearts, breaking us and revealing our pride."

Christ for Greater Los Angeles, a group of local businessmen, had organized the rally — the term *crusade* was not used until later — which was held in large Ringling Bros. circus tents erected on a vacant parking lot at the intersection of Washington and Hill Streets. With a capacity of six thousand people, it was believed to be the largest revival tent ever set up and became known as "the Canvas Cathedral." Nervous and nail-biting as ever, Graham urged the businessmen's group to spend freely on pre-meeting publicity: flyers and posters touting "America's Sensational Young Evangelist" and "Visit the Canvas Cathedral and the Steeple of Light." The musical couple Cliff and Billie Barrows was on hand, along with soloist George Beverly Shea, and, of course, Grady Wilson, Graham's boyhood friend. Graham himself was dressed only slightly less flamboyantly than in the Youth for Christ days, a silk handkerchief invariably hanging out of the breast pocket of his dapper, usually double-breasted suits. In those early days, dazzling ties, colored shirts, and blue suede shoes were the mainstay of Graham's attire.

The Christ for Greater Los Angeles revival was originally scheduled for three weeks, but so many people either had to be turned away or had to settle for listening to the rally from outside the tents that the meetings were extended by four weeks, and then extended again, to a total of eight weeks altogether. The interest of local and national newspapers was piqued when Stuart Hamblen, a big Texas radio personality and a heavy drinker and gambler as well, announced on air that he had been converted at the Canvas Cathedral. His conversion was followed by that of convicted felon and wiretapper Jim Vaus and former Olympian Louis Zamperini, who had survived a World War II combat plane crash in the Pacific Ocean and internment in a Japanese POW camp. Publishing magnate William Randolph Hearst instructed his local and national newspapers to give the revival blanket coverage, leading to the celebrated quote of one reporter saying to Graham as they surveyed the gathering press hordes at the tent's entrance, "You've been kissed by William Randolph Hearst," and the oft-repeated anecdote that Hearst had cabled his editors with the terse instruction, "Puff Graham." (Hearst's son, William Randolph Hearst Jr., later denied the anecdote.) But Graham had been kissed by more than just Hearst: the *New York Times, Time, Life,* and *Newsweek* all ran stories on the Los Angeles revival phenomenon.

By the time of his closing sermon at the Canvas Cathedral on November 20, 1949, Graham had preached sixty-five full sermons and given hundreds of other talks, and he had basically run out of sermon topics. He pressed into service every clergyman he knew to provide him with sermon material. An estimated 350,000 Angelenos heard him preach, and 3,000 people had come forward to indicate "decisions" for Christ. "I do not believe that any man, any man, can solve the problems of life without Jesus Christ," Graham said in his closing sermon. "There are tremendous marital problems, there are physical problems, there are problems of sin and habit that cannot be solved without the person of our Lord, Jesus Christ. Have you trusted Christ as your savior? Tonight I am trying to tell you as we close that the Lord Jesus Christ can be received, your sin forgiven, your burdens lifted, your problems solved, by turning your life over to Jesus Christ."[18] It sounds today idealistically simple, but in 1949 the sheer directness of it all won over thousands.

The power of Billy Graham's evangelistic appeal lay in good measure in his transparent sincerity, his obviously guileless passion to preach salvation to all who would listen. But even Billy was not immune to the pull of Hollywood. Despite the pressures of the revival, the demands of sermon preparation, and the toll of sheer exhaustion — he said he lost twenty pounds during the Los Angeles revival — Graham took time off to meet with Hollywood stars, including Jimmy Stewart, and even to take a screen test for movie mogul Cecil B. DeMille. For Gra-

113

ham, at thirty going on thirty-one, it was all a bit heady.

Two characteristics of Billy Graham's lifelong preaching pattern were apparent in Los Angeles: repeated citations from the Bible, invariably prefaced by the words, "The Bible says . . . ," and references to national and international headline-grabbing events that prompted discussion of serious issues. Graham sounded a strong anti-communist theme several times in his sermons, warning that Los Angeles was the third American city, after New York and Chicago, to be marked out as a target for Soviet nuclear weapons, the existence of which President Truman had announced a few days earlier. "Do you know that the Fifth Columnists, called Communists, are more rampant in Los Angeles than any other city in America?" he thundered at his audiences, his hands slashing down in a karate chop-like move. "God is giving us a desperate choice, a choice of either revival or judgment. There is no alternative! If Sodom and Gomorrah could not get away with sin, if Pompeii and Rome could not escape, neither can Los Angeles! Judgment is coming just as sure as I'm standing here."[19] While in Los Angeles, Graham developed a theme to which he would return many times in the 1950s, and which, admittedly, many other preachers also took up in that decade and later: communism was itself a religion, an anti-God religion. "Western culture and its fruits had its foundations in the Bible, the Word of God, and in the revivals of the seventeenth and eighteenth centuries," he stormed, pacing up and down on the platform. "Communism, on the other hand, has decided against God, against Christ, against the Bible, and against all religion. Communism is not only an economic interpretation of life — communism is a religion that is inspired, directed, and motivated by the devil himself who has declared war against Almighty God."[20]

Graham's theatrical style of preaching recalled some of the greatest preachers of past revivals: Jonathan Edwards, George Whitefield, and, of course, Billy Sunday. He was variously called "Barrymore of the Bible," "Gabriel in Gabardine," and "Beverly Hills John the Baptist." His thespian leaps, which caused Ruth to roll her eyes and good-naturedly mock him, probably peaked a few months later, at rallies in Boston, but eventually he did tone down the theatrics. Graham's delight in using anecdotes, however, as well as frightening headlines and statistics (sometimes snatched with only partial accuracy from news reports that he had only half-digested), and story-telling as a way of enrapturing his audiences, remained features of his preaching throughout his life.

He meticulously planned and prepared his sermons, the occasional misquoted news facts notwithstanding. He would listen to tapes of his earlier messages, sometimes the one given just the night before, looking for some point that could have been phrased better. He became extraordinarily attentive to his audiences, able to see, from several yards away, a listener's eyes blink and know then that he needed to speed up or slow down the tempo of his delivery to keep the audience's attention. The description of Graham as "God's machine gun" was first used by journalists who wrote about him in Los Angeles.

For all of the intense prayer backing, the preparation, the publicity, and the serendipity of high-profile conversions, Graham was dumbfounded by the success of the Los Angeles rallies. With characteristic piety and humility, he acknowledged again and again that the work must be God's and that he was merely a fortunate participant. Ruth shared this view. "We felt we were just spectators," she said. "God was doing something, and Billy and I were just watching."[21] When the crusade was over, and as their train back to Minneapolis was pulling out of the Los Angeles station on November 21, husband and wife sank to their knees in gratitude. In Billy's case, it was also exhaustion.

The return to Northwestern Schools, however, was again brief. At the very end of 1949, Graham was off to a series of meetings in Boston. Some of Boston's liberal mainline denominations and its Unitarian churches sniffed that the young zealot was setting Christianity back a hundred years. Graham's reply — which he has repeated countless times in response to the same complaint in the years to follow — was that he wanted to set Christianity back 1,900 years, to the zeal of the first-century church. In contrast to the reception from Boston's Protestant churches, the Roman Catholic Church, in a generous foreshadowing of the Vatican's later outreach to other branches of Christendom, responded warmly to Billy's presence. "Bravo Billy!" the *Pilot,* the official archdiocese publication, cheered in the headline of one of its editorials.[22] What had been scheduled as a single New Year's Eve service in Mechanics Hall attracted a crowd of six thousand. Additional meetings were hastily added, but even so, thousands had to be turned away.

In Boston, Graham took one theme to an extreme that was to haunt him five years later, when the British media mocked him mercilessly at the beginning of an ultimately triumphant crusade in Harringay, England. He somewhat rashly plunged into detailed descriptions of heaven, telling his Boston audience that it was "sixteen hundred miles long, sixteen hundred miles wide, and sixteen hundred miles high." How would the saints spend their time there? He knew the answer: "We are going to sit around the fireplace and have parties and the angels will wait on us and we'll drive down the golden streets in a yellow Cadillac convertible."[23] He continued, too, on the theme of the apocalyptic menace of communism, predicting that Joseph Stalin was about to be deified, with his birthday as celebrated as Christmas in Christian countries. Communism itself was described as "a fanatic religion supernaturally empowered by the devil to counteract Christianity."[24]

Even more tellingly, Graham raised the premillennialist, dispensationalist teaching of the end times, saying that the Rapture might occur within ten to fifteen years (Hal

118

Lindsey, author of *The Late Great Planet Earth* a quarter century later, also predicted that it might come within a decade or so) and vividly depicted the scene. "Wait till those gravestones start popping like popcorn in a popper," he told mesmerized Bostonians. "Oh boy! Won't it be wonderful when those gravestones start popping?"[25] Graham was now preaching the same dispensationalist doctrine that his mother had adopted when she became more pious in her religious beliefs.

The doctrine was first introduced by J. N. Darby (1800–1882), an Irish clergyman in the Church of England. In many ways the father of Protestant fundamentalism, Darby was the founder of the denomination called the Plymouth Brethren, but his main influence, which was profound on fundamentalism, was his doctrine of dispensationalism. Darby's dispensationalism was also to profoundly influence evangelical Protestantism as a whole through *The Scofield Reference Bible,* an annotated version of the King James Bible that was first published in 1909 and contributed to the growing influence of premillennial dispensationalism, that is, the view that the millennial rule of Christ would be preceded first by the Rapture of the saints, and then by the Second Coming.

Darby believed that the Rapture would be followed by a period called the Tribulation (a term denoting great persecution and referred to in the last book of the Bible, Revelation), Armageddon (a great battle in which Christ would be victorious over all his enemies), and then Christ's millennial rule of one thousand years. In effect, all dispensationalists are premillennialists — they believe that the Millennium has not yet arrived — but not all premillennialists are dispensationalists. The doctrine of the secret Rapture was not entirely new to Christian history, but had been rare until Darby rendered it mainstream.

The Scofield Reference Bible quickly came to be the annotated version of the Bible by which fundamentalists defined their faith. Later, it became one of the teaching hallmarks of Dallas Theological Seminary, founded in 1924 and probably the most influential seminary in the world for teaching dispensationalism. Among its students was Hal Lindsey, the previously mentioned author of the 1970s bestseller, *The Late Great Planet Earth.* The more recent blockbuster, the *Left Behind* novels, is also based on this view of end-of-the-world events, and its coauthor, Tim LaHaye, was exposed to a full range of fundamentalist teaching when he was a student at Bob Jones University.

Though Billy Graham has modulated major elements of his fundamental beliefs over the years — causing some fundamentalists to charge that he has betrayed Christianity itself (a controversy to be examined in Chapter Six) — in Boston in 1950, the imagery of the premillennialist, dispensationalist approach to Christ's second coming was very real to him, and he was still very much rooted in the fundamentalist worldview. Hell, for example, he believed in the early 1950s to be an actual place, and certainly some of the power of his preaching may have derived from his willingness to talk about it in his sermons. Later in his career, especially when questioned by journalists on the subject of hell, he sounded much more equivocal about describing it as an actual place of burning fire. In one of his first books, *Peace with God,* published in 1953, Graham acknowledged that the traditional teaching on hell was "one of the hardest of all teachings of Christianity to receive." But, he insisted, "scores of passages of Scripture could be quoted to support the fact that the Bible does teach there is hell for every man who willingly and knowingly rejects Christ as Lord and Savior."[26]

In Boston, the original New Year's Eve

meeting was immediately extended to nine days to accommodate the record numbers, but because of the great interest and, indeed, curiosity that Billy Graham evoked, the meetings were extended again to eighteen days. Graham hammed up his performances, interpreting Bible stories with slangy modernisms (calling an Old Testament feast "a shindig," for example) and acting out various biblical roles with theatrical flair. Preaching one night on the prodigal son, he role-played tossing slops to the hogs as if he had been raised on a hog farm. Ruth was not impressed. "As an actor," she opined, "I'm afraid he is pretty much a ham. When he starts that kind of acting sermon, I usually start to squirm."[27] One of Ruth Graham's many considerable contributions to their marriage has been a healthy irreverence when Billy has seemed on the point of taking too seriously some of his own adoring publicity.

Graham left Boston for a scheduled series of meetings in Toronto, but with a deep feeling of discomfort. Had he missed God by not extending the New England meetings even further? He wasn't sure, and the question of how much to plan and how much to leave to God's spontaneous response was one that plagued him for many years.

Perhaps he wondered whether more Graham meetings might have reignited a spiritually dead New England in the way that George Whitefield and Jonathan Edwards ignited America's Great Awakening of the 1730s and 1740s.

Whatever the case, the momentum of the Billy Graham crusades was now gathering steam. After the breakthrough in Los Angeles, invitations were coming in thick and fast to the fledgling Graham team. When he went to South Carolina in March 1950 for the first of several visits over the next few decades, he discovered the fascination of association with political power, though later he was also to experience its perils. Governor Strom Thurmond, who had run for president against President Truman in 1948 and won four Southern states and thirty-nine electoral votes, treated Graham as something of a Protestant pope for South Carolina. Thurmond insisted that Graham stay in the governor's mansion, arranged for him to speak to the state assembly, and invited as guests on Graham's platform a host of prominent political and journalistic figures.

One of the journalists was Henry Luce, the founder and publisher of *Time* magazine, as well as the co-founder of the Time Inc.

empire that then included *Life, Fortune,* and *Sports Illustrated.* Luce had already ensured that Graham's Los Angeles phenomenon was given full coverage. Now the publishing magnate, who certainly appreciated Graham's strongly anti-communist views, was interested in whether the evangelist might be the herald of a major change in mind-set in America. The son of a prominent missionary to China, Luce was a keen Presbyterian, and although not a fundamentalist, as a journalist he was a perceptive observer of trends in religion worldwide. He spent hours with Graham in the governor's mansion, talking about what later was to be called the "new evangelicalism."

Staying with Strom Thurmond was one thing, but being received at the White House was another. Graham pushed hard for an invitation to meet President Truman, and was finally successful in July 1950. The meeting, however, was a disaster and ensured that, if Billy Graham was a friend to many presidents, Truman was not among them. The president, although a solid Baptist like his parents and grandparents and raised with a thorough knowledge of the Bible and a high emphasis on ethics, did not like public displays of religion and was suspicious of the motives of famous evangelists. He agreed to see Graham, Cliff Barrows, Grady Wilson, and Graham's newly appointed press aide, Gerald Beavan, only after intense lobbying by Billy.

The four young men, all dressed in light-colored suits — biographer Martin brilliantly described them as looking like "hospital orderlies at the racetrack"[28] — met with the president for the scheduled thirty minutes, at the end of which Graham asked if they could pray together. "I don't suppose it could do any harm," Truman responded with characteristic dryness. But when the four men exited the Oval Office and promptly informed the waiting press corps that they had prayed with the president, then allowed themselves to be photographed kneeling on the White House grounds, Truman was furious. He later denounced Billy as "one of those counterfeits" and made clear that Graham's claims of friendship with several presidents did not apply to Truman himself.[29] Although Truman, long after he had left office, softened toward Graham, the gaffe taught Billy a hard lesson: never tell the public about your private meetings with world leaders.

The year 1950 marked another milestone in Billy Graham's career: the creation of the Billy Graham Evangelistic Association.

While preaching at a crusade in Portland, Oregon, in July, Graham was approached by advertising mogul Walter Bennett and by Graham's future son-in-law Ted Dienert with a proposal to go on nationally syndicated radio on a weekly basis. Doing so, however, would require an initial outlay of $25,000 to buy air rights for the program. In another of those hagiographical moments recounted repeatedly in biographies, Graham decided that he would only go ahead with the proposal if the entire amount could be collected by midnight that day as unsolicited offerings, without any announcement of the need. It was. But in order not to be subject to heavy taxes, the money needed to be deposited in a not-for-profit account. Thus was born the Billy Graham Evangelistic Association, an organization that in 1950 had only one employee in a tiny office in Minneapolis. By the time its headquarters was relocated to a sixty-three-acre site in Charlotte, North Carolina, in 2003, it had grown into a diverse cottage industry that employed 450 people. *The Hour of Decision,* the show that was the trigger for the creation of the association, became the most popular radio religious broadcast ever, and within months was being aired on all 350 ABC network stations. The show's name had been Ruth's idea.

The creation of the BGEA came none too soon for Billy Graham's reputation. He had long known of the suspicion many Americans held toward traveling evangelists, some of whom had indeed been plain hucksters. The stereotype had been fixed for all time in the American imagination by the Sinclair Lewis novel, *Elmer Gantry,* in which the Baptist minister of the book's title is both a philanderer and a crook. One afternoon in November 1948, while still with Youth for Christ, Billy had invited George Beverly Shea, Cliff Barrows, and Grady Wilson to his Modesto, California, hotel room to discuss a thorny problem: how to avoid the great snares that had befallen so many evangelists and indeed men of the cloth in general. They quickly concurred that sex, money, and worldly glory were the greatest, ever-present temptations. To deal with sexual temptation, the four men decided that, as long as they were in association with each other, none would ever be alone in a room or travel alone in a vehicle with a woman who was not his wife. With regard to money, they agreed that the "love offerings" usually taken during evangelistic meetings were necessary to pay for local expenses, but they also agreed that these would not be emphasized during the meetings. To avoid the pitfalls of worldly glory, the four men decided to accept, as far as possible, the crowd estimates of local police or other officials, so as to forestall any suggestion of exaggeration. Finally, Graham himself suggested that none of them should make public criticism of any other Christian pastor or leader, in order to overcome the legacy of men, such as Mordecai Ham, who made a point of criticizing local clergy when they arrived in a town to preach.

The "Modesto Manifesto," as it came to be called, proved its worth as far as keeping at bay sexual temptation and exaggeration of numbers. But it took an embarrassment in December 1950, when a photograph of a broadly grinning Graham appeared in a local newspaper alongside a photograph of happy crusade workers holding up big bags of "love offerings" from the just-concluded Atlanta meetings, to make him realize that he needed to be on a fixed salary to avoid any suspicion that he was profiting from the large crowds drawn to his preaching. He selected the initial figure of $15,000, the salary of a senior pastor at any large church of the time. By 2005, his salary had risen to close to $200,000, which, though on the high end, was still well within the salary range for a senior pastor in a large church.[30]

The "Modesto Manifesto," however, failed to foresee another, more subtle temptation for the young evangelist: proximity to the allure of political power. Graham had first experienced this in Columbia, South Carolina, when Governor Strom Thurmond accorded Billy the reverence appropriate to a church prelate. The following year, 1951, was the year before a presidential election, and it brought to Graham the first whiff of the lure of national political power. He was aware of the power and influence his anti-communist crusading was having, particularly now that the United States was in the second year of the Korean War. He had been stung by the debacle of the meeting with President Truman, but he continued to hold out hope that he could persuade Truman to lend his prestige to a crusade by showing up at one. He grew increasingly critical of the president, however, in Truman's final year in office, albeit indirectly. In words that hinted at the force that years later would be called the Religious Right, Graham warned, "The Christian people of America will not sit idly by in [the presidential election of] 1952. [They] are going to vote as a bloc for the man with the strongest moral and spiritual platform, regardless of his views on other matters."[31] Truman was not impressed. In one final effort to enlist the president in his evangelization efforts, Graham sought Truman's support for his January–February 1952 crusade in Washington, DC, either in the form of a presidential endorsement or a presidential appearance for at least one session. The White House politely but firmly declined. Though Graham succeeded in getting permission, through a special Act of Congress, to address a mammoth crowd — estimated to be bigger than the turnout at most inaugurations of the time — on the steps of the Capitol, Truman declined to lend his presidential prestige to any of Graham's activities.

Graham himself made statements in 1951 and 1952 that could be interpreted as a bid for political office. As the political atmosphere in the United States began to heat up, his remarks raised the eyebrows of those with keen political antennae. "If I could run as president of the United States today on a platform of calling the people back to God, back to Christ, back to the Bible, I'd be elected," he said in February 1952.[32] A few months later, he said that several congressmen had suggested he run for the Senate from North Carolina in the 1952 election.

The implication: it wasn't such a far-fetched idea.

Graham's political interests, however, were focused more on who would next occupy the White House. In November 1951, at the prompting of a Texas oil tycoon, Sid Richardson, who was on close terms with several political figures, Graham wrote to Dwight Eisenhower, then in Paris where he was Commander at the Supreme Headquarters Allied Powers Europe, urging the popular general to consider a 1952 presidential bid. Eisenhower, already under pressure from multiple sources to enter the race, was intrigued by the letter and invited Graham to visit him when he was next in Europe. This Graham did in March 1952, and the two men spent two hours in warm conversation. Eisenhower had not publicly indicated whether he would enter the presidential race already fast approaching, but the two men did talk about the November election. Graham indicated that, privately, he strongly supported the general on moral issues, even though he would be unable to give him a public endorsement.[33] This early association with Eisenhower was the start of Graham's decades-long ties to the heights of national and international power. Although he never did run for any political office, Graham's impact on the American political scene perhaps was greater than if he had been an elected — or even appointed — government official, a notion that will be considered in more detail in later chapters focusing on the evangelist's political influence.

Graham's travels and increasing proximity to power, however, were taking a heavy toll on his family. The task of raising a growing brood of children more than ever fell upon his wife, Ruth. Their first child, Gigi, was born in September 1945, when Billy Graham was still officially employed as pastor of Western Springs Baptist Church. The others followed in quick succession: two more girls — Ann (1948) and Ruth Jr., also called "Bunny" (1950) — followed by Franklin (1952) and finally Nelson, also called Ned, in 1958.

Once Graham burst upon the national scene after the 1949 Canvas Cathedral rallies in Los Angeles, the modest home the family occupied in Montreat, North Carolina, became something of a pilgrim destination for America's faithful, hoping to get a glimpse of the nation's most famous evangelist. Sometimes the family resorted to crawling across a room below the windowsill to avoid the hordes of curious gawkers. At other times, Ruth saw strangers peering in the bedroom window. In 1954, the couple took measures to ensure genuine privacy for the family by purchasing two hundred acres of mountain land — for which they paid $12.50 to $14 an acre at the time — that they could entirely fence in and protect from the inquisitive. The house, creatively designed and decorated under Ruth's direction, became a comfortable rural retreat called Little Piney Cove, and was ready for occupation in 1956.

By 1953, Billy Graham was hitting his stride as America's dynamic young evangelist, preaching annually in crusades in a half dozen cities across the country, a pattern he was to continue steadily for nearly five more decades. In June 1953, he achieved something of a milestone in a crusade in Dallas, filling the 75,504 seats in the Cotton Bowl Stadium in what at the time was the largest evangelical meeting in American history. Reporters were constantly at his side, prodding him for opinions on a range of topics, many of which he had little expertise in. He was such a focus of media attention that for two years in the mid-1950s, more newspaper and magazine space was devoted to coverage of Billy Graham than to anyone else in the country, including the president.[34]

When Eisenhower took office in January 1953, the new president said he hoped the nation would undergo a spiritual renewal. And indeed, renewal began even during his first term in office. Did Billy Graham play a major role in this? Very likely. Among other outward indicators of this transformation, which will be examined in greater detail in Chapter Eight, devout Christians in Congress gathered in 1953 to start up what was at first called the Presidential Prayer Breakfast but later, in the 1960s, became the National Prayer Breakfast. Both President Eisenhower and Billy Graham were present at the inaugural breakfast, setting a precedent that has secured the attendance of every US president since then, on an annual basis, early in February. For most of those years, Billy Graham's attendance has been *de rigueur* as well.

By emerging quite suddenly on the national scene and preaching a fiery brand of Christianity not delivered with such power since the days of Billy Sunday, Billy Graham had succeeded in returning personal spiritual salvation to a conspicuous place in American national life. The French historian Alexis de Tocqueville in his 1835 book *Democracy in America* had written of his astonishment at the prominence of religion in American society, but as Woodrow Wilson experienced, many had reacted with jaded cynicism — as many Americans and foreigners continue to do — to expressions of personal piety on the part of the American chief executive. Graham had succeeded in rendering an evangelistic, not to say fundamentalist, version of Christianity more respectable in the United States than at any time since before the 1925 Scopes trial. The challenge he now faced was a simple though daunting one: could the "hot gospel" formula, apparently so successful in his home country, be exported? In 1954, Billy Graham took it to a country that seemed, initially, dismally unsympathetic to it: England.

FIVE:
HARRINGAY AND THE WORLD

Billy Graham's thirteen-week Harringay crusade in London in 1954 remains an epochal experience in the evangelist's life. It was a career milestone both in terms of attendance at his speaking engagements and in the number of people who signed cards indicating a "decision" to receive Jesus Christ. The crusade had a lasting impact on Britain, altering the composition of the clergy of the Church of England in ways that would influence the country for decades to come. Probably only the Australia and New Zealand Southern Cross crusade in 1959 had a similarly huge national impact, but Harringay was the first instance of Graham's astonishing appeal outside the United States.

The experience changed Billy Graham in an equally profound way, by broadening his concept of what constitutes Christendom and enabling him to recognize fellow Christians among those whose backgrounds, upbringing, and even theology differed profoundly from his own. In the two decades to follow, Graham's increasingly extensive world travels would solidify these new views and bring about an evolution in his theology that would render him broadly open to the widest variety of historically orthodox Christian traditions. In 1954, at the outset of his foreign travels, Graham was still very much a fundamentalist. That began to change as a result of his experiences in England, where he met Christians with whom he recognized a commonality of Christian spirit but who were neither fundamentalist nor even part of the emerging neo-evangelical movement. This change was evident in the way Graham described himself just a year later, for example, he said in Scotland that he was not a fundamentalist or a modernist.

By 1954, Billy Graham thought that he knew Britain well, having first traveled there in 1946 — twice, for Youth for Christ rallies. Other visits had followed, most recently on the same 1952 trip to meet General Dwight D. Eisenhower in Paris. Stopping in London following that meeting, he addressed seven hundred clergymen who wanted to know if his dramatically successful crusades in the United States could be replicated in the United Kingdom. Graham, with his instinctive enthusiasm for all new and adventurous Christian projects, assured them that success was certain. After all, he himself, in his sermons in the United States, had frequently bemoaned England's sorry spiritual condition, so how could he respond otherwise to an opportunity to have a spiritual impact on the United Kingdom? Graham was not alone in holding a dire view of Britain's spiritual condition; it was shared by some in high levels of power. None other than US Secretary of State John Foster Dulles had opined, "Britain must have a spiritual renaissance to survive."[1]

The invitation to conduct a crusade in London had been extended by Britain's Evangelical Alliance, an association of evangelically minded clergy and laypeople, founded in 1846, but it was personally conveyed by two men who traveled all the way from England to meet with Graham in 1952. The meeting took place in a hospital in Asheville, North Carolina, where Ruth was about to give birth to their first son, Franklin. The two emissaries from Britain were F. Roy Cattell, the Evangelical Alliance's secretary, and John Cordle (1912–2004), the treasurer of the World Evangelical Alliance and a man who was to become a disparaging critic of what he saw as a growing immorality in British public life. Elected to Parliament in 1959, Cordle was later overtaken by both personal tragedy — both his grandson and granddaughter were killed in separate accidents — and personal scandal. He went through two bitter divorces and was found guilty of contempt of Parliament by a House of Commons committee for accepting money from a company whose interests he had promoted in the Commons. But Cordle in the early 1950s was scandal-free and an advocate of spiritual revival in Britain. He had met Billy on one of Graham's 1946 trips to England with Youth for Christ, and Cordle had bigger things in mind for the American evangelist than freezing churches in the mountains of Wales. The British organizing committee took a three-month option on the twelve thousand-seat Harringay Stadium, a somewhat down-market indoor venue of greyhound races, boxing matches, and occasionally, the circus in north London.

Back in the United States, fund-raising began for the substantial sum needed to finance the crusade. Though many on Graham's team were willing to go to London with only their expenses covered, Billy, with his characteristic passion for publicity, had pushed for $50,000 to be spent on crusade promotion, an absolutely astronomic sum by British standards of the time. Posters with nothing more than "Hear Billy Graham" and a photograph of him were slapped on walls and columns all over London.

Carelessness in the fund-raising very nearly sank the crusade before it had even started. A calendar given to BGEA financial supporters bluntly stated, "What Hitler's bombs could not do, socialism with its accompanying evils shortly accomplished." The calendar, which Graham later claimed had erroneously used the word "socialism" instead of "secularism," fell into the hands of Hannen Swaffer (1879–1962), a sometime-theater critic and columnist for the left-leaning *Daily Herald* newspaper and a leading figure in British journalism of the day. Swaffer, who once called playwright George Bernard Shaw "a tiresome old driveler," shared the strange bedfellow enthusiasms of socialism and spiritualism. As a socialist, he would surely have caught wind of Billy Graham's fulminations against communism and his unflattering comments about Britain's first Labour government (1945–1951). As a spiritualist, he would have harbored a visceral hostility toward any

Christian evangelist, because spiritualists completely reject the divinity of Jesus Christ, the biblical notion of sin, and, for that matter, the existence of hell. "Wild fanaticism," he called Graham's appeals to conversion. "Apologize — or stay away!" thundered the headline for Swaffer's column.[2]

Taking up the same cudgels, Labour Party Member of Parliament Geoffrey de Freitas announced plans to challenge Graham's right to be admitted to Britain at all. The American, he claimed, was "interfering in British politics under the guise of religion."[3] The British press, never in a hurry to pass up a good controversy, licked its chops in anticipation of the fun it would have at the expense of the earnest young evangelist. London's *Evening News* grunted that Graham was "an American hot gospel specialist." "Like a Biblical *Baedeker*," it said, hitting its stride, "he takes his listeners strolling down Pavements of Gold, introduces them to a rippling-muscled Christ, who resembles Charles Atlas with a halo, then drops them abruptly in the Lake of Fire for a sample scalding."[4] Shades of Billy's Boston dramatics were coming back to haunt him.

The ship that Billy and Ruth took to Britain in March 1954, the SS *United States,* stopped briefly in Le Havre, France, where a horde of British reporters, smelling blood, boarded. The reception was even worse on arrival in Southampton, when one reporter crassly asked Ruth if Billy carried around his personal pitcher of water for baptisms. (The question, of course, belied the reporter's ignorance about Baptists: a reference to a personal water tank would have been more apt.) Even before the ship docked, however, Graham had sent out meek apologies to both de Freitas and Swaffer, and the crusade's advance team in London was busy putting out fires too.

If Billy Graham thought his arrival was off to a desultory start, he was mistaken. Maurice Rowlandson, the BGEA's British representative, remembers pleading with the stationmaster at London's Waterloo station to assign a bigger platform for the Graham's train arriving from Southampton. "No way," the stationmaster responded. "I've coped with the arrival of hundreds of film stars, and none of them have had more than a handful of fans to meet them. The platform we have chosen will be quite adequate." As Rowlandson despairingly left the stationmaster's office, a policeman came bounding up the stairs shouting excitedly that thousands of people had gathered and the boat train, as it was called, would have to come in to a larger platform or someone would surely be injured. The stationmaster capitulated.[5] As the train pulled in, a crowd of four thousand people jostled each other for a view of the Grahams and sang the traditional hymn "To God Be the Glory." It was the largest crowd at Waterloo in thirty years, since the 1924 arrival of screen legends Mary Pickford and Douglas Fairbanks. A station official on seeing the turnout for the evangelist, cracked, "If these are the Christians, it's time to release the lions."

In fact, the "lions," in the form of the establishment of the Church of England and Britain's irreverent tabloid press, were already prowling about. The British Council of Churches, representing the majority of Christians and church organizations in the United Kingdom, had not joined with the Evangelical Alliance in inviting Graham, and the archbishop of Canterbury at the time, Geoffrey Fisher, let it be known that he did not care for the American evangelist's theology, style, or approach to evangelism. Only one prominent Anglican, Suffragan (i.e., deputy) Bishop of Barking Hugh Gough, was on the platform with Graham at the evangelist's first press conference in London. He dryly noted, "Well, Billy, if you are to be a fool for Christ's sake, I'll be a fool with you."[6]

The press was determined to paint him as that "fool." A typical Fleet Street broadsheet, the *People,* ran a headline calling Graham "Silly Billy," and griped that "being bulldozed into loving God by ecstatic young men who talk about Him with easy familiarity is something which makes the biggest British sinner shudder."[7] Despite these growls from prickly Brits, however, and despite Graham's own first-night terror that the crusade might be a terrible flop, it was anything but. Even on that first night, March 1, 1954, a damp, rainy evening, the stadium was jam-packed, and 178 people came forward. The second night had a few spare seats, because the rain had turned to snow, but for the next three months the stadium was packed every night. The faithful, the undecided, and the just-plain-curious came in numbers that astonished not just the Brits but Graham and his aides as well.

One of those who attended the first night was the prominent British television journalist Sir David Frost. When I interviewed him in London in 2001, Frost, whose father was a Methodist minister, said he had gone with the youth group of his father's church to hear Graham and would have gone forward as an "inquirer" if he had not been afraid that the church bus might leave without him. Recalling that he was fifteen at the time and "at a crossroads," he said, "I was deeply affected by what I heard."[8] "That first rally at Harringay made religion come alive for me, really," he told Mark Elsdon-Dew, the editor of *Alpha News*, a newspaper published by the worldwide evangelism program called Alpha. He said of Graham, "Through the years, I have found him a tremendously wise man, a great example to people."

The impact of the Harringay crusade during its three-month run was palpable. On the London subway, better known as "the tube," crowds returning home from the crusade in the late evening broke into spontaneous hymn singing. Stephen Olford, who had led Graham to a new understanding of the role of the Holy Spirit eight years earlier, had suggested that church members riding church-rented buses to the crusade each commit to bring along with them one non-churchgoer. It was called Operation Andrew, and it brought to Harringay a much wider swathe of society than would normally attend crusades.

The press softened too, metamorphosing from hostile and irreverent at the outset to attentive, then sympathetic, and then openly supportive. It was one of the most remarkable transformations of media attitudes in Britain's recent history. One of Graham's most biting detractors had been William Connor, a columnist who wrote under the name Cassandra for the pro–Labour Party tabloid, the *Daily Mirror.* Stung by Connor's sniping, yet determined to love his enemies, Graham wrote a letter to the columnist, expressing admiration for his way with words and suggesting that they meet. Connor replied with the witty suggestion that they meet in a pub called "The Baptist's Head." "You could drink what you choose," Connor wrote, "while I sin quietly with a little beer." Graham accepted.

Connor wrote after the meeting, "He came into the Baptist's Head absolutely at home — a teetotaler and abstainer able to make himself completely at ease in the spit and sawdust department, a difficult thing to do. He has a kind of ferocious cordiality that scares ordinary sinners stone-cold. I never thought that friendliness could have such a sharp, cutting edge. I never thought that simplicity could cudgel us sinners so . . . hard. We live and learn. The bloke means everything he says. And in this country he has been welcomed with an exuberance that makes us blush behind our precious Anglo-Saxon reserve."[9]

Connor's about-face reflected two features of the Harringay crusade: Billy Graham demonstrating once again his astounding personal humility in the face of sometimes vitriolic criticism, and, on the part of Britons from all walks of life, an almost desperate openness for any way out of the drab, pinched existence of the postwar years. Graham's approach clearly struck a chord. "We have not come here to the city of London to save England," he told the crowds at Harringay. "We haven't come with any great ideas that we are going to tell you how to do it. We haven't come to reform you."[10]

David Winter, a British evangelical who trained to be a counselor at Harringay, wrote much later in reflecting on the whole experience that the response was hard to account for in terms of Graham's actual performance as a preacher. He still spoke too fast — though critical comments at Harringay taught him that he definitely *had* to slow down — and, according to Winter, "he was not particularly eloquent, certainly not profound, seldom ever memorable."[11] (This view that Graham's preaching was not memorable is challenged by my sister,

Susan Philips, who a half century after attending one of the Harringay meetings can still quote from Graham's sermon on 2 Kings 9, about the judgment on Ahab's family, executed by the army officer Jehu.) Nevertheless, Winter adds, almost in bewilderment, "he talked in the language of ordinary people and related the gospel message to the world in which I lived. He read the newspapers and kept up with world events. He understood and could employ for his own purpose the insecurity and latent terror of that first nuclear generation."[12]

The phenomenal success of the Harringay crusade secured for Graham invitations to address audiences at Oxford and Cambridge universities as well as other academic institutions. When a student in a monkey suit crashed through a window high up in the auditorium at the London School of Economics during Graham's address, in an obvious attempt to mock fundamentalist opposition to the theory of evolution, Billy had the wit to quip, "He reminds me of my ancestors." Then, as the audience of students laughed appreciatively, he added the zinger, "Of course, all my ancestors came from Britain." His audience roared and seemed won over from that point on.[13]

As the British media turned completely around, so did the British establishment. On the last day of the crusade, in Wembley Stadium, the venue of international soccer and rugby games, the archbishop of Canterbury agreed to sit on the platform in front of a crowd estimated at more than 185,000. Though his oral blessing on the crowd was, in the view of some, rather perfunctory, even he became caught up in the enthusiasm of the event and, turning to Grady Wilson, a key member of the Graham team, said, "I don't think we'll see a sight like this again until we get to heaven."[14]

The icing on the cake as far as the British establishment's acceptance of Graham, however, was not the approval of the archbishop of Canterbury, nor even that of the Queen, who, less than two years into her reign, had an aide write to Graham to say that she had been touched by what had been happening at Harringay, although she was counseled against meeting with him. The icing on the cake was a meeting with the ultimate British lion, Prime Minister Winston Churchill.

Churchill, who while in political exile in the 1930s had solemnly warned against the rise of Adolf Hitler, and then as prime minister had defied the Nazis during World

War II, was in his seventy-ninth year, an old man. He had been in political opposition from 1945 until 1951 as leader of the Conservative Party, and, though no one knew it at the time, would resign as prime minister in less than a year because of poor health. He had watched the Harringay phenomenon from the sidelines, first with bemusement, and then with amazement, as the young American evangelist seemed to captivate Britain, at least for those three months in the spring of 1954. Graham had invited Churchill to come and lend his considerable prestige to the crusade, just as he had — in vain — invited Harry Truman to attend the Washington crusade two years earlier. Churchill, on the advice of sober aides, declined. Nevertheless, he wanted to meet the American, and so, on the morning of May 25, the day of Graham's departure from London for Scotland, Billy received a call from Downing Street. It was John Colville, Churchill's private secretary, calling to tell Graham that the prime minister would at least like to meet him, though only a mere five minutes in Churchill's schedule had been allotted for the encounter.

In fact, the meeting lasted forty-five minutes, and the man kept cooling his heels outside the Cabinet Room while Graham and Churchill conversed was none other than the Duke of Windsor, who, as King Edward VIII, had abdicated the throne in 1936 so he could marry American divorcée Wallace Simpson. "Let him wait!" barked Churchill at one point when Colville interrupted to remind him of his luncheon appointment.

"I am an old man," Churchill said several times during the conversation, "without any hope for the world. What hope do you have, young man?" Churchill pointed to the newspapers lying on the table and remarked that they were filled with reports of things that he said rarely happened when he was young: murders, rapes, and other major crimes.

Graham had learned after three months in England to be cautious about saying anything political and merely nodded when Churchill described problems in world affairs. For instance, the French less than three weeks earlier, on May 7, had been defeated in Indochina by the Vietnamese Communists, the Vietminh, at Dien Bien Phu. The French defeat marked the beginning of the end of France's colonial empire and the beginning of American involvement in Southeast Asia. Graham, evangelist to the core, could not pass up an opportunity to share the gospel with the Western world's most famous leader. "Are you without hope for your own soul's salvation?" Graham asked, perhaps surprising himself with his boldness.

"Frankly, I think about that a great deal," replied Churchill.

"Mr. Prime Minister, I am filled with hope," Graham said exuberantly.

Producing his pocket New Testament, Graham then went through various verses pointing to salvation through faith in Jesus Christ. Churchill listened attentively. Then, exactly forty minutes after the meeting was scheduled to end, Churchill indicated that it was time to bring things to a close. Getting up, he shuffled toward the door, concluding his own melancholy reflections with the pronouncement, "I do not see much hope for the future unless it is the hope you are talking about, young man. We must have a return to God." In contrast to his disastrous media encounter following the Truman meeting five years earlier, Graham told the waiting press this time simply that he had just met "Mr. History."[15]

The three-month Harringay run took a physical toll on Graham, who by his own estimate lost thirty pounds. Though Harringay depleted him less than the 1957 New York Crusade, which Graham was later to say had so taxed him that he never physically recovered his former vigor, it was still an ordeal. To cope with the demanding schedule, he began a practice he adopted for later crusades as well, of simply taking to bed to sleep or rest for much of the day if he was scheduled to preach in the evening. There were other important changes. He had slowed down his rapid-fire delivery and abandoned the loud ties, and by the end of the crusade, he had learned to finesse political comments that, two years earlier, he might have fired off without any qualification or second thought.

The numbers at the crusade were certainly impressive, with 38,447 "inquirers" filling out decision cards. Some British evangelicals declared the level of interest in religion in England to be comparable to that at the outset of World War I. Graham himself seemed swept up in the euphoria, telling the magazine *US News and World Report* that Britain might be on the brink of "what could be the greatest spiritual awakening of all times."[16] He wondered in a conversation with the archbishop of Canterbury whether he should stay on and build on the momentum already created. Archbishop Fisher advised him to come back in a year.

In fact, though, aside from the public piety

during the three-month crusade — the hymn singing, the almost other worldly politeness of the crowds — there was no discernible lasting impact on ordinary British life. Three years later, Archbishop of Canterbury Fisher said rather uncharitably that there had been little to show from the massive evangelistic effort. But this was not at all the case. The real impact of the crusade was in the numbers who entered the ministry as a result of Harringay and in the type of Anglicism they preached. In 1966, when Billy Graham returned to Britain for another crusade, sitting on the crusade platform at Earl's Court stadium one evening were fifty-two Anglican clergymen, every single one of whom had made the decision to become Christians during the 1954 Harringay crusade.[17] Even more strikingly, twenty-three of the thirty-three Anglican clergy ordained in 1956 were evangelical — nearly 70 percent compared with a mere 7 percent before the Harringay crusade. Despite the overall low rate of British church attendance — in 2005, only 7 percent of the population attended church on any given Sunday, compared with 40 to 45 percent in the United States — ever since Harringay, the number of evangelical clergy in the Anglican church has grown faster than has that of mainline liberal clergy.

As a result of the church-based evangelism program called Alpha, now widely known throughout the United Kingdom and spreading worldwide, the Church of England has seen a slight turnaround in its declining rate of attendance. Even the Alpha program itself can be traced indirectly to the Harringay crusade, for the principal architect and speaker for the course in its present format, Rev. Nicky Gumbel of the Anglican church Holy Trinity Brompton in London, was converted to Christianity while at Cambridge University through a fellow student who had himself been profoundly affected by listening to Billy Graham preach.

The Harringay crusade had originally been cautiously planned as the first stop of a European tour to Helsinki, Stockholm, Copenhagen, Düsseldorf, Frankfurt, Berlin, and Paris. These stops were intended to be a series of one-day meetings, not full-scale crusades like Harringay. Word of the Harringay phenomenon, however, preceded Graham and his team to all seven cities, and the crowds were astonishingly large, even in the pouring rain in the main city square of Copenhagen and in Amsterdam, where

40,000 people showed up. The biggest impact was in West Germany, where Billy Graham also faced the harshest criticism from German clerics. One called him "a salesman in God's company" who "advertises the Bible as if it were a toothpaste or chewing gum."[18] In Berlin, in the same stadium where Hitler had presided over the Olympic Games in 1936, Graham drew a crowd of 80,000, as many as 20,000 of whom had crossed over from East Germany. The construction of the Berlin Wall was still seven years in the future, so there was still relatively free movement between the two halves of the city in 1954. The East German authorities were profoundly irritated and embarked on what for a while appeared to be a vindictive campaign against Graham. The East German Communist-controlled press called him a spy, a demagogue, and an envoy of American imperialism, and concocted a ludicrous tale that Graham and his team had visited East German nightclubs and been thrown out of them for not paying their bills.

Graham returned to the United States from Paris in July with a keen taste for crusades overseas; the experience had given him a vision for what might be accomplished abroad that he had not had before

Harringay. He had discovered that the version of the gospel he had preached with such effect at home could indeed be preached overseas, with little more than an accurate translation and some careful study of a country's cultural traditions. Graham now clearly began to see himself as an evangelist to the world at large. For the remainder of the decade, he focused most of his energies on his overseas trips, holding only eight full-scale crusades in the United States. He spent much of late 1954 planning a return trip to the United Kingdom — to Scotland this time — and ventures even farther afield: to India, for example, and five years later to Australia and New Zealand.

Graham's return to Britain in 1955 was something of a triumphal one. The main crusade was in Kelvin Hall in Glasgow for six weeks, but he also had a weeklong return engagement at Wembley Stadium in London. He preached to even more people on Good Friday, April 29, when the BBC carried his sermon live to an audience believed to be the largest since the young Queen's coronation in 1953. This time, the British royal family was not so cautious about meeting with Graham as it had been the previous year. Queen Elizabeth invited Billy and Ruth to meet her at her London apartments at Clarence House and then asked Billy to speak at the Royal Chapel in Windsor Castle. On May 22, he was the first American ever to preach there, and it was a signal honor. This first audience with the Queen was also the beginning of a tradition of a private visit with her on almost every occasion that Graham passed through London.

At the Scotland crusade, despite the enthusiasm and large numbers of "inquirers," no lasting effect upon the Scots was discernible. In fact, though, as at Harringay the year before, the long-term impact on the clergy was remarkable. When the Moderator of the Church of Scotland, the Right Reverend Hugh Wiley, the highest ecclesiastical leader in the Scottish church, introduced Billy Graham via satellite TV hookup for a Scottish evangelism school program in 1993, he said that his own conversion could be traced back to Graham's Glasgow crusade nearly two decades earlier.

At Cambridge University, Graham encountered highly critical clergy but enthusiastic students. Billy had anticipated a lukewarm response on the part of Cambridge faculty, which held generally liberal scholarly views of Christian doctrine, but he discovered the students were wide-open to his neo-evangelical approach. He also was introduced to the celebrated English Christian writer C. S. Lewis, author of *The Chronicles of Narnia* as well as classics of Christian apologetics, such as *Mere Christianity.* The introduction was made by John Stott, who was probably the best-known living writer on evangelical themes and whom Graham had first met only a year earlier when in London before the Harringay crusade. Lewis and Graham got on well, with the famous writer bluntly telling the famous evangelist that he had heard much criticism of Graham's evangelistic style but never from anyone who had personally met Graham.[19]

The week at Wembley Stadium in London was followed by another rapid European tour, this time of twelve cities, during which Graham made another of his blundering generalizations. "France is like a watch without its mainspring. It has run down," he said at a press conference during his four-day evangelistic effort in Paris. "The French just sin and sin, and get weaker." French journalists badgered Graham about this comment at subsequent stops until he lamely apologized, saying that he had been quoting the observations of an Asian diplomat. Despite that *faux pas,* though, the left-leaning newspaper *Le Monde* displayed both graciousness and some perspicuity in telling Parisians, "His technique may offend European intellectuals, but the fact remains he is successful. French Protestants who, despite some reservations, did not hesitate to ask him to come to our country, made no mistake."[20]

The visit to France was but a short jump from England, but wider travels were in the offing. He had been approached in 1955 by an English Anglican clergyman familiar with India, Rev. Jack Dain, with the suggestion that he visit that subcontinent. Apart from a 1952 trip to provide pastoral care to US troops in Korea, this would be the farthest from the United States that Graham had hitherto traveled. Not only that, political stakes were high too. Indian Prime Minister Jawaharlal Nehru had just started to implement his policy of nonalignment in the Cold War between the United States and the Soviet Union. Though India was a democratic nation, Nehru had been profoundly influenced by Fabian socialism and, in fact, was sympathetic to Marxism. His concept of "nonalignment" and "neutralism" made him unwilling to be a pawn of Washington against Moscow. India, however, was by far the most important of the nations of the "third world" (another Nehru coinage) that had not yet succumbed to Communist Party rule, and Delhi's sympathy toward Moscow not only rankled Secretary of State John Foster Dulles, but also it frankly worried him. With Graham's India crusade following by just two months the triumphant visit to Delhi by Soviet leaders Nikolai Bulganin and Nikita Khrushchev, the religious event also had important implications for American diplomacy.

President Dwight D. Eisenhower sent Graham a greeting before his January departure, and Secretary of State Dulles himself summoned Billy for a private briefing at his home. Dulles told Billy that he hoped the evangelist would not make any political mistakes in India and indeed might be an advocate of American interests. This was but the first of many occasions US administrations found it useful to capitalize or piggyback on Graham's evangelistic activities and indeed his prominence as a worldwide evangelist. In decades to come, not only did his crusades have the indirect effect of helping to bring down totalitarian regimes, but, on occasion, Graham served as an unofficial emissary for American presidents to world leaders with whom the

US government was unable otherwise to have direct contact.

As if Dulles's warning was not pressure enough on Graham, when he arrived in Bombay in January 1956, riots had broken out across the country over Delhi's plan to redraw state border lines, an issue over which the Indian states perennially squabbled. Graham handled this situation with aplomb by brushing off any suggestion that his visit might have political implications.

The India crusade had some strange moments in it, ones that the Graham team would remember for years afterwards. In north India, few of the Muslim majority showed up to hear Graham's message, and those who did listened attentively but coolly. In the south, however, where there had been Indian Christian communities since the first and second centuries of the Christian era, the response to Graham's presence was reverential almost to the point of idolatry. Christians attending his meetings sometimes tried to touch him as though he exuded the powers of a "holy man" common to the Indian religious experience. In Kottayam, a small city of 50,000 in the heavily Christian state of Kerala, teams of schoolgirls fashioned a temporary amphitheater out of the hillside surrounding the athletic field of a church school to accommodate the crowds. By the time the evening meeting started, 75,000 people had arrived, nearly all of them dressed in white. The majority of them had walked up to sixty miles to attend the event.

At Palamcottah, in southernmost India's Tamil Nadu state, Graham found himself in prayer battling strange Hindu forces that were threatening to turn an orderly evangelistic meeting into a riotous assembly. People in the audience had started to shout and scream, partly because the loudspeaker system was proving unreliable. Biographer Martin describes Graham bowing his head and "praying a prayer of authority," silently "commanding" any troublesome spiritual elements to be quiet, somewhat as Jesus had commanded the evil spirits to be silent.[21] "Oh God, stop the noise; quiet the people now," Graham urgently prayed. Jack Dain, the English preacher who had first suggested the Indian crusade to Graham, recalled, "Immediately, a deathlike hush came on the crowd, and it became the quietest, most reverent meeting we have had in India yet. It was like the breath of God had suddenly fallen. You couldn't hear a sound."[22]

Both Eisenhower and Dulles hoped that the Graham visit to India might counterbalance the considerable publicity splash created by the visit the previous November of the Soviet leaders Bulganin and Khrushchev. Dulles, through US ambassador to India John Sherman Cooper, had pushed strongly for Nehru, who in 1956 was emerging as one of the leaders of the world's nonaligned nations, to meet with Graham. It was an honor that Graham himself, never averse to being in the presence of powerful political figures, also looked forward to eagerly. Nehru, however, was India's most secular-minded premier and probably considered American evangelicalism a combination of Yankee boosterism and spirituality for the simple-minded. He did finally consent to a meeting, which by happenstance took place immediately after a scheduled visit from UN Secretary-General Dag Hammarskjold. The UN chief apparently either did not recognize Graham as he left the prime minister's office or chose to ignore him.[23]

For Graham, an affable conversationalist, the meeting with Nehru did not start well. As he chatted about how much he admired both India and Nehru and about how much he had learned about the country on this trip, the Indian leader came close to displaying open boredom, looking at the ceiling or fiddling with a letter opener. Finally Graham fell back on the best way he knew to evince interest on the part of other people: he talked about how Christ had changed his life. Nehru immediately became alert and, according to Graham, began to ask questions. The meeting concluded with Nehru saying that he had nothing against Christian missionaries so long as they avoided politics.

Somewhat to his surprise, Dulles discovered that Graham's crusades often created ripples of goodwill in countries whose governments were actually quite skeptical of Washington. The Indian trip proved Graham's value as an unofficial White House envoy. This was rendered all the easier by Graham's general desire to keep in touch with the administration of the day and to keep it apprised of both his plans for future overseas trips and his impressions of those trips on his return.

Graham's India trip lasted four weeks and was followed by brief visits to the Philippines, Hong Kong, Taiwan, Japan, and Korea. In Taiwan, Graham met Generalissimo Chiang Kai-shek, who had been ruler of the island since the Nationalists retreated there after its defeat by the Communists on the Chinese Mainland in 1949. Chiang, a Christian for many years, smiled through the entire meeting with Graham, causing the evangelist to gush, "I doubt if there are two statesmen in the world today that are more dedicated to Christ and His cause than Generalissimo Chiang Kai-shek and his wife."[24] Graham may not have known how draconian Chiang's rule at that time was as strongman in one of the most authoritarian non-Communist regimes in the world.

In 1958, Graham visited the Caribbean for a series of crusades, but the highlight of overseas crusades in the 1950s, after the success of Harringay and India, may well have been his three-month visit to Australia and New Zealand from mid-February to the end of May 1959. The irreverent Australians had treated visits by the American evangelists Aimee Semple McPherson, Billy Sunday, and (more recently) Oral Roberts with a combination of indifference, ribald mockery, and outright opposition. Graham, however, confounded the most skeptical critics and the rather modest expectations of his own staff. At crusades in Melbourne and Sydney, he drew larger crowds even than had gathered at his final rally at Wembley Stadium in England in 1954.

In August 2005, in Cairns, far to the north of Sydney, I met an Australian who had attended one of the Melbourne crusades forty-six years earlier. For Bryan O'Connor, then just fifteen years old, the recollection of Graham speaking still loomed large in his memory. "I was just blown away at the way he could control a crowd. To listen to this man speaking was something I've never forgotten. How alive he was just struck me." But O'Connor, now a car rental clerk, had not "gone forward" in Melbourne, and, in fact, having spent several months of 2005 in Thailand, was of the opinion that a mild dose of Buddhism would be good for everyone.

This view certainly was not shared by the Right Reverend Peter Jensen, archbishop of Sydney. Jensen, who also was fifteen at the time, was converted in April 1959 while listening to Billy Graham in the Agricultural Showground of Sydney. "It was the most important event of my life," he recalled in 2005. "I went a total of twenty-three times to the crusades, and my parents were beside themselves. Church had always been a dreary experience. Church halls were dingy and the singing turgid. But when you came into the arena where Billy Graham was preaching, everything worked." Jensen recalled in vivid terms the impact of Graham's message: "Has there ever been a voice like his? There was the utter sincerity of it. He was transparently sincere, personally attractive. He was a prince among God's people."[25]

Through actual crusade attendance and through landline radio linkups of the crusades that were broadcast to other parts of Australia, an estimated 50 percent of the entire population of ten million in 1959 heard the American evangelist. The total number of Australians who indicated having made a commitment or a recommitment to Christ during the crusades was more than 130,000, a remarkable 1.2 percent of the entire country. The impact on future clergy was even more remarkable. An estimated 50 percent of theology students in Australia in the following ten years were influenced by Graham's presence in the country.[26]

The Australian crusade of 1959, in fact, may well have come as close as anything in Graham's entire career to precipitating a national revival. According to Stuart Piggin in his study of Christianity in Australia, the sociological impact of Graham's Australia crusade was significant: a lower crime rate in the months after the crusade, a reduction in out-of-wedlock births, even the closings of several pubs, an unlikely occurrence in a country that enjoys social drinking with no small enthusiasm. The sheer numbers of Australians whose lives were changed by the crusade no doubt whetted Graham's appetite to repeat the success, if possible, in other countries. As at Harringay, Graham seemed to have discovered that cultural anti-Americanism was usually eclipsed by the effect of straight-out preaching of an evangelical gospel message. Thus, in his broadening view of the global possibilities of evangelism in general, no country was likely to be impervious to the effect of well-organized crusades.

Early the following year, 1960, he toured nine African countries for eight weeks, from Liberia in the west to Kenya in the east, from Egypt in the north to Zimbabwe (then known as Southern Rhodesia) in the south. Although his position on race in the United States had, up to this point, seemed ambivalent (see Chapter Six), in the two British-ruled Rhodesias, Graham was unequivocal in insisting that blacks be admitted to the services and that his sermons be translated into local languages. He often repeated the message that Jesus had not been a white man at all, but had been distinctly dark-skinned. On that trip to Africa, he refused an invitation to go to South Africa, because he had by then promised African Americans at home that he would never again preach to a segregated audience. Besides, even if he had made an exception for a foreign audience, Graham did not want to go to a country where his associate evangelist Howard Jones, an African American, would be subjected to the humiliations of apartheid, South Africa's policy of enforced racial separation that was abolished in the early 1990s only after years of intense and persistent international pressure. In Ethiopia, the Christian emperor Haile Selassie joined the list of famous foreign leaders who received Graham. The final stop of the Africa trip was a meeting in a huge red tent in Cairo, Egypt, believed to be the first such public Christian rally since the arrival of Islam in Egypt in the seventh century.

Then it was on to Jordan and Israel. The Jordanian visit, though brief, gave Graham an opportunity for a quick visit with the young King Hussein. The visit to Israel was considerably more colorful. Graham had to enter the country via the Allenby Bridge across the Jordan River. As this was seven years before Jerusalem and the West Bank came under Israeli control following Israel's victory in the Six-Day War of 1967, the bridge was technically in Jordan, and anyone wanting to visit either East Jerusalem, also under Jordanian control, or the Israeli-controlled West Jerusalem had to go through elaborate security screening on both the Jordanian side and the Israeli side.

Golda Meir, then foreign minister and later Israel's prime minister, wanted to meet with Graham immediately upon his arrival on Israeli territory in West Jerusalem, an indication of her awareness of how potentially important this American evangelical might be in taking home a positive image of Israel. (In that, Graham apparently did not disappoint, for on her last visit to the United States, she brought and gave to Graham a Bible in which she had written: "Billy Graham, a friend of Israel."[27]) Meir summoned Graham also because she wanted to make sure that he knew the Israeli position on various international issues before he spoke to the press. It turned out, however, that the Israeli media was not especially interested in Graham's thoughts on international affairs, even though he held some rather interesting views about Israel. In an interview in 1957, he had told an American Jewish reporter that Israel was destined to expand its territory until all the lands promised to Abraham's descendants, from the Nile to the Euphrates rivers, was in its hands.[28] In his autobiography, he added this thought that he said he had not shared at the press conference in Israel, "I have always believed that the Jews were God's special people, chosen to preserve the Hebrew Scriptures through the centuries and to prepare the way for the coming of Jesus."[29]

Israel's media, in fact, was not overly friendly at first, with the English-language *Jerusalem Post* worrying that Graham had come to proselytize among the Jews. Concern about Graham's possible motivations for visiting Israel had also spilled out from an off-the-record meeting Graham had with Israel's founding prime minister, David Ben-Gurion. According to *Time* magazine, Ben-Gurion had pointedly asked Graham to avoid mentioning Jesus in any of his meetings with Jewish audiences.[30] As he was to do with great skill many times throughout his life, Graham turned potential suspicion and hostility to his personal advantage at the press conference that had caused so much worry. On the day after his meeting with Meir, Graham told the astonished reporters assembled at the King David Hotel that he wanted to thank the Jewish people for doing to him what they feared he would do to them. "I want to thank you for proselytizing me, a Gentile who has committed his life to a Jew who was born in this country and reared up here in Nazareth," Graham said. "I want to thank you for being the nation through which Jesus was brought to this earth in the divine plan of God. And I want to thank you as one who has given my life to a Jew, who, living upon this earth, claimed to be God." For a rare moment in Jerusalem, the often garrulous and opinionated Israeli press corps was stunned into silence.[31]

Graham expanded his knowledge of the world with two Latin American tours in 1962, encountering some political opposition there because of US actions against Fidel Castro's rule of Cuba since 1959. It was, after all, barely more than a year after the disastrous US-backed effort to dislodge Castro in the 1961 Bay of Pigs incident. Many countries in Central and South America, sensitive to the sometimes heavy-handed American interference in their internal affairs, were more upset by an abortive US attempt to unseat a regime in the region than by the fact that Castro seemed to be providing a platform in Cuba for a whole new series of subversive operations against their own governments.

These Latin American trips were followed by efforts to build on Graham's first great successes in the United Kingdom and in Australia and New Zealand with return visits, to the first in 1966 and to the latter two in 1968 and 1969. In each instance, the results were statistically satisfying but the reception less than stellar. Britain had moved on economically, socially, and politically since the 1950s. The 1960s saw the apogee of London's glitzy reputation as a "swinging" city, the Vietnam War was already surfacing as a focus of anti-American feeling, and mass evangelism was, well, passé in England. The British press, which in 1954 had at first been hostile but then was won over by Graham, twelve years later either ignored the evangelist or tried maliciously to embarrass him. When Graham was speaking to a crowd through a bullhorn from atop a car in London's Soho district, a woman was passed over the heads of the throng toward him. The plan was that she would unzip her dress in front of him while news photographers captured the embarrassing scene on film. As soon as Graham saw her approaching, he jumped down from the car roof and his entourage sped away, the woman trying to follow. "She was on drugs, she was demon possessed — she had the strength of ten men," Graham recalled later to biographer Marshall Frady.[32] The stunt had apparently been orchestrated by a Fleet Street tabloid.

A more typical response, however, was the cynically clever turn of phrase in London's *Daily Mail,* evoking Rex Harrison's song in the musical *My Fair Lady,* which had had a triumphant run in London a few years previously, "We've grown accustomed to his faith." Paradoxically, the very familiarity of Graham's style and message secured him a permanent place in the hearts of Britain's royal family. Tea with the Queen at Buckingham Palace went well, and on his subsequent trips to Britain, the British royals often invited Graham to visit them.

In Australia and New Zealand in 1968 and 1969, though the crusades themselves attracted large crowds, Graham and his team encountered a rough reception. Questions about the Vietnam War and Graham's relationship with President Nixon — who was already beginning to enter the pantheon of figures that students around the world loved to hate — were sharp. There were disruptions of some meetings, a bomb threat in New Zealand, and belligerent heckling of Graham's brother-in-law Leighton Ford, a member of the Graham team, when Ford preached at the University of Adelaide. Public opinion in many parts of the Western world seemed to be turning against the United States, and in some respects against the concept of evangelism itself. Nonetheless, Graham visited American troops in Vietnam in 1966 and 1968, and was publicly supportive of his friend President Lyndon Johnson and indeed of American foreign policy overall.

The major international event in Graham's career in the 1960s decade was the ten-day World Congress on Evangelism, held in Berlin in late October to early November 1966. Graham's far-flung travels and meetings with evangelicals in diverse countries of the world had convinced him that there was no forum for evangelicals comparable to the World Council of Churches. That body, comprising mainstream Protestant churches around the world, had been founded in 1948, and Graham, at the time a Youth for Christ evangelist, had been on hand at its establishment as an observer. In 1961, also as an observer, he had attended its meeting in New Delhi. In theology and politics, however, the WCC had been moving steadily to the left, eschewing any concept that Christianity had exclusive claims to religious truth, and at a meeting early in 1966, the council even espoused violence as a valid means of bringing about needed changes in the "structures" of society.

The Berlin Congress, which brought together twelve hundred Christian leaders from 104 nations, offered the antithesis of this point of view. Congress organizers set up a thiry-foot-tall digital clock in the lobby of Berlin's Kongresshalle that methodically counted the babies being born in the world — at a much faster rate than the expansion of Christianity — to vividly illustrate the urgent task of world evangelism. The congress's theme was "One Race, One gospel, One Task," and the delegates were challenged to aim for "nothing short of the evangelization of the human race in this generation."[33] To provide the Congress with a measure of international prestige, and to avoid the appearance of a gathering dominated by Westerners, the keynote address was given by the Ethiopian emperor Haile Selassie, whom Graham had met in 1960. Selassie, the leader of one of the world's most ancient Christian nations, exhorted the delegates to "arise and, with the spiritual zeal and earnestness which characterized the Apostles and the early Christians," take the gospel to everyone in the world.[34] Graham challenged his audience in his opening address to recall the zeal of an earlier evangelistic conference in Edinburgh in 1910. God would hold the delegates responsible "at the Judgment Seat of Christ," he sternly told them, "for how well we fulfilled our responsibilities and took advantage of our opportunities."[35] The Berlin Congress was the first example of Graham's efforts to build on his own personal successes in international evangelism as a way of galvanizing further efforts by others in the field. In the view of some church historians, the Congress helped create a new worldwide ecumenical movement which was evangelical and distinct from the liberal World Council of Churches and the Catholic Church.

Graham's international travels continued in 1970 with a crusade in Dortmund, West Germany, followed by visits in 1972 to war-torn Belfast, Ireland, and meetings later that year in the tense state of Nagaland, India. It was, however, the crusades in 1973 in South Africa and in South Korea that, after Harringay and Australia, had the greatest impact in terms of overall global influence.

Graham had finally agreed to accept an invitation to South Africa only after being assured that his audiences would not be racially segregated. Thus he made history in Durban by speaking to the first fully racially integrated public gathering ever in South Africa. "Christianity is not a white man's religion," he told the crowds, "and don't let anyone tell you that it's white or black. Christ belongs to all people!"[36] This was a potentially provocative statement because it undermined the entire premise of South Africa's racist policy of apartheid. But instead of following up with a more detailed assault, Graham characteristically drew back from mentioning the word apartheid in any of his subsequent addresses. In so doing, he disappointed many who had hoped the evangelist would peel open South Africa's closed society. Characteristically, Billy Graham just did not like upsetting people, and he knew he would if he used his crusades to make the political points many wanted him to make. Nonetheless, the main Durban newspaper's headline the day after Graham's address predicted, "Apartheid Doomed." In 1985, Bishop Alpheus Zulu of Zululand said that "the spirit of reconciliation we sense in many of South African hearts can be traced back directly to the Billy Graham meetings held in Durban and Johannesburg in 1973." Because of

Graham's demand for integration, "from that moment on, we were on the road to reconciliation," he recalled.[37]

In South Korea, Graham made history of a different sort. At a mile-long open space on Seoul's Yoido Island, Graham in early June 1973 addressed what was then the largest gathering to hear a sermon in a single place: 1.12 million people, as measured by paper grids glued to the ground with each square estimated to be large enough for six to twelve people. Though Pope John Paul II later would address larger audiences, nothing of this size had ever been seen before in Christian history. Even more significantly, the event took place not in a nation traditionally associated with Christianity, but in Korea, where Buddhism had until recently been the dominant religion. Not only was this Asian nation even in the 1970s turning into a significantly Christianized society, where by 2005 about 28 percent of the population was Christian, but it has become one whose brand of Christianity overflows with evangelistic zeal. Thirty years after the Yoido gathering, the South Koreans have become the world's second-largest missionary-sending nation, after the United States itself. Even the North Korean media could not ignore the historic nature of Graham's crusade, and, commenting hatefully on the proceedings, speculated that Graham had exercised in Seoul an unusual kind of witchcraft.

The Korean selected by Graham to be his interpreter had initially been reluctant to be involved. Dr. Billy Kim had been taken under the wing of an American soldier during the Korean War, converted to Christianity, and sent to college at Bob Jones University, Graham's one-time alma mater, where he heard an earful from Dr. Bob Jones on what a catastrophic scourge to Christianity Billy Graham was. Back in Korea when Graham contacted him, Kim's animosity was softened by the need for all Christians, still a minority of the Korean population, to stick together. Besides, Kim had attended the 1966 Berlin Congress, where he had heard Graham preach, and he had been impressed.

"He was so sensitive to the needs of the Korean people. He was preparing to preach on [the notoriously wicked Israelite king and queen of the Old Testament] Ahab and Jezebel, and I said it might be offensive to President Park," Kim recalled in 2005, referring to South Korea's authoritarian then president. "So he preached on blind Bartimaeus" (Mark 10:46). Commenting on the wide impact Graham had on Korean society, Kim said, "I meet people from all walks of life who say they were converted in the 1973 crusade." Kim himself was disarmed by Graham's humility and approachability. He remembered, "The first thing he did was ask me about my children, what their names were, and how each was doing."[38]

The Korean triumph in 1973 was a fitting prelude to by far the most important Graham-initiated event of the 1970s: the follow-up to the Berlin Congress of 1966. Graham had not been content to rest on his laurels after the impact made by the 1966 meeting, which spawned several "mini-Berlins" in different parts of the world. Nor would global Christian developments allow him to. The center of gravity of Christendom worldwide was moving inexorably eastward as the gospel continued to lose ground in traditional strongholds such as Western Europe and to gain ground in Africa, Latin America, and Asia. Global Christian leadership was changing too. Christians in the newly Christianizing parts of the world were no longer content to defer to the missionary and church elder statesmen of the West. It is one of Graham's most remarkable achievements that he was not only the first world-famous Christian leader to recognize this but was willing to lend his prestige and reputation to moving the process forward. In so doing, Graham provided what must have been welcome support and encouragement to Christian leaders laboring in these new Christian frontiers, and he would later also assist them in practical ways through training sessions and seminars to equip them with evangelistic skills he had honed over several decades.

The historic Berlin gathering of eight years earlier was dwarfed in both size and ambition by the International Congress on World Evangelization in Lausanne. More importantly, it set in motion developments that are still continuing on the global Christian scene today. A total of 2,473 delegates gathered in the Palais de Beaulieu conference building in Lausanne, Switzerland, for ten days in July 1974. This time, they came from 150 countries, many of them at the epicenter of world news. One delegate was the president of the Supreme Court of Cambodia, a former Buddhist who ascribed his conversion to reading Billy Graham's 1953 book, *Peace with God*. (When the Khmer Rouge rebels took Phnom Penh the following April, driving out of the capital into the countryside almost every single member of the urban populace, they shot many others on the spot in the national stadium, including this judge.) As at Berlin in 1966, there was a "population clock" in the lobby of the conference building, digitally ticking away the world's population increase for the duration of the Congress. On the last day, July 25, the tally exceeded 1.8 million.

Lausanne broke precedent with previous global conferences on world evangelism not just in terms of the number of delegates or the diversity of the countries they represented, but because it was clear for the first time that delegates from "white nations" were not driving the agenda. In fact, many delegates from first world countries were astonished to discover how vigorous were the third world adherents of the faith. The Congress was emphatic about the importance of "cross-cultural" evangelism, a concept that contradicted the emerging intellectual orthodoxy in the developed world that all cultures and beliefs are inherently equal. In fact, many delegates at Lausanne were resentful of what they saw as efforts by Western missionaries to impose Western culture on the non-Western countries they were evangelizing. Ralph Winter, the American who later founded the US

Center of World Mission in 1976, made it clear, however, that he was not at all advocating Western cultural imperialism. As he observed, if African Christian converts from Islam wished to make Friday — the traditional Muslim holy day of the week — a special worship day, why should they be discouraged from this? Winter furthermore made clear that by "cross-cultural" he did not at all mean just the efforts by Western missionaries to export the Christian gospel to the non-Western world, but also attempts by non-Western Christians to do the same.[39] The Lausanne Congress may have been the first major international gathering to bring forward the concept of "people groups" — that is, distinct ethnic communities whose existence is not decided by political boundaries — rather than nations as missionary targets.

There was more discussion even than at Berlin of the social responsibility of Christians, as well as a determined effort by many of the delegates to ensure that global Christian evangelization not be dominated by the political conservatism of American evangelicals. The delegates seemed to want to make the point that condemning global dictatorships of the left was justifiable, but, they said, those of the right should be criticized too. What emerged from this mode of thinking was the Lausanne Covenant, a three thousand-word document compiled under the leadership of Britain's leading evangelical intellectual, John Stott. The Lausanne delegates were not required to sign the covenant, but many did, including Billy Graham.

His wife, Ruth, however, objected to Stott's wording in the section of the covenant that called on signatories "to develop a simple life-style in order to contribute to both relief and evangelism." "What is 'simple'?" she asked Stott in person. "You live in two rooms; I have a bigger home. You have no children; I have five. You say your life is simple, and mine isn't." Stott, a bachelor, refused to change "simple" to "simpler," and Ruth Graham refused to sign the covenant.[40] As an indication of the intellectual respect with which he regarded her, Billy did not try to change his wife's mind.

Lausanne was undoubtedly one of Graham's greatest contributions to Christianity worldwide. Though it made far less of a visual impact than such grandiose events as the massive 1973 Korean gathering, or major crusades like Harringay in 1954 or Sydney in 1959, the long-term fruits of the Congress were far more significant. Graham, whose BGEA covered most of the costs of Lausanne, had not wanted any follow-up institution to be founded at the Congress, but delegate demand created the Lausanne Committee for World Evangelization (LCWE), which organized subsequent conferences such as "Lausanne II" in Manila in 1989 and the Forum for World Evangelization in Thailand in 2004. Literally dozens of spin-off evangelization conferences were seeded by Lausanne, starting with the Kenya Congress for Unreached Peoples the following year, no fewer than seven Chinese Congresses on World Evangelization between 1976 and 2006 (though it's important to note that these "Chinese Congresses" had no connection with official church authorities in Communist-ruled China nor with representatives of China's many unregistered "house churches"), and several conferences on such diverse and perplexing topics as "contextualization" and even "nominalism." Conferences on evangelization have been held in Africa, India, Hong Kong, and Singapore. Overall, Lausanne created a profound, universal consciousness among the world's evangelical Christians not just of the importance of who they were but of the impact of where they were.

Whereas Berlin and Lausanne had focused on the big names of global Christianity and focused efforts on recasting Protestant Christianity worldwide into an evangelical mold in the Billy Graham style, two conferences for "itinerant evangelists" in Amsterdam in 1983 and 1986 may have had far more wide-reaching and longer-lasting significance. For these two conferences, the BGEA expended strenuous efforts to identify "the little guys out in the bushes," that is, the modest, usually very poor, but highly motivated Protestant Christians who tried to live out lives of evangelism under trying circumstances. At Amsterdam in 1983, and then on a larger scale in 1986, little-known preachers from all over the third world attended workshops and plenary sessions specifically designed to equip them to carry the gospel into the remotest parts of their countries, with maximum effectiveness. The two International Conferences of Itinerant Evangelists in Amsterdam not only illustrated the incredible diversity of the Protestant Christian experience the world over, but also significantly enhanced the skills of those invited to attend. To identify the "itinerant" evangelists whom the Amsterdam organizers considered most eligible for an invitation to the conference, the

BGEA sometimes sent teams of investigators to particular countries to check up on the background of the invited preachers. Throughout the two conferences, Graham was generously available, not only granting interviews to a wide variety of news organizations, but enthusiastically plunging into the throngs of sometimes overawed third world visitors.

The singular impact, therefore, of Billy Graham's leadership on global Protestant Christianity is impossible to overestimate. Before Graham's emergence as a world figure of public evangelism, Protestant Christianity, though lagging far behind the Roman Catholic Church in membership, had been the fastest-growing component of global Christendom. In 2007, the generally accepted figure for Protestants worldwide was about 590 million to 600 million, versus 1.1 billion Roman Catholics.[41] But what kind of Protestantism was it? It comprised a colorful tapestry of creeds ranging from the "embrace-all-religions" ecumenicism of the World Council of Churches to the "circle-the-wagons" exclusivism of Bob Jones and other American fundamentalists. Once Billy Graham began to bestride the world scene, however, that started to change. The dominant strand within global Protestantism became something entirely new, sharing many of the beliefs of traditional fundamentalism while seeking to maintain a relationship with any in the traditional Protestant denominations — Presbyterians, Methodists, Episcopalians, Baptists, and others — who nonetheless viewed Christian evangelism as a good thing.

The new brew became known as the "new evangelicalism," and over time it became the hallmark of Billy Graham's theological worldview and of his willingness to deal open-handedly with Christians from a wide variety of traditions. Certainly Graham had started his Christian life under the preaching of hard-core fundamentalists such as Mordecai Ham and Bob Jones, both of whom were characterized by an exclusivist conservative theology. But by 1957, Graham's own theological positions had clearly altered, so much so that the old patriarch Bob Jones, founder of Bob Jones University, Billy's alma mater, publicly denounced him and read him out of the fundamentalist movement with great bitterness. How that happened is worth looking at.

Six:
THEOLOGY AND RACE

At the beginning of his national fame as an evangelist, Billy Graham was a preacher solidly in the fundamentalist tradition that had its roots in the twelve-volume theology text, *The Fundamentals: A Testimony to the Truth,* compiled by conservative Christian scholars and published between 1910 and 1915 to counter the tide of theological liberalism and modernism that was rising in American churches, seminaries, and universities. As stated earlier, the core beliefs of the fundamentalists include the "inerrancy" of the Bible, the virgin birth, the deity of Jesus Christ, and the bodily resurrection of Jesus.

The understanding of the term *fundamentalist,* however, has recently become problematic, mainly due to imprecise usage of the word in several ways. First, it started to be used in the early 1980s to describe followers of radical interpretations of Islam.

The more precise way to refer to members of Al-Qaeda, for example, would be "Islamist," because Al-Qaeda's doctrines emphasize Islamic teachings interpreted as a triumphalist political ideology. Second, many journalists and even scholars have used the term "fundamentalist" to refer to anyone who takes literally Christianity's claims to historical truth, such that the "fundamentalist" net in this usage covers every form of Christianity from the doctrinal pronouncements of the Vatican in Rome to media-savvy megachurches in California to storefront New York Pentecostalism. By this definition, an Anglo-Catholic Episcopalian priest who cherishes a retreat to practice the "spiritual exercises" of Ignatius Loyola, founder of the Jesuits, and who happens to hold a Harvard divinity degree is as much a "fundamentalist" as the late Jerry Falwell (1933–2007), one of the few prominent American Christians who actually identified himself as a "fundamentalist." Third, what was an identifiable early twentieth-century historical movement focused on reforming Christian doctrine has broken up into so many different groups — of which "neoevangelicalism" is merely the most prominent — that using "fundamentalism" to refer to all of them risks serious confusion.

That said, groups which to this day identify themselves with what they call "fundamental" Protestant Christian doctrines are usually characterized by these features: suspicion of Roman Catholicism and of Protestants who express sympathy for it; emphasis on restrictions on certain behavior in their communities (banning consumption of alcohol, dancing, and sometimes even the wearing of pants by women); opposition to all theories of Darwinian evolution; belief in a premillennial, dispensationalist view of the end times; and susceptibility to conspiracy theories involving the United Nations, a putative World Government, and "the New World Order" (first mentioned by President George H. W. Bush in 1990 to suggest a global partnership of the Soviet Union and the United States in the wake of the collapse of Communism in Eastern Europe and the rise of challenges to world peace posed by Iraqi leader Saddam Hussein).

Early in his career as an evangelist, Billy Graham's conspicuous dispensationalism, with its graphic speculation about end time events and how heaven would function, his vivid descriptions of heaven and hell, and his conviction that only faith in Christ guarantees entry into heaven put him squarely in the tradition of Billy Sunday and, in the context of the early 1950s, on the same team as such fundamentalist firebrands as Bob Jones, the fundamentalist patriarch who founded Bob Jones University.

Two subtle but important developments, however, began to draw Graham away from the fundamentalism that characterized his preaching at the 1949 Los Angeles and 1950 New England rallies. These developments eventually would not only cause him to withdraw from the fundamentalist camp but would make him the target of vehement attacks by the fundamentalists, foremost among them being Bob Jones himself. The first of these developments was Graham's growing friendship with Roman Catholic prelates. The other was his experience at the Harringay crusade in London when he decided that he could successfully cooperate with Christian traditions that were quite liberal theologically.

The first prominent Roman Catholic prelate Graham was known to have been close to was Bishop Fulton J. Sheen, a silver-tongued dispenser of comfortable wisdom, who was famous on American TV in the 1950s through a weekly, half-hour show called *Life is Worth Living.* The show was immensely popular, and Sheen's polished delivery, elegant bishop's robes, and hypnotic gaze won him an Emmy, a *Time* magazine cover, and a spot on a list of the "most admired" Americans. Graham described Sheen as "the greatest communicator of the 20th century,"[1] and when he died in 1979, Billy said that he had known and been friends with the bishop for thirty-five years. If that is accurate, it would mean the two men met in 1944, before Graham was generally known outside a rather narrow band of American evangelicals. Graham, however, may have been mistaken about the time frame, and he is more likely to have met Sheen after the 1949 Greater Los Angeles Crusade that catapulted him to national fame. According to Graham's account, Sheen introduced himself to Billy on a train journey between Washington and New York, and the two men "talked about our ministries and our common commitment to evangelism, and I told him how grateful I was for his ministry and his focus on Christ . . . We talked further and we prayed; and by the time he left, I felt as if I had known him all my life."[2]

The Catholic Church in the United States, to be sure, was ambivalent about Graham in those early years. Wary because of past experiences with fundamentalists, who often fulminated from the pulpit against Rome, some priests and bishops warned their flocks against attending Billy Graham crusades. Cardinal Richard James Cushing (1895–1970), however, had not been one of these. In 1950, when Graham was holding a crusade in the heartland of American Catholicism — Boston — Cushing, the archbishop of Boston, was the one who wrote the editorial for the diocesan newspaper with the headline, "Bravo, Billy!" When Graham returned for another Boston crusade in 1964, he and Cushing engaged in a forty-five-minute public lovefest of mutual admiration on a Boston TV station.[3] Later, Graham was to say of Cushing and Catholicism, "He and I became close, wonderful friends. That was my first real coming to grips with the whole Protestant/ Catholic situation. I began to realize that there were Christians everywhere. They might be called modernists, Catholics, or whatever, but they were Christians."[4]

In fact, Graham's evolution from plain-speaking fundamentalism had not occurred in a vacuum but rather against a backdrop of important trends in Protestantism. When he had been president of Northwestern Schools from 1947 to 1949, he had bluntly stated, "We do not condone nor have any fellowship with any form of modernism."[5] That was a normative sentiment for anyone in the fundamentalist fold. But it was a view also held by many American Protestants of another sort: those who shared most of the core fundamentalist beliefs about biblical inerrancy and other theological points central to evangelical Protestantism but were unhappy with the way fundamentalists seemed to have absented themselves from many of the social concerns of American life. This group came to call themselves the "New Evangelicals," a term coined by an influential evangelical theologian who emerged in the 1940s as the movement's leader. He was Dr. J. Harold Ockenga (1905–1985), and in 1942 he had formed the National Association of Evangelicals, in effect, the conservative Christian equivalent of the distinctly liberal National Council of Churches. Ockenga had become troubled by fundamentalist Christianity's growing social disengagement from issues such as race relations and poverty. That alienation would have been unthinkable to the prominent evangelical British and American social reformers of the nineteenth century, who, in the tradition of John Wesley, sought the immediate expression of Christian "enthusiasm" — followers of Wesley's evangelical revival in England were often called "enthusiasts" — in the problems of daily life. Ockenga was offended by fundamentalism's "notorious lack of concern for social reform" and in particular by its almost hypnotic fixation on eschatology, that is, end time questions, that had flowed into fundamentalism under the influence of the dispensationalists. One of Ockenga's close friends was Edward John Carnell (1919–1967), who, like Ockenga, was a man of strong evangelical conviction and was concerned that the fundamentalists had abandoned attempts that Carnell thought could still be made to recapture mainline denominations from the hands of theological modernists and liberals.

In 1947, Ockenga and others founded Fuller Theological Seminary, in Pasadena, California, as a vehicle to train evangelical leaders who did not want to be removed from social affairs. Ockenga was named its founding president even though at the time he was pastor of the Congregationalist Park Street Church in Boston. Fuller Seminary, as envisioned by the founders, was to be "the Caltech of the evangelical world." In short, it was to enable evangelical Christianity to reengage with society instead of drawing increasingly distant from it, which was what the new evangelicals thought the fundamentalists were doing.

It was Ockenga who had invited Billy Graham to Boston for the 1949–1950 meetings, and he soon joined the board of the BGEA. Carnell became a Fuller faculty member, and when it became clear that Ockenga could not be president of a seminary in California while resident in Boston, Carnell succeeded him as president. The two men shared the desire for Fuller to be accepted by the non-evangelical theological establishment of American Protestantism as a legitimate institution from a scholarly and teaching perspective. But it was Carnell who first formulated the notions of evangelical inclusivism that Graham himself was later to embrace wholeheartedly. "God has true believers in every professing church," Carnell wrote. "Whenever there are genuine signs of faith and repentance, we must presume the gospel is at work." It was the Christian's duty, he added, to love Christians everywhere, not simply those in agreement with evangelicals.[6]

Ockenga was also an influential force behind another major achievement in Billy Graham's career, the founding in 1956 of the magazine *Christianity Today.* Graham, in his own version of the events, said he had originally been seized by the idea of an evangelical equivalent of the liberal Christian magazine *Christian Century* in 1953 and was up until the wee hours one night sketching out the format and likely future contents of the magazine. In the event, the financial angel for the project was J. Howard Pew, president of the Sun Oil Company. When *Christianity Today* was launched in mid-October 1956, its editor was Carl Henry (1913–2003), who had been Fuller's first acting dean, and Ockenga was the chairman of the board. Dr. L. Nelson Bell (1894–1973), Graham's father-in-law, served as executive editor from the magazine's founding until his death.

Graham wanted the magazine to be conservative theologically but liberal on social issues — liberal, that is, at least by the standards of the day. Of its overall tone, Graham later wrote in his autobiography, "It was my vision that the magazine be pro-church and pro-denomination and that it become the rallying point of evangelicalism within and without the large denominations." Theologian Iain Murray notes that it is scarcely conceivable that Graham could have written this, say, six years earlier,[7] when he was still firmly fundamentalist in his views. Graham's objective with *Christianity Today* accorded very much with what Ockenga hoped to accomplish at Fuller, which was to equip young men (women were admitted only later) to return to mainstream denominations and infect them with the evangelical view of the Bible and of the Christian message in general.[8] The approach proved to be a success. By the ninth issue, *Christianity Today* matched the liberal *Christian Century* in its paid subscription list, and it is now widely regarded as the leading serious religious magazine.[9]

A main impetus for Graham's evolution away from fundamentalism almost certainly was his experience in England in 1954. Though the invitation to preach at Harringay had been extended by the Evangelical Alliance, a diverse band of evangelicals from many different British church traditions, the Graham team had often found itself working with Christians from far outside the orbit within which most fundamentalists would have been comfortable. Indeed, some Anglican clergy did not believe in a literal heaven or hell or even in the physical resurrection of Jesus. A judicious observer of conservative Christianity in the United States, George Marsden, wrote later:

During his campaign in England in 1954, Graham received broader church support than his fundamentalist supporters would have allowed him in the United States. Such successes in culturally influential religious circles were leading Graham toward the conviction that he could make marvelous inroads into America's major denominations if he could jettison the disastrous fundamentalist image of separatism, anti-intellectualism, and contentiousness.[10]

Graham in England in 1954 and in Scotland in 1955 associated publicly with prominent American and British clergy who had gone on record as believing neither in the virgin birth, nor the Trinity, nor even Christ's resurrection. Yet to Scottish reporters who seemed to have a nose for theological controversy, Billy had responded, "I am neither a fundamentalist nor a modernist."[11]

One prominent American fundamentalist who followed Graham's career closely apparently overlooked Billy's "neither fundamentalist nor modernist" statement and was greatly cheered by Graham's success in England and Scotland. He was John R. Rice, whose magazine, *The Sword of the*

Lord, proclaimed on its masthead that it stood for "the Verbal Inspiration of the Bible, the Deity of Christ, His Blood Atonement, Salvation by Faith, New Testament Soul Winning and the Premillennial Return of Christ, Opposes Modernism, Worldliness and Formalism."[12] Rice, who later was prominent in the fundamentalist charge against Graham, personally attended a week of the Scotland crusade meetings in 1955 and proclaimed the experience to have been "seven miracle days."[13]

Some American fundamentalists could perhaps excuse Graham's hobnobbing with liberals in Britain, where evangelicals did unthinkable things such as drink wine and beer and where, in any case, a skeptical press had apparently been won over by Graham's guileless charm and obvious good-heartedness. It was quite another thing back on home turf in the United States and, above all, in that center of worldly iniquity, New York City. Thus it was that the New York crusade of May to September 1957, which in many ways was the high-water mark of Graham's American evangelistic crusades of the 1950s, also became the point of final and definitive rupture between Billy Graham and the fundamentalists, with whom he had begun his life as an evangelist.

The break was neither quick nor clean, for on the fundamentalist side bitterness arose over what they considered a betrayal of fundamentalist principles, a bitterness that still smolders on in angry Web sites on the Internet today.

The invitation to conduct a crusade in New York had come in 1955 from the Protestant Council of New York City, a body that represented seventeen hundred churches and thirty-one denominations. The very breadth of the invitational group turned out to be one of the major points of contention for the fundamentalists. For example, the women's prayer group for the crusade was headed up by Ruth Stafford Peale, wife of Norman Vincent Peale (1898–1993), whose 1952 book *The Power of Positive Thinking* has sold 20 million copies. By 1957, the book had already made Peale, a member of the Reformed Church of America, something of a guru of "positive mental attitude." In 1957, he had been a pastor for some three decades of the well-attended Marble Collegiate Church in Manhattan, and though in no way a modernist, Peale certainly was not a fundamentalist either. "Positive thinking," after all, is not sufficiently spiritual to be included in a worldview acceptable to fundamentalists.

In the run-up to the New York crusade, Graham did not help matters by adopting what seemed a breezy, almost casual approach to Christian evangelism with regard to the "inquirers" who might come forward at his crusades. "We'll send them to their own churches — Roman Catholic, Protestant or Jewish . . . The rest is up to God," he said.[14] From the moment that crusade preparations got under way, Graham was full of trepidation. New York had a decades-old reputation of being a particularly hard nut for evangelists to crack; it was urbane, sophisticated, cynical, and averse to religious enthusiasm in general and to "revealed truth" in particular. "From the human viewpoint and by human evaluation it may be a flop," Billy wrote in his diary before the crusade. "However, I am convinced in answer to the prayers of millions that in the sight of God and in heaven's evaluation it will be no failure."[15]

In fact, the first major opposition to the New York crusade came not from fundamentalists, but from prominent figures theologically and politically to the left of Graham. Reinhold Niebuhr, the thoughtful, respected mainstream Protestant theologian whose break with former leftist Christian theologian colleagues in the 1930s over how to deal with fascism and communism had impressed many Americans, probably spoke for the non-evangelical establishment of American Protestantism when he was invited to write a column for *Life* magazine. Graham's preaching, he asserted, "neglected the social dimensions of the gospel,"[16] and his message of a solution to every human problem through an encounter with Jesus Christ was "not very convincing to anyone — Christian or not — who is aware of the continual possibilities of good and evil in every form of civilization, every discipline of culture, and every religious convention."[17]

Graham's public response to Niebuhr's criticism plucked the characteristically humble chords he had earlier used with the British journalist William Connor, who had invited Billy for drinks in The Baptist's Head pub in London. He told reporters, "When Dr. Niebuhr makes his criticisms about me, I study them, for I have respect for them. I think he has helped me to apply Christianity to the social problems we face and has helped me to comprehend what those problems are."[18] But despite earnest appeals, Niebuhr refused to meet with Graham in any setting, perhaps fearing he would succumb to Billy's formidable double canonry of humility and charm. Criticism of what was going to be attempted in New York came also from some local Roman Catholics. Rev. John E. Kelly, of the National Catholic Welfare Council, forbade Catholics to attend crusade services, listen to or watch radio or television broadcasts of the crusade, or read any of Graham's books. Billy Graham was a purveyor of heretical beliefs and was simply "a danger to the faith," he warned.[19]

Niebuhr was not the only voice among American Protestants critical of Graham. The magazine *Christian Century,* which had tended to criticize the boisterous, extrovert evangelistic methods traditionally favored by fundamentalists, editorialized: "The Graham procedure . . . does its mechanical best to 'succeed' whether or not the Holy Spirit is in attendance. At this strange new junction of Madison Avenue and Bible Belt, the Holy Spirit is not overworked; he is overlooked."[20]

Despite these pre-emptive swipes of criticism and Graham's own misgivings — the product of a lifelong tendency to take a "glass half-empty" view of situations — the New York crusade broke records from the moment it opened in Madison Square Garden on May 15, 1957. The sheer size of the undertaking must have helped: a 4,000-

member-strong choir, 3,000 ushers, and 5,000 counselors trained in the proven techniques of counseling those who "came forward." In his opening address, Graham told the audience of 18,000, "I want you to listen not only with your ears, but the Bible teaches that your heart also has ears. Listen with your soul tonight."[21] In the weeks that followed, attendance reached a total of nearly 2.4 million people, and more than 61,000 came forward. Among those who attended the Madison Square Garden meetings was Dr. Henry Kissinger, though whether the then-recently minted PhD and junior member of the government department at Harvard University "came forward" is not publicly known.

The crusade meetings were all in the evenings, but Graham's days were packed with requests to speak to groups large and small, both from the media and from Christian organizations. He also addressed lunchtime crowds on Wall Street, accompanied by George Beverly Shea's singing.

At what had originally been planned as the closing night event on July 20 at Yankee Stadium, a record crowd of 100,000 turned out, exceeding attendance at the previous record-holding Yankee Stadium event, the Joe Louis–Max Baer fight in September

1935. The night was historic for another reason: Vice President Richard Nixon was on the platform, the first time such a high-ranking national political leader had attended a Billy Graham crusade. When Graham introduced him to the crowd, Nixon in turn relayed greetings from President Dwight D. Eisenhower, whom Nixon described as a "good friend" of Billy Graham. The final night of the crusade was held not in Yankee Stadium but in Manhattan's Times Square on 42nd Street, by reputation the very heart of "sinful" New York. Crowd estimates for the September 1 finale of the sixteen-week crusade varied wildly, from an initial 200,000 to a more generally accepted 60,000–75,000.

Whatever the actual numbers in Times Square, Graham's audience had already expanded dramatically through television coverage. On June 1, about a month into the New York crusade, ABC Television broadcast the first of fourteen weekly one-hour programs of the crusade. It was a turning point in Graham's career. This first exposure to a national television audience expanded by multiple factors Graham's exposure across the country, and thirty-five thousand letters — "many from people who had made a decision for Christ right in their own homes"[22] — poured into the Minneapolis headquarters of the BGEA after the first telecast alone. Within three months, that figure had swollen to more than 1.5 million. By mid-1957, Graham's national name recognition had reached a phenomenal 85 percent, and 75 percent of those who recognized his name viewed him positively. Perhaps more significantly, even the *New York Times* printed verbatim full texts of some of Graham's Madison Square Garden sermons, as though he were some international dignitary addressing the United Nations. The *New York Herald Tribune* gave Graham space to write a daily column called "Billy Graham Says." The first installment ran on the front page the day after the crusade's opening night. Graham started the column with: "In this opening day of the New York Crusade, we are very certain of our expectations in this regard: We do not expect to see a city transformed, but we do expect to see individuals transformed."[23] Never before had a more favorable reception been given a Christian evangelist in the city's history.

The very success of the New York crusade, however — the fact that people and groups considered by fundamentalists anathema to Christendom seemed comfortable about accepting Graham — helped poison the relationship between Billy and his erstwhile fundamentalist mentor, Bob Jones Sr. When Graham was in Scotland two years earlier, he had endured some sniping for his alleged fraternizing with theological liberals, and he had poured out his hurt to Ruth in letters home. "Some of the things they say are pure fabrications," he wrote. "I do not intend to get down to their mud-slinging and get into endless arguments and discussions with them . . . We are too busy winning souls to Christ and helping the church to go down and argue with these . . . publicity-seekers . . . If this extreme type of fundamentalism was of God, it would have brought revival long ago. Instead, it has brought dissension, division, strife and has produced dead and lifeless churches."[24] In April 1957, before the New York crusade opened, Graham had responded to a query from the National Association of Evangelicals with these words, "I would like to make myself clear. I intend to go anywhere, sponsored by anybody to preach the gospel of Christ if there are no strings attached to my message. I am sponsored by civic clubs, universities, ministerial associations, and councils of churches all over the world. I intend to continue."[25] This was pure neo-evangelicalism, the message of Edward Carnell. At another point in the preparations for the New York crusade, he said, "The one badge of Christian discipleship is not orthodoxy, but love."[26] This likely was the last straw for the fundamentalists.

An extended dispute ensued between the BGEA, often represented by Dr. Nelson Bell, and Dr. Bob Jones. To his death, Jones never once let up in his conviction that Billy Graham had betrayed Christian orthodoxy and had in effect delivered a major setback to the cause of Christ. Bob Jones University for several years distributed to new students copies of letters back and forth between supporters of Graham and those of Jones. From these, it is not difficult to understand what the heart of the disagreement was. Quite simply, it was over who was hosting Graham's events. Jones himself never disputed that Graham was an authentic evangelical who loved Christ. What he objected to was the fact that, at almost all of Graham's crusades from the mid-1950s onwards, people who were modernists or liberals were invited to sit on the platform. In an article entitled "Is Billy Graham's sponsorship by modernists, infidels, and unbelievers justified in the scripture?" probably written during the spring 1957 debate between

212

neo-evangelicals and fundamentalists, Jones argued, "God expressly forbids the granting of Christian recognition to unbelievers and false teachers." On March 19, 1957, Bell wrote to Jones, wondering if a report he had heard that Bob Jones University would expel any student known to be praying for the Graham New York crusade was true. Jones' reply a week later denied the report, but affirmed nevertheless that the New York crusade "was not according to Scripture." Moreover, he warned, if Billy persisted in his association with liberals and modernists, within two or three years he would "lose completely all of his contact with the un-compromising, orthodox preachers and lay-men." Jones added ominously, "I have been in touch with this country for sixty years, and I know what I am talking about."[27]

The correspondence heated up in the next few weeks. Bell had apparently inquired if a particular Bob Jones University student had been expelled because of his support for Graham. Jones denied it, and tartly noted that the reason for the unfortunate student's expulsion was "none of your business." Then Jones got personal. "Your letter is, I think, one of the most illogical letters I have ever known an intelligent man to write," he said condescendingly. He reiterated that sponsorship of Graham's New York crusade was "unscriptural."[28] The correspondence became even more rancorous, and the Bob Jones faculty chimed in with a letter under the dean's name expressing "resentment and indignant displeasure at [Bell's] unethical letters." Apparently, Bell had sent copies of his original letter to Jones to several students and faculty members at the university. On May 16, 1957, Jones' son, Bob Jones Jr., now president of the university, jumped into the squabble with an even more sharply worded letter of his own to Bell, saying Bell's letter was "asinine," full of "pious hypocrisy," and had "earned the contempt" of everyone at the school.[29]

The dispute over the sponsorship of the New York crusade spread beyond Graham's family and in-laws to other supporters. Bob Jones University withdrew its advertising from *Evangelical Christian*, a Toronto magazine, because of a raging debate between the Jones family and the magazine's editor, Dr. J. H. Hunter, who refused to print an article by Bob Jones Jr. clarifying his criticism of Graham. In the correspondence between Jones Jr. and Hunter, Jones reiterates the charge that Graham was sponsored in New York by "modernists of various stages of heresy and apostasy"[30] and had thus done "untold harm in breaking down the lines between orthodoxy and heresy."[31] In August 1957, Jones Jr., in the continuing dispute with Hunter, wrote of Graham, "I have never seen any firm declaration on his part against heresy, any firm denunciation of those who deny the fundamentals of the Faith, or any firm warning to young Christians against modernism and infidelity."[32] Particularly galling to the fundamentalists was the fact that the inquirers at the New York crusade were sent to a great variety of churches, many of which were indeed pastored by clergy who were modernist or liberal. The "setup" in New York was "unscriptural," thundered Jones Jr. in yet another statement from this period. Every time Graham asked a modernist or a liberal on the platform to lead in prayer, Jones argued, Graham was "giving the same recognition to an anti-Christ that is given to a Christian; *and this is forbidden in the Word of God* " (emphasis in original).[33]

The fundamentalists were further outraged by Graham's crusade in San Francisco in May 1958, in part because it was endorsed by the Oakland and San Francisco Councils of Churches and the Episcopal Diocese of California, the latter of which, at the time, was headed by a bishop, James Albert Pike (1913–1969), who resigned from his position in the Episcopal Church in 1966 after being censured by fellow bishops for doctrinal unorthodoxy. Pike later dabbled in spiritualism when he used mediums to try to contact his dead son, who had committed suicide. Graham, aware that the fundamentalists were still lobbing broadsides, released a twelve-page open letter defending his association with theological liberals. He said that he had met hundreds of men wrongly labeled liberals and found them to be "warm, Godly men, who hold to the essentials of the Christian faith but who for various reasons do not want to be associated with modern-day evangelicalism, its organizations and institutions." The problems caused by liberalism, he said, were no more harmful than the "bitterness, jealousy, rancor, division, strife, hardness, a seeking after revenge, and vindictiveness that characterizes a few fundamentalists."[34]

This counter-fire, only enraged Bob Jones and his son even more. When a crusade was scheduled in Greenville, South Carolina, in March 1966, Jones Jr. warned Bob Jones students in a university chapel talk more than a year prior that no student would be given permission to attend and that any who cooperated with the crusade would be expelled.[35] Bob Jones Sr. in early 1966 made probably his most fire-breathing criticism of Graham. Billy Graham was "doing more harm to the cause of Jesus Christ than any living man," Jones asserted in his warnings to stay away from the South Carolina crusade, which he claimed were being held in his home state for the sole reason of giving Graham a chance to embarrass and attack Jones.[36]

By the early 1970s, the Bob Jones camp had elaborated on its objections to Graham's new evangelicalism with a full-blown, pamphlet-length argument entitled "Why we do not support Billy Graham." All the familiar arguments about sponsorship were in the document, along with some additional epithets. Graham was now a "modern-day Jehoshaphat," a reference to the biblical king of Judah who allied himself with Ahab, the wicked king of Israel. There was also some interesting, substantive criticism of the methodology of the crusades themselves. Referring to the Oakland crusade of 1971 in which 21,670 people had "come forward" and signed decision cards, Jones noted that the sponsoring churches had done a follow-up and found that a full one-third of these "inquirers" had signed fictitious names or given incorrect addresses. Jones gleefully reported that the sponsoring churches had concluded that there was no lasting fruit from the ten-day crusade.[37]

Graham made one attempt in person to heal the breach with his erstwhile mentor in the late 1950s when, by coincidence, they were both staying in the same hotel in Birmingham, Alabama. Billy asked permission to call on Jones in his room and tried to warm the atmosphere by commenting favorably on the appearance of the older man. The old fundamentalist patriarch, though, refused to reciprocate in the same warm good nature. "You're on your way down, Billy," Jones reportedly said. Graham responded, "If that's the way God wants it, then it's settled." Billy was, in effect, turning the other cheek, but no reconciliation took place. When Bob Jones Sr. died in 1968, his son took the trouble to inform a member of Billy Graham's team that no Graham representative would be welcome at the funeral.[38] Today, the dispute with Graham continues on the Internet,[39] principally with the charge that his ecumenicism, that is, his warm relations with Roman Catholics and with Protestant figures considered severely unorthodox, has made him a traitor to Protestant Christianity itself and

218

an advocate of everything from the New World Order to universalism. In the view of most fundamentalists, however, the point of definitive split was the New York crusade of 1957.

The same New York crusade was a milestone for another reason: it was the first crusade at which Graham publicly recognized civil rights leader Martin Luther King Jr., inviting him on the crusade platform one evening in July to give the opening prayer. By so doing, Graham finally came down off the fence in his public support of the civil rights movement. He had been prevaricating in the first half of the 1950s, frequently expressing personal opposition to racism in America, but often failing to challenge head-on the institutions in the South that practiced segregation. Characteristically, Graham avoided for as long as possible making any decision that would cause any significant social group, in this instance white Southern segregationists, to dislike him. After all, he wanted them to come forward too at his crusades in the Southern states, and he was uncomfortable doing and saying anything that might antagonize them.

Born in South Carolina, Billy Graham was, of course, a child of the South and of Southern attitudes about race. Though he mixed freely with the children of his father's dairy farm foreman, a black man named Reese Brown, who often invited him home to dinner, the easy social interplay ended in Billy's early teenage years when he inherited a typical white Southern attitude toward blacks. "It was sort of an unspoken assumption that we were in a different class," he said, looking back on his upbringing. "Whether it was master/servant I don't know. It was with some people, I'm sure. I don't think I ever analyzed it when I was a boy."[40] At the Mordecai Ham rally in 1934, where Graham dedicated his life to God, there had been no prohibition on blacks attending, but few did so. No blacks were enrolled at the Florida Bible Institute when Graham was a student, and blacks were barred from Bob Jones University until the early 1970s.

It was not until Billy arrived at Wheaton in 1940 that his personal attitudes about race began to undergo significant change. Wheaton stood squarely in the tradition of nineteenth-century evangelical agitation against slavery, and Graham was influenced both by its historical role in the struggle to end slavery and by the black students he met there. "At Wheaton College I made friends with black students, and I recall vividly one of them coming to my room one day and talking with great conviction about America's need for racial justice," he writes in his autobiography.[41] Years later, at a 1983 crusade in Tacoma, Georgia, an African American woman told of a personal encounter with Graham more than forty years earlier, when he was a Wheaton undergraduate preaching in local revival tents. She had been a child then, attending the revival with her mother, and was playing with a white girl when a white woman tried to propel the black girl toward the "colored" section at the back. Graham's large hand descended on the white woman's shoulder. "You're going the wrong way, sister," he said. "She belongs down front — all the children belong down front so God can smile on them." Graham then disentangled the child from the white woman's grasp and had all the children, black and white, move to the front. The woman recalls that the rope separating the colored section was removed at Graham's request "because Billy Graham refused to speak to a segregated audience."[42]

The race question was not an issue when Graham made his national debut at the Christ for Greater Los Angeles revival in 1949, nor the following year in meetings in

New England. Segregation was only practiced in the American South, and the audiences at the Los Angeles and New England rallies were all racially integrated. When he preached in South Carolina in 1950, however, a separate section labeled "colored" was marked off in the stadium seating for African Americans. The same was true of several subsequent crusades in the South from 1950–1952: in Fort Worth, Memphis, Greensboro, and Raleigh, organizers ensured that the audiences were segregated. Graham rationalized this by saying that he acceded to the local norms wherever he preached. "We follow existing social customs in whatever part of the country in which we minister," he explained in Jackson, Mississippi, in 1952. "I came to Jackson to preach only the Bible and not to enter into local issues."[43] Earlier, though, in Portland, Oregon, in 1950, he had proclaimed, "All men are created equal under God. Any denial of that is a contradiction of holy law." Yet in Atlanta two months later, he had not objected that his audiences were segregated. In 1951 in California, when pressed for an explanation for why he had not spoken out against segregation, Graham said that he thought the Communists were behind most of the civil rights agitation in the United

222

States.[44] This was a view expressed by then head of the FBI, J. Edgar Hoover, and eagerly repeated by many Americans who either opposed desegregation or did not want to be bothered by the inconvenience of ending it.

Although Graham at this time in his career preached no sermons on the evil of racial segregation, there is little doubt that it not only made him uncomfortable but that it also challenged him theologically in a very deep way. At the same crusade in Jackson, Mississippi, where, under pressure to say more about the race issue, Graham had backed away on the grounds that he did not want to interfere in local issues, he had himself stirred the pot by saying, "There is no scriptural basis for segregation. It may be there are places where such is desirable to both races, but certainly not in the church . . . The ground at the foot of the cross is level . . . [and] it touches my heart when I see whites stand shoulder to shoulder with blacks at the cross."[45] This was to remain Graham's standard theological objection to racism in all institutionalized forms until the end of his preaching career. In an address to the Southern Baptist Convention in 1952, he did challenge the accepted practice of the time by saying that every Christian college had an obligation to accept all academically qualified students, regardless of race.

It was not until March 1953 in Chattanooga, Tennessee, however, that Graham took decisive crusade action against segregation, denouncing it at an evening preparatory meeting of the crusade organizing committee and later personally removing the rope divider that marked off the "colored" section. The head usher, deeply offended, resigned. At a 1953 crusade in Detroit, he rejected as unbiblical the assertion that blacks had been consigned to a lower rank than whites because Noah had cursed Canaan, the son of Ham (Gen. 9:22–27). Later, in his syndicated column, he answered a question about whether the Bible had anything to teach about racial inferiority or superiority, saying, "Definitely not. The Bible teaches that God hath made of one blood all the nations of the world."[46]

Although there is little doubt that Graham was sincere in expressing these views, biographer Martin nonetheless suggests that in responding to the rising national clamor against segregation while also trying to avoid offending the white Christians at whom he was primarily aiming his crusades in the South, Graham in the early 1950s appeared to be waffling. In Martin's assessment, "consistent with his pacific and conciliatory nature, Billy would always prefer decorum to bold example, and he would never be comfortable with violent protest or even with non-violent socially disruptive measures aimed at changing the standing order."[47]

Pacific and conciliatory or not, Graham was getting plenty of abusive letters from white segregationists accusing him of meddling in their affairs and no small amount of criticism from Protestants in the political center and left — Reinhold Niebuhr, for example — for not speaking out like a prophet against racial prejudice. Meanwhile, events in the United States were propelling the debate forward. In May 1954, the Supreme Court handed down its milestone *Brown v. Board of Education* ruling that segregated schools anywhere in the nation were unconstitutional. In December 1955, African American Rosa Parks boarded a bus in Montgomery, Alabama, and sat in the front, which by city ordinance was for whites only. Her refusal to move to the back of the bus resulted in her arrest and trial and precipitated a boycott of the Montgomery city buses. That boycott thrust to the forefront of national and international attention the black civil rights leader Martin Luther King Jr., pastor of Dexter Avenue Baptist Church in Montgomery, Alabama.

By spring 1956, the civil rights struggle was developing into a crisis of national proportions, and Graham began a correspondence with President Eisenhower, punctuated by a White House meeting with Ike, to see if he could help to defuse the rising tensions. Eisenhower hoped that Graham might influence Southern white evangelicals to admit more qualified blacks to school boards and graduate schools and to develop flexible seating plans on buses in order to avoid confrontations in the process of integration. Graham in turn said that the church "must take a place of spiritual leadership" in promoting "racial understanding and progress." He would do all in his power, he told Ike, "to urge Southern ministers to call upon the people for moderation, charity, compassion, and progress toward compliance" with Supreme Court decisions.[48] Later, Graham was to play a significant role as a supporter of Eisenhower's decision to send federal troops into Little Rock, Arkansas, in the summer of 1957 to carry out the desegregation of Little Rock Central High School.

Graham's most significant public identification with the civil rights movement, however, was inviting King to give the opening prayer at the New York crusade on July 18, 1957. King was anathema to many Southern white Christians who supported Graham but opposed desegregation, so Billy's decision to invite King onto the speaker's platform at Madison Square Garden brought a predictable torrent of abusive letters and threats to his family. King, however, in his prayer, expressed gratitude for the public display of support by white Protestant Christendom's most prominent American figure: "O God, we ask Thee to help us to work with renewed vigor for a warless world and for a brotherhood that transcends race or color. We thank Thee this evening for the marvelous things which have been done in this city, and through the dynamic preachings of this great evangelist. And we ask Thee, O God, to continue blessing him. Give him continued power and authority. And as we look [unto] him tonight, grant that our hearts and our spirit will be opened to the divine inflow."[49]

King briefed the Graham team during the summer of 1957 about the ongoing civil rights struggle. Graham, who clearly liked and admired King, recounts in his autobiography that the civil rights leader explained to him the philosophy and methodology of his campaign of civil disobedience against segregation but cautioned Graham not to pursue racial justice by the same means. Graham wrote later, "He urged me to keep on doing what I was doing — preaching the gospel to integrated audiences and supporting goals by example — and not to join him in the streets." King, in this account, also said to Graham, "You stay in the stadiums, Billy, because you will have far more impact on the white establishment there than you would if you marched in the streets. Besides that, you have a constituency that will listen to you, especially among white people, who may not so much listen to me." King offered the additional counsel that a leader should never get too far out in front of his own people. Billy writes, "I followed his advice."[50]

A few weeks later, King, apparently still moved by his experience at the New York crusade, wrote to Graham: "I am deeply grateful to you for the stand you have taken in the area of race relations. You have courageously brought the Christian gospel to bear on the question of race in all its urgent dimensions. I am sure you will continue this emphasis in all of your preaching, for you, above any other preacher in

America, can open the eyes of many people in this area." Then he added: "Although we have a long, long way to go in solving the internal problem of race facing our nation, I still have faith in the future. We are gradually emerging from the bleak and desolate midnight of injustice into the bright and glittering daybreak of freedom and justice. This remains true because God is forever at work in His universe."[51]

Graham remained in periodic contact with King, and says that, en route to the 1960 Baptist World Alliance meeting in Rio de Janeiro, the two men did "a lot of swimming and praying together" at the Hilton Hotel in San Juan, Puerto Rico. Once in Rio, he gave a dinner in King's honor. In his autobiography, Graham mentions almost casually that he had known King for "several years" and that King had asked Billy to call him "Mike," as King's family members did. Graham pointedly notes that in Rio in the days following the dinner honoring King, white Southern Baptist conference attendees from Mississippi noticed how friendly and informal relations were between the civil rights leader and Graham's top aides.[52]

Despite King's historic appearance at the New York crusade in July 1957, it was painfully obvious after just a few weeks that black New Yorkers were staying away in droves. In an attempt to correct the impression that his evangelistic message was just for white people, Graham invited onto his evangelistic team, while the crusade was still in progress, his first African American associate evangelist, Howard Jones. The immediate task Jones was charged with was organizing venues for Graham to preach at in black areas of the city, notably Harlem. He succeeded in doing this so well that the number of African Americans attending the Madison Square Garden crusade grew as the crusade continued.

Jones's success did not come easily, though. When word of the plans for the first appearance in Harlem got out, Graham got nasty phone calls and letters full of curses and predictions that his crusades would be destroyed. On the day of the outdoor event, pouring rain began to fall as the Graham team drove to Harlem, and Billy wondered out loud if anyone would come. To everyone's relief, a crowd of five thousand was waiting inside the packed church, which was unable to accommodate any more people. Just as Graham was ready to start speaking, the sun came out, and the event was moved outside again — where the numbers swelled to eight thousand. Jones, recounting the story in 1984, recalled, "It was right out there in these tall apartment houses, and thousands of people opened their windows" so they could hear. "The next week we went to Brooklyn, and we had ten thousand there. And then they started coming, our people started coming, by the droves. Just that one visit," Jones said.[53]

The personal toll on Jones, however, for his courageous willingness to be associated with Graham's team was great. "It was difficult," he recalled later. "I was usually the only black person around. I received piercing stares, and I often sat isolated on campaign platforms because people refused to sit next to me. After Billy preached, we associate pastors would leave the platform to help counsel people. There, too, I got dirty stares from people. I'd go ahead and talk to people about Christ, but it was difficult for me. There were times during that New York crusade when the stress was so great. I remember one time when I lay awake, weeping in bed. I prayed, 'Lord, I can't take this pressure. It's too much.' "[54]

Jones nevertheless stayed with the BGEA for more than three decades, and Graham never again waffled on the race issue. Still, he did not take any resolutely unpopular stands to denounce segregation. About a year after the New York crusade, King protested that Graham was honoring Southern white segregationists by inviting them onto the speaker's platform at crusades in the South. The complaint, in effect, was the same as Bob Jones's criticism of Graham for inviting apostates and heretics to sit on his crusade platform.

When King was assassinated in March 1968, Graham was in Australia, too far away to attend the funeral. He sent flowers and made a statement to the media that "in the eyes of the world [King] has become one of the greatest Americans." It was a less-than-ringing eulogy, one that suggested that while Graham himself favored civil rights, he was all too aware of how many white Americans in the South remained deeply suspicious of King — and Billy Graham just did not want to say anything that might alienate them.

With the perspective of hindsight, it is easy to say that Graham could have done more in support of the civil rights movement. He did not need to march with King, but he could have been more outspoken, and he could have been more forceful in dissociating himself from segregationists. Rev. Jesse Jackson is one of a number of African American leaders who believes Graham failed in furthering the cause of civil rights for African Americans. "I have seen him at great rallies in Europe, in Russia, and all around the world," Jackson told me in a 2001 interview. "If he had [used his evangelistic crusades] to bring down walls in this country, it would have elevated his powerful evangelism to another level."[55] On the other hand, after King's death, the late Senator Daniel Patrick Moynihan (1927–2003) sent Graham a message describing him as equal to King in the fight against racism. "You and Rev. King, more than any two men — and surely with God's help —," he wrote, "brought your own South out of that long night of racial fear and hate."[56] Graham, born in the land of Dixie, certainly made his own emphatic break with the racism that pervaded much of the South. In confronting the evils of racism, however, his dominant impulse had been that of evangelist and pastor, and not of prophet.

SEVEN:
COMMUNISM:
A NEW APPROACH

When Billy Graham burst onto the national scene in the 1950s and started leaving his mark on the United States and the world, his politics, ideology, and rhetoric reflected the mood of the times. During the 1949 Los Angeles crusade, he had already expressed a visceral anti-communism in his doomsday predictions about the looming Soviet threat, and in the decade following he stayed the course as a distinctly hawkish, sometimes fire-breathing American patriot. In the 1960s, when many Americans were protesting the Vietnam War, Graham urged his listeners to allow the White House to conduct diplomacy, war, and peace as it saw fit, which first under John F. Kennedy and then under Lyndon Johnson showed no hesitation about prosecuting a massive war in a distant part of the third world.

By the late 1970s, however, Graham's worldview had changed profoundly, and that change in turn would, in the view of some observers, play a role in transforming the political structure of the world. Not only had he become willing to talk about "peace" in a way that previously might have been associated with a political liberal or even a pacifist, but he was enthusiastically venturing into Communist countries that had hitherto considered him little more than a propagandist for warmongering imperialists. In the 1980s, Graham's apparent zeal to preach the gospel in the very heart of communism led to one of the most controversial foreign visits of his entire career: his presence in 1982 at a Soviet-sponsored peace conference in Moscow. Despite angry criticism of that trip by foreign policy specialists and journalists, he continued his preaching forays into Eastern Europe throughout the decade, and also ventured into China.

The transformation of Graham's views on communism, war, and peace was truly momentous, and by the end of his preaching career, he was someone much closer in attitude to Pope John Paul II, Soviet dissident and writer Aleksandr Solzhenitsyn, and a handful of other major world thinkers who hold worldviews that largely transcend tribal and national constraints. This transformation highlights and reflects some of the same aspects of Billy Graham's character that were apparent in his response to the race question, to his conflicts with the fundamentalists, and to the various occasions when critics slammed him for what he had said or done. Billy Graham had an overarching desire to offend no one, which sometimes resulted in pleasing few. He unhesitatingly seized all opportunities to preach the gospel, no matter the venue, regime, or possible fallout. He also developed an uncanny knack for disarming his critics.

During this evolution of his views, Graham certainly made mistakes, above all in the occasional comments on religious freedom in various parts of the Communist world that, at best, made him sound naïve and, at worst, made him appear to be an apologist for authoritarian regimes. In taking the major political risks that he did, however, he may also have achieved something unique in American religious history: attaining the status of a truly international statesman, and in the process playing a significant role in pushing the international political landscape forward into the postcommunist world of today.

Graham's international endeavors have

always been fueled by his religious motivations. In the mid-1970s, he seemed at times genuinely pessimistic about the impact of international political developments on Christian freedom around the world. He even speculated openly about the possibility that Christians in the West might be persecuted for their faith at some near-future time.[1] Graham's pessimism may have been due to the triumph in 1975 of Communist armies in Indochina, the Horn of Africa, and in the former Portuguese colonies of Angola and Mozambique. A few years later, however, Graham's concerns had evolved from alarm over the threat to Christian freedom posed by repressive political movements such as communism to the apparently growing danger of global nuclear war.

During the Carter administration, a high-ranking Defense Department official briefed Billy and Ruth in their Montreat home on the consequences of nuclear conflict. Presumably the briefing was unclassified and therefore would have contained information available to anyone researching the subject. But "the grim facts . . . appalled the Grahams," according to biographer Pollock.[2] In his autobiography, Billy says that he had been talking about "peace" for several years, though the media had paid little attention to his statements.[3]

Graham had visited the Soviet Union for a few days in June 1959 as a tourist, and in July 1967 he had preached in Yugoslavia, which, though Communist-ruled, was not part of the Soviet bloc. A visit to Poland planned for 1966, to celebrate the millennium of Polish Christianity, was cancelled by the Polish government because the Vatican tried too hard to secure an invitation for Pope Paul VI, and Polish authorities did not want to make the controversial decision of inviting a Protestant religious leader from America but not the pope. Despite these early Communist contacts, his first trip to any Warsaw Pact nation in Eastern Europe — to Hungary in 1977 — required five years of diligent planning, diplomacy, and sheer scheming by an extraordinary Hungarian-born American Protestant, Alexander S. Haraszti (1920–1998). An ordained Baptist minister and a medical doctor in his native Hungary, Haraszti was also the translator of a bootlegged 1955 Hungarian version of Billy's book *Peace with God*. Haraszti escaped from Hungary at the very beginning of the abortive Hungarian uprising against Soviet control in 1956 and eventually arrived in the United States. Once in America, he furthered his medical training with degrees in general medicine and surgery while on the side zealously pursuing ways to encourage evangelical Protestantism in his former homeland and in other parts of Eastern Europe. He met Graham for the first time in 1972 when Billy was conducting a crusade in Cleveland, Ohio, and introduced him to Sandor Palotay, then president of Hungary's evangelical Council of Free Churches, and Dr. Janos Laczkovszki, who headed a large association of Hungarian Baptists. It was Palotay who invited Graham to come and preach in Hungary.

It required five years of painstaking further negotiations by Haraszti, however, to nail down the arrangements. Graham biographer Martin describes the Hungarian as being "equipped with apparently inexhaustible energy, monomaniacal tenacity, and virtually total recall," qualities entirely necessary to overcome complex internal rivalries within the murky world of church-state relations in Eastern Europe.[4] He had to coax Palotay, for example, to share control over the itinerary not only with the Hungarian government — for obvious reasons — but also with Lutherans and Roman Catholics, in whose churches Graham also wanted to preach. The Hungarian government, for its part, wanted a *quid pro quo* from the US government for agreeing to let Graham visit Hungary. Conveniently, two issues were lying on President Carter's desk at the beginning of the fall of 1977: the return of the Hungarian royal crown, which had been moved to the United States for safekeeping at the end of World War II, and the issue of Most Favored Nation trading status, which Congress grants to normal trading partners of the United States. Graham, without promising anything to the Hungarians other than his willingness to discuss these issues positively with US officials, helped move forward US-Hungarian relations in the process of securing his invitation. The crown was returned shortly after Graham left Hungary, and the MFN trading status was granted in 1989.

Before the formal invitation to Graham was finally extended, much effort went into convincing the Hungarian authorities that Billy was neither a "burning anti-communist" ignorant of Eastern Europe nor a warmonger.[5] For a time, they even held against Graham the fact that he had visited Yugoslavia a decade earlier. The problem was that by visiting Yugoslavia, which, though Communist, had refused to join the Moscow-led Warsaw Pact, Graham might have been perceived as thumbing his nose at the Soviets. Opposition to the visit, though, did not just come from the Hungarians. Many American evangelicals were similarly aghast at the prospect of America's leading evangelist accepting an invitation from a Communist regime.[6] Haraszti received angry and bitter complaints from fellow-Hungarians in the United States, and Graham himself was criticized by US-based Hungarian exile groups. The objections to the visit were understandable: Graham's very prestige would lend credence to the appearance of "tolerance" of Christianity by a regime that provided only limited outlets for expressions of religious faith, and this false impression would in turn be used as propaganda by the Communist authorities to bolster their legitimacy.

Graham's motivation for preaching in Hungary was exactly the same as stated in his response to the National Association of Evangelicals in 1957 when the group criticized his willingness to associate with non-fundamentalist Christian groups: "I intend to go anywhere, sponsored by anybody, to preach the gospel of Christ if there are no strings attached to my message." He was well aware that the Hungarian government would seek to derive propaganda value from his visit, the very reason some of his BGEA associates opposed the trip. Graham took the view, however, that the seeds of the gospel he preached would bear greater fruit than the temporary ideological advantage the Hungarian Communist government might gain. In light of developments resulting from the visit, he was surely correct.

Graham preached in Hungary in Lutheran, Baptist, and Reformed churches, always to overflow crowds, and often, at the conclusion of his sermons, the sanctuaries echoed with a chorus of clicks as scores of tape recorders were turned off. The climax of his visit was probably a talk at the conclusion of a Baptist youth camp meeting in Tahi, about sixteen miles north of Budapest. The audience estimated by police at thirty thousand had traipsed in not only from all over Hungary, but from other parts of Communist-controlled Eastern Europe as well, for example, from Czechoslovakia, Romania, and Bulgaria. A Soviet Baptist delegation had even arrived from Moscow, and it turned out that they had an invitation of their own: would Graham be willing to come and preach in Soviet Baptist churches? The camp event was Hungary's largest post–World War II Christian assembly, and when Graham finished, there was prolonged applause.

Graham had certainly fulfilled part of his ambition to preach the gospel without restrictions on the content of his message to any audience in Hungary that was willing to listen to him, but the Hungarian government got what it wanted as well. "Things are far more open than I had supposed," Graham said on leaving. "There is religious liberty in Hungary . . . The church is alive in Hungary." Then, perhaps wanting to deflect in advance criticism he knew such comments were sure to elicit, he added, "I have not joined the Communist Party since coming to Hungary, nor have I been asked to. But I think the world is changing, and on both sides we're beginning to understand each other more."[7]

Almost unnoticed in these events was an ability Graham had frequently displayed of disarming the criticism and doubts of fellow Protestants about his brand of evangelicalism. Although fundamentalists of the Bob Jones variety back home had two decades earlier come to the conclusion that Billy had supped with the devil by associating with so many ecumenically minded clergy in America, it was not known by many overseas that Graham was becoming increasingly broad-minded in his under-

243

standing of Christian fellowship. In Hungary, for example, two leading Budapest Protestants, Bishop Zoltan Kaldy of the Lutheran church and Bishop Tibor Bartha of the Reformed church, had initially opposed his visit, but they, like so many others, were won over. Bartha later said that he had been impressed by Graham's "warmth, his Christian spirit, his honesty, and his humility in saying, 'I have come to learn.' " He added, "I took him to my heart."[8]

Like dominoes falling one by one, so did the other regimes of Eastern Europe. In October 1978, Graham added Poland to his list of Eastern European states willing to receive him. His ten-day October 6–16, 1978, tour coincided, ironically, with the Vatican deliberations that resulted in the election of Polish Cardinal Karol Wojtyla of Krakow to be Pope John Paul II. In fact, the future pope's Rome-bound plane was waiting to take off as the one carrying Graham and his party landed at Warsaw airport.

As in the case of the Hungarian visit a year earlier, it had required all the considerable skills of Alexander Haraszti to smooth ruffled feathers in advance. Poland's Catholic primate, Cardinal Stefan Wyszynski, the archbishop of Warsaw, had sent an envoy to Atlanta in the spring of 1978 to complain to Haraszti that the hierarchy of Poland's powerful Roman Catholic Church had not been consulted in advance of the invitation to Graham. Furthermore, the envoy suggested, the visit would be an embarrassment because Poland had so few Protestants who would show up to hear Graham's sermons. Haraszti shrewdly countered that the presence of an overwhelming array of Western journalists would guarantee that the visit would grab international news headlines for Poland.

In the event, it was Karol Wojtyla, whose appointment as auxiliary bishop of Krakow in the late 1950s Wyszynski had opposed, who played a major role in opening up Poland's powerful Roman Catholic Church to Graham's influence. Because of the Vatican deliberations to select a new pope, Wojtyla was unable to meet Graham for tea as planned, but he not only granted permission for a large church in his diocese, St. Anne's, to be made available for the American evangelist's preaching, but he also personally invited Billy to preach there. In fact, Graham was doing just that, to an overflow crowd, just four days before Wojtyla's election as pope.

It was in Katowice, however, a Polish mining town whose Communist leadership had done its best over the years to limit the Catholic presence, that Graham preached his most powerful sermon to a Catholic audience. An astonishing crowd of as many as thirteen thousand showed up at Christ the King cathedral, including three hundred priests and nuns. When Billy ended his sermon by asking those wishing to indicate a new commitment to Christ to raise their hands, all the priests and nuns did so. The bishop of Katowice, Herbert Bednorz, called Graham's visit "the greatest ecumenical event in the history" of his diocese.[9] Sales of Bibles in Poland rose significantly after the ten-day visit.

While he was in Poland, Graham toured some of the most desolate parts of the former Nazi–death camp Auschwitz and, as attested to both by his BGEA associates and by his autobiography, he was profoundly impacted, nearly to the point of tears. The Auschwitz visit "made me reflect long and hard on the hawkish sentiments of my youthful years," he wrote. "I felt that I needed to speak out even more concerning the need for efforts toward international peace in the nuclear age."[10] Addressing his Polish hosts and the accompanying press corps at the Wall of Death in Auschwitz, he added, "The very survival of human civilization is at stake . . . The present insanity of a global arms race, if continued, will lead inevitably to a conflagration so great that Auschwitz will seem like a minor rehearsal." Graham called on world leaders to put the survival of the human race above national pride and power, and he called on all Christians to rededicate themselves "to the Lord Jesus Christ, to the cause of peace, to reconciliation among all the races and nations of the world." He added, "The issues we face are not only political; they are also moral." Graham says in his autobiography, "The incredible horror that took place there will always be burned into my heart and mind."[11]

The Auschwitz visit became a milestone in a transformation in Graham's thinking that had begun after the Defense Department briefing several years earlier in his home. Graham said that that briefing had caused him to decide that "peace was a moral issue and not just a political issue, and we were to be instruments of His peace whenever possible."[12] In biographer Pollock's view, Auschwitz marked a turning point in Graham's entire approach to world peace. He began to speak out with increasing fervor not only in favor of nuclear disarmament but also against all weapons of mass destruction. He had, in fact, ceased to be a conservative Protestant patriot urging military readiness against the Soviet threat. Although he had always eschewed the role of a prophet on domestic policy — after all, as we shall see, he was strangely silent during Watergate — on issues of war and peace Graham was imperceptibly assuming the role of a Jeremiah to the nations. In that role, he would eventually play a significant part in turning the world upside down, as preachers of the gospel since apostolic times have often done.

A few months after his Polish tour, a campaign by mostly liberal Protestant churches in America urging the US administration to sign the SALT 2 agreement between the United States and the Soviet Union on nuclear arms reductions was gathering momentum. Abandoning any further inhibitions about being associated with such theologically liberal organizations as the National Council of Churches, Graham joined the chorus. "Why can't we have peace?" he asked. He denied he was a pacifist and said he did not favor unilateral disarmament, but added that he approved of disarmament in general. "I'm in favor of trust," he said. "I'm in favor of having agreements, not only to reduce but to eliminate.

Why should any nation have atomic bombs?" In his writings and speeches in the late 1970s, Graham even began to refer approvingly to "SALT 10," a sort of future mythic agreement under which all nuclear weapons owned by all the major powers would be abolished. Referring to the only use by any nation of nuclear weapons, he now said, "As I look back — I'm sure many people will disagree with me on this — but as I look back, I think Truman made a mistake in dropping that first atomic bomb. I wish we had never developed it . . . I have seen that we must seek the good of the whole human race, and not just the good of any one nation or race."[13]

It was a view of the bombings of Hiroshima and Nagasaki that certainly would not have found support among the vast majority of Americans who had fought in the Pacific against the Japanese during World War II. What is striking is that this major sea change in Graham's historical outlook appears to have gone unnoticed by his countrymen. In fact, over many years, Americans — with the notable exception of the fundamentalists — have tended to overlook in Graham anything with which they disagreed while fastening onto those attributes they found comforting; Graham, in effect, is something of a Rorschach test for American Christianity

The visit to Poland was significant not only in reinforcing Graham's evolving views on world peace. It also built up his confidence that he could deal satisfactorily with Communist governments and with the often-harassed Protestant and Catholic church leaderships in Eastern Europe. He returned to Poland and Hungary in 1981 to receive honorary theological degrees, but he was already seeing the glimmerings of the real prize of his first, tentative foray into the Communist world: an invitation to Moscow.

According to Graham, during his first visit to the Soviet capital, as a tourist in 1959, he had knelt in Red Square and prayed that one day he would be able to conduct a crusade there in the Soviet Union's most important public square and in Moscow's largest sports stadium. It would take thirty-three years for that prayer to become reality. The Soviet Baptist delegation to Hungary in 1977 had indeed brought a modest invitation for Graham to come and preach in their churches, and a provisional schedule for the Soviet visit was arranged for September 1979. Greater world affairs, however, forced the cancellation of those plans: the visit of Chinese leader Deng

Xiaoping to the United States in January 1979, which irritated the Soviets, and the Soviet invasion of Afghanistan in December 1979, which alarmed the Americans. Now, in 1982, Graham faced a far more daunting challenge: whether to accept an invitation to a conference in Moscow that was likely to be a transparent propaganda jamboree staged by the Soviets. If he went, he would almost certainly be savaged by the Western media as a dupe of Soviet foreign policy. If he stayed away, he would probably forego any future opportunities for ministry in the Soviet Union, and even in parts of Eastern Europe that he had not yet visited.

Graham was in some anguish over the decision. Though he sensed deep down it was the right thing to do, many of his senior advisors, as well as his wife, Ruth, did not, and they urged him to stay away. He turned to his old friend Richard Nixon, by now largely rehabilitated from the Watergate scandal, for advice. Nixon told him, "There is great risk, but I believe for the sake of the message you preach, the risk is worth it." In a 1986 account of his role, Nixon told Graham biographer Pollock, "I frankly told him that I had no illusions whatsoever that he was going to be able to convert the atheistic Communist leaders of the Soviet Union,

Romania, etc. to Christianity, but that it was important to let the people in those countries see and hear an American religious leader who could give them at least a glimmer of hope that there was a better spirit life for them than the dull, drabness of Marxist/Leninist societies."[14]

As ever, Graham wanted to be absolutely sure that the White House did not oppose his visit. He knew the State Department vehemently did, and Vice President George H. W. Bush, while not actually saying that he was against the Moscow trip, in a phone conversation shortly before his departure made sure that Graham knew how strongly most of the US government opposed it. But at a short-notice luncheon at the vice-presidential residence, surprise guest President Ronald Reagan himself provided the ultimate *imprimatur.* "Now Billy, don't you worry about this trip. God works in mysterious ways," he said. He then gave Graham a handwritten note with the words, "We'll be praying for you every mile of the way."[15]

In 1982, the year of the Moscow conference, the Cold War was approaching its climax as the Reagan presidency gathered momentum. Within months, the Soviet Union's own leadership would be grappling with the long and difficult transition from the era of Leonid Brezhnev, which ended with Brezhnev's death in November 1982, to the era of *glasnost* and *perestroika* introduced by the new secretary-general of the Soviet Communist Party, Mikhail Gorbachev, when he assumed the reins of power in March 1985, following the deaths in quick succession of Brezhnev's successors Yuri Andropov in 1984 and Konstantin Chernenko in 1985.

When Billy Graham finally arrived in Moscow, President Reagan had just castigated the Soviet Union as an "evil empire" in a March address to the National Association of Evangelicals in Orlando, Florida. Even before that famous speech, though, the whole tenor of American strategic attitudes toward the Soviet Union had already been defined by Reagan's generic anti-Soviet rhetoric and in his defense policies of conventional military buildup and the development of the "Star Wars" missile defense program. On the part of the Soviets, meanwhile, there was talk that the global "co-relation of forces," that is, the global balance of power, was nevertheless moving in the Soviet Union's favor, even as the autocratic regime that Stalin in the 1920s had hammered into shape out of the old

Russian empire was showing signs of serious internal weaknesses. In the early 1980s, government propaganda lecturers fanned throughout major Soviet cities, warning that war with the United States might really be in the offing.

Graham flew into this cauldron of tension on May 7, 1982, with his staff and accompanying journalists to attend the cumbersomely named "World Conference of Religious Workers for Saving the Sacred Gift of Life from Nuclear Catastrophe" in Moscow. The name itself was enough to cause eyes to roll among Sovietologists and American diplomats from Moscow to Washington. Obviously, the conference was intended to score propaganda points against the United States: which of the two superpowers, Moscow or Washington, was more dedicated to eliminating the danger of nuclear war?

Graham, in fact, had been developing his emergent theme of opposition to nuclear weaponry and had already been speaking of peace in the spring of 1982 at colleges in New England. At Harvard, he had called for an end to the arms race, to apartheid in South Africa, to racial discrimination anywhere on earth, and to "America's exploitation of a disproportionate share of the world's resources."[16] The problem was, nobody seemed to take him seriously as a peace activist. Part of his motive for accepting the Moscow invitation was to draw attention to his new cause. "I had started speaking out against nuclear weapons and calling for the elimination of all weapons of mass destruction, whether chemical or nuclear, but it was never in the press," he told biographer Martin. "So I decided the only way I could make my statement known was to accept the invitation to come to the peace conference in Moscow. 'Then they will listen to me,' I thought."[17] In reality, few Americans paid much attention to what he said in Moscow.

As with all of Graham's previous visits to Eastern Europe, the ground had been prepared by the ever-resourceful Alexander Haraszti. During the preparations for the visit originally scheduled for 1979, Ambassador Anatoly Dobrynin had invited Graham to the Soviet embassy to discuss the plans. Why did he want to come? Dobrynin bluntly asked. Billy deftly turned to Haraszti, who was with him, and asked him to explain. Haraszti told Dobrynin that Billy Graham wanted to express gratitude to V. I. Lenin, founder of the Soviet state, for breaking the religious monopoly in Russia of the

Orthodox Church. It was probably the most disingenuous reason for wanting to visit his country that the astonished Dobrynin had ever heard. But Haraszti was just warming up. He reminded Dobrynin that there were 40 million to 50 million Christian believers in the Soviet Union. "If you do not make peace with them, sir," warned Haraszti, "you are going to face a very serious problem."[18] Dobrynin faithfully reported back to Moscow the purported conversion of America's favorite evangelist into an admirer of Lenin, and when US–Soviet relations had recovered from the hiccups of Deng Xiaoping and Afghanistan, the long-sought invitation was extended.

Graham's willingness to attend a Soviet-sponsored religious peace conference, even though he had agreed to come only as an "observer," was but one problem he faced on arrival. A far more troublesome matter was the case of the Siberian Seven, Pentecostal Christians from Chernogorsk who had darted past Soviet guards to enter the US embassy in Moscow, been granted asylum within the embassy, and were demanding permission to go abroad. The Siberians, on learning of Graham's plans, asked him to stay away as long as they were not being permitted to depart the country.

The US ambassador, Arthur Hartman, meanwhile, was sympathetic to their case and campaigned hard with State Department officials against Graham's plans to attend the conference.

In Graham's and Haraszti's negotiations with Moscow over the terms of the visit, Billy, to his credit, insisted on seeing the Siberians holed up in the embassy despite strong disapproval from the Soviets. At the same time, extremely reluctant to further embarrass his hosts, Graham demanded that the visit be private, without the presence of reporters or photographers. Hartman was annoyed about the exclusion of the press. In the event, it was probably one of the chilliest "pastoral" visits of Billy Graham's career. The Siberians peppered Graham with questions about biblical interpretations, essentially wanting him to agree with them that the red horse in the book of Revelation referred to Soviet Communism. When Graham tried to defuse the tension by suggesting they pray, they were stonily silent while he prayed, asking God to give wisdom to the Pentecostals. Finally, after a pause, Graham and his party got up and took their leave.

The Graham group had arrived on a Friday and were scheduled to visit a Baptist church, where he would preach, on Sunday evening. But Billy's insistence on issuing a press release about his schedule, which was then relayed back to Moscow by the US government radio broadcast, the *Voice of America,* annoyed his Soviet hosts so much that they demanded the schedule be changed, fearing a mob scene at the Baptist church. They moved the church visit to 8 a.m. Sunday morning, instead of Sunday evening, when Baptists from all over the Soviet Union had prepared to come and hear the visiting American. After the re-scheduled Baptist church visit, the visitors were hustled off to Moscow's Orthodox patriarchal Cathedral of the Epiphany for a greeting to worshippers during the regular Sunday liturgy.

The Baptist church appearance provided a foretaste of further controversy. While Graham was preaching, a woman in the balcony unfurled a banner which read, "We have more than 150 prisoners for the work of the gospel," a reference to the number of Baptist pastors believed then to be held in prison or labor camps. Graham apparently did not see the protest sign, but the attentive Western reporters did. The demonstrator was hustled quickly out of the balcony, whether by Baptist church officials or KGB plainclothesmen isn't clear. When Graham was asked at a later stop on his Soviet tour what he thought about the incident, he lamely replied, "We detain people in the United States if we catch them doing something wrong." A disappointed Soviet Baptist later told a reporter, "I don't see any difference between Dr. Billy Graham and our own timid churchmen, who are scared to death to offend the authorities. We hoped for better things from him. He could be very helpful if he wanted to be."[19]

Graham was now firmly in the maw of both the Soviet bureaucracy and the hierarchy of the Russian Orthodox church, who were determined to move him from one event to another with minimal interruption. At the Orthodox cathedral, it was time for the service of the Divine Liturgy, and Billy waited for his turn to be introduced and to speak briefly while standing next to Patriarch Pimen, the head of the Orthodox Church, and Orthodox dignitaries from other parts of the Soviet Union as well as from Romania, Bulgaria, and the Egyptian city of Alexandria. There were no microphones, and Graham's interpreter was barely audible in the cavernous stone building. Shouts of "Louder, louder" came from the back, which Billy — now informed of the incident in the Baptist church — anxiously feared was another demonstration. Graham spoke louder, as did his interpreter, as he reiterated his commitment to the notion of international peace, no doubt pleasing his Soviet hosts. He said he had gone through three conversions in his life: first, to Jesus Christ as Lord and Savior; second, to the principle of racial justice; and third, to work for world peace for the remainder of his life.[20]

This seemed an odd, albeit spontaneous formulation. While his initial conversion through Mordecai Ham was well known to all who knew Billy Graham's story, neither sympathetic whites nor sympathetic blacks would have said that he had actually undergone a "conversion" to the black civil rights movement. That, after all, would have implied that he had at one time opposed racial justice, a notion that neither he nor any of his supporters would have wanted to promote. True, Graham had moved over a period of a few years from a friendly neutral position on desegregation to one openly supportive of it. But "conversion"? This was an unlikely notion.

On the other hand, in the context of his efforts to be taken seriously as a worldwide peacemaker, "conversion" would indeed apply to the change in his worldview from a once ardent anti-communist crusader to a Christian leader willing not only to publicly criticize the United States for its failings on the international scene but to attend a conference where the entire tone would be essentially anti-American.

The conference began on Monday morning and, as expected, delegate after delegate made it clear that the onus for endangering world peace rested with the United States. In the negotiations over his participation, Graham had threatened to walk out if the conference turned into a hate fest against the United States. In the event, when a Syrian delegate launched into an anti-America diatribe, Graham did not walk out but obviously and conspicuously removed his headphones at his seat on the platform. After a flurry of notes were exchanged among Russian Orthodox and other officials, the attacks ceased.

When Graham's turn to speak came, he was eloquent and cogent.

"No nation, large or small, is exempt from blame for the present state of international affairs," he said. "If we do not see our moral and spiritual responsibility concerning this life-and-death matter, I firmly believe the living God will judge us for our blindness and lack of compassion."[21] To the irritation of his Soviet hosts, Graham did not refrain from calling for the protection of religious freedom in every country of the world, using the exact wording of the 1975 Helsinki Accord, to which the Soviets were signatories. His reason for doing this, however, is curious. It was not, as one might have supposed, to balance the one-sided anti-America rhetoric at the conference. Rather, he had raised the Helsinki wording in the hope that "it might stir the conscience of the Soviet government, which had signed the agreement but was widely judged to be ignoring some of its provisions," Graham later wrote.[22] This, surely, showed real naiveté. Had the Soviet government ever given any indication that, on matters of freedom of conscience, it even had a conscience?

Press coverage of Graham's visit paid scant attention to the conference, presumably discounting the whole affair as a Soviet propaganda sideshow. Graham certainly acquitted himself effectively and with dignity at the conference and was rewarded with a three-minute ovation from all the delegates. But the accompanying journalists were loaded for bear for the remainder of the six-day trip. At an impromptu meeting outside the Zagorsk monastery, Western reporters asked if he had seen any evidence of persecution. "No, I have not personally seen persecution," Graham replied, even though he had already met with the Siberian Seven in the US embassy. At a predeparture press conference, Graham was asked whether he thought the reports of Soviet suppression of religious freedom were a myth. "Not necessarily," he responded, which was a reasonable reply and left open the possibility that he knew more than he was letting on. But foolishly Graham did not stop there; he compared what he had seen at three completely packed Orthodox churches on Saturday evening with what one might find on a Saturday night back home. "You'd never get that in Charlotte, North Carolina," Graham said to laughter. Of course not, his critics replied; churches in Charlotte are free to hold worship services without restriction any day of the week, and on Sunday they are indeed packed. Then Billy really sounded like a total naïf when he added that life in the Soviet Union was not as grim as many people thought. "In the United States," he said, "you have to be a millionaire to eat caviar, but I've had caviar with almost every meal I've eaten."[23] It was gratuitously insulting to the intelligence of both American and Soviet journalists for Graham to have ignored the fact that he happened to be a VIP visitor on whom the Soviet spared no expense to impress for the sake of gaining kudos on the international front. Ordinary Soviet citizens themselves, he ought to have known, ate caviar only on the very rarest occasions, if at all.

Graham's remarks on the Soviet treatment of religion, albeit sometimes quoted out of context or even maliciously misquoted, caused a furor back home. At his alma mater, Wheaton College, some fifty demonstrators marched outside the Billy Graham Center with placards that read, "BILLY GRAHAM HAS BEEN DUPED BY THE SOVIETS" and "GRAHAM EATS CAVIAR AS RUSSIAN CHRISTIANS SUFFER IN JAILS."[24] American network TV news programs and talk shows were only too eager to label him a sucker for Moscow's propaganda and an ignoramus in Soviet affairs. Radio Moscow even mischievously misquoted him as saying there was more religious freedom in the Soviet Union than in England. What Graham had in fact said was that there was no "state church" in Russia as there was in England, and in that sense the Orthodox Church was a *free* church. Of course, this use of the word "free" was misrepresented by American critics too.

Public Broadcasting Service documentary show host Bill Moyers acerbically summed up what many Americans regarded as a Graham diplomatic debacle in the Soviet visit. "He's a popular and pleasant fellow who doesn't like offending his hosts, whether in Washington or Moscow," Moyers said, accurately describing one of Graham's prevailing personality traits. "But it's never easy to sup with power and get up from the table spotless. That's why the prophets of old preferred the wilderness. When they came forth, it was not to speak softly with king and governors, but to call them to judgment."[25] Moyers' observation, though, was not entirely fair, as Billy had never said that he was going to the Soviet Union as a prophet.

Not all critics of that day, however, held to their original views as events in the Soviet Union and Eastern Europe unfolded. In a 2001 interview with me for a documentary on Billy Graham's life, CBS news anchor Dan Rather reflected on his 1982-era harsh criticism of that Moscow trip: "Graham's efforts contributed to the fall of communism, and in no small way. Graham believed that the so-called new Soviet man and woman was a façade, that beneath it there remained a depth of faith that I did not believe existed. I thought that sixty-five-, seventy-odd years of Marxist-Leninism had really pushed it down to a bedrock of only older people. But Graham was a true believer. He believed that the Russians remained a deeply religious people, that they were only being forced to hide it, keep it in the shadows, by this dictatorial regime." Rather concluded simply, "He was right; I was wrong, big time."[26]

Though he paid a high cost in terms of criticism back home, Graham kept his word to the Soviets that he would not be two-faced, saying one thing while in Moscow and another when safely out of the country. In retrospect, this integrity profoundly impressed the Soviets. It may not have "stirred their conscience," as Graham had hoped, but there is little doubt that it not only paved the way for subsequent visits to the Soviet Union in 1984 and 1988 and to Eastern Europe, but it also created something of a fascination with Graham among Soviet leaders that seemed to last well into the Gorbachev era. When Mikhail Gorbachev made his first visit to the United States in 1987, Graham was invited to a state dinner at the White House and was seated next to the leader's wife, Raisa, despite the fact that in earlier press interviews in Moscow she made no secret of her religious unbelief.

Graham's Soviet visits yielded some touching personal contacts that may have impacted Sino-Soviet relations. During his 1982 trip, Graham was invited to meet with candidate Politburo member Boris Ponomarev, also chairman of the Communist Party Central Committee's International Department. The meeting, during which Graham says he spoke with great confidence and forcefulness on the need to understand America's religious convictions in order to understand the United States, seems to have impressed Graham profoundly. "That meeting with Mr. Ponomarev was one of the most unexpected events of my life," he wrote with little apparent exaggeration. "He was gentle, courteous, thoughtful, and well-informed on America and its views."[27] We may never know what Ponomarev reported back to his Politburo and Central Committee colleagues or whether Graham's words carried any weight in the formulation of Soviet policy toward Washington, but they might well have. In fact, Graham met with Ponomarev again, in 1984, when he returned to the Soviet Union for a twelve-day tour of four cities. Once again, Billy reiterated to Ponomarev that Moscow would never really see improved relations with the United States until it moderated its treatment of both Christians and Jews under its rule. Ponomarev again listened politely and carefully. Four years later still, in 1988, Graham ran into Ponomarev while in Moscow, and the Russian greeted Billy with great warmth. "He said, 'I will never forget the things that you said,' " Graham recalled. " 'We have deeply appreciated it and have discussed it many times.' "[28]

The American evangelist's extraordinary capacity for forging friendships in unlikely places also yielded fruit in his first contact in 1982 with the head of the Russian Orthodox Church, Patriarch Pimen. When he returned in 1984, Graham reinforced their friendship, and when he returned for his 1988 trip, Billy visited Pimen as the priest lay dying in a bedroom at Zagorsk monastery. "I sat by his side for a long time and held his hand," Graham recalled in his autobiography. "He told me again, as he had on an earlier visit, that he wanted his priests to learn how to preach evangelistic sermons. I prayed with him as my brother in Christ."[29] In essence, one of the major accomplishments of that first Moscow visit in 1982 was to establish the fact that Graham now saw his own brand of Protestant Christianity as entirely compatible with one of the major Christian faith traditions, Eastern Orthodoxy. He had, of course, by then already made his peace with Roman Catholics through meetings with Pope John Paul II.

The real reward, though, for Graham's entirely moderate — critics would say "compliant" — behavior in Moscow was that doors opened up to him in East Germany, Czechoslovakia, and Romania, hitherto three of the most hard-line of the Eastern European states. In October 1982, he was in East Germany, preaching from Martin Luther's very own pulpit in the *Schlosskirche* of Wittenberg, the town's castle church. It was on the door of this very church that Martin Luther in 1517 had nailed his "95 Theses," marking the start of the Protestant Reformation. In honor of Martin Luther, Graham picked for his sermon Luther's favorite verse, "The just shall live by faith" (Rom. 1:17).[30] His East German audiences were overwhelmingly young.

That same month, he was also in Czechoslovakia for four days and offended some people by laying a wreath at a war memorial for Soviet troops who had liberated

Czechoslovakia in 1945 from Nazi control. But when Czech TV broadcast his words in that evening's newscast, it was the first time since the Communists came to power in that country in 1948 that a Christian message was openly aired on national television. "Those of us who are Christians," Czech TV showed him saying, "are reminded of the greatest sacrifice of all, the sacrifice of Jesus Christ who gave his life on the cross so that we might be freed from slavery of sin and death."[31]

In the case of Romania, the indefatigable Haraszti had been working on the government for several years, dangling the potential reward of the granting of MFN status by the US Congress. Yet again, Graham was far more effusive to his hosts than he needed to be. On his arrival in September 1985, he insisted on thanking the government of Romania for being one "which gives full and genuine freedom to all religious denominations."[32] In fact though, Romania at the time was held in the grip of one of the most repressive regimes in the world, ruled by a megalomaniac dictator who had imprisoned political opponents by the hundreds and at that very moment had embarked on an egotistical architectural project that was laying waste to whole historic sections of Bucharest.

Interestingly, Graham's over-the-top praise did not endear him to his hosts. The Romanian authorities displayed their irritation throughout Billy's trip, limiting attendance at important preaching events and cutting wires to loudspeakers at several locations. The popular response to Graham, a Protestant, in a predominantly Orthodox country was nevertheless astounding. Billy's greatest success was in Timisoara, a city of predominantly Hungarian ethnic composition, where Protestants were strong. The streets were totally blocked by crowds gathered to hear him or simply be near him. Throngs estimated at 150,000 sang and cheered as Graham walked among them. At the Timisoara Orthodox Cathedral, where Billy spoke, the surge of well-wishers seriously frightened many in Graham's party. Graham himself was jostled about by the crowd trying to mob him, and the police became alarmed, worried about whether they could extricate him from the scene.

The overwhelmingly enthusiastic response of ordinary Romanians so angered the country's Communist Party leader and dictator, Nicolae Ceausescu, that he canceled a scheduled meeting with Graham in a huff. Perhaps he had a premonition of how his political end would unravel. The collapse of Communism in Romania in the last days of 1989 and the overthrow of Ceausescu, followed by his and his wife's executions, had their beginnings in Timisoara when crowds gathered around the apartment of Pastor Laszlo Tokes, a Protestant clergyman who had criticized the Ceausescu regime to the international media. The initial protest around Tokes's apartment was broken up by police, but the protestors regrouped around the Orthodox Cathedral, the very church where four years earlier Graham had attracted equally huge crowds. That initial protest turned into a weeklong series of demonstrations and clashes with military forces that culminated with the Romanian ruler and his wife fleeing the raging crowds by helicopter.

Three years after the Romanian visit, Graham fulfilled a longstanding wish to visit China. The seventeen-day, five-city trip took place in April 1988, during which he preached in several churches. Ruth, who accompanied him, had spent the first seventeen years of her life in east China on her father's medical missionary base in Qingjiangpu, now part of the city of Huaiyin in coastal Jiangsu province. The timing of the 1988 visit was serendipitous. The country was still trying to come to terms with the impact on its political and social system of the "open door" and modernization policies inaugurated in 1978 by Chinese leader Deng Xiaoping. Christianity was growing rapidly, and it flourished in something of a legal no-man's-land. The draconian repression of religion during the 1966–1976 Cultural Revolution had been decisively ended, and several officially sanctioned Protestant churches were allowed to reopen. Yet the government authorities still were unsure precisely what policy to adopt toward Christianity, which had surged clandestinely in the countryside during the Cultural Revolution and was in effect completely outside the control and influence of officially approved Protestant churches.

The Communist Party revealed its uncertainty about how to handle religion when newly installed Premier Li Peng met with Graham for fifty minutes in Zhongnanhai, the Communist Party's sealed enclave next to Beijing's Forbidden City. Li admitted to the Graham team that China needed "moral power" in its struggle to develop and modernize. Then, in a display of candor never to be repeated by any Chinese government figure, he further admitted that the constitutional right to religious belief had not always been honored. The import of this admission apparently was lost on Graham, as well as on most of those in his party, and on those who have recounted this meeting in news reports and Graham biographies. Now that nearly two decades have passed, the significance of Li's statement is even more apparent to observers like me who have taken a close interest in China and in Christianity there for many years: other Chinese leaders have spoken of the moral vacuum in modern Chinese society, but no one before or since has forthrightly admitted that authorities have failed to uphold constitutional rights in their handling of religious affairs in China.

Even while Graham was still in Beijing, authorities were violating these constitutional rights of Christian believers. A prominent Chinese Christian who led a network of unregistered "house churches," Peter Xu Yongze, was arrested in Beijing as he made his way to a scheduled meeting for tea with Graham and several other house church leaders in Graham's hotel. Xu was to spend several years in prison before finally leaving China and winning asylum in the United States.

As for Graham's own schedule, in a display of independence from his Chinese hosts that was fiercely debated among Graham's advisors prior to the trip, Billy and Ruth in Shanghai visited Wang Mingdao, the retired patriarch of Chinese Christians, then eighty-seven, who had resisted the Communists and paid for it with nearly twenty-three years in a labor camp. In Guangzhou, they also visited the feisty house church leader Lin Xiangao, better known in English as Samuel Lamb, also a two-decade survivor of labor camps. Ruth wrote in her diary of their visit of more than an hour at Lamb's "church," in a small network of rooms at the top of a steep, narrow staircase in a house situated down a crowded alley in a dingy section of the city, that she felt she had been in the catacombs of the early Christian church.[33]

Journalists who covered Graham's visit were deeply affected by it. Adi Ignatius, then the *Wall Street Journal*'s Beijing correspondent, said Graham's contact with Chinese Christians was "strangely moving." He recalled later, "What I remember is the elderly women who were just thrilled, talking enthusiastically about Graham's visit. The year 1988 was really a thrilling period, to me the *most* thrilling period. It kind of led to what happened later . . . It was just something you didn't anticipate. I cared what happened in China even though I'm not a religious person myself."[34] The reference to "what happened later" was, of course, to the Chinese army's ruthless June 4, 1989, crackdown on prodemocracy protestors demonstrating in Beijing's Tiananmen Square. Obviously, neither the substance nor the timing of Graham's China visit had anything to do with the Communist Party's decision to suppress the demonstrations. Graham's visit, however, had coincided with deliberations by China's policy-setting State Council on possible changes to the system of control of religious worship, changes that would have led to significantly more freedom.[35] Had the Tiananmen crackdown not taken place, it is possible that Graham's visit might in retrospect have been seen as one important event that helped to promote religious freedom in China.

With regard to Eastern Europe and the Soviet Union, the question is, of course, whether Graham's forays played a role in the collapse of Communism in those countries. Undoubtedly, religious faith played *some* role in the collapse of Communism there, if one considers merely the vigorous resistance by Poland's Roman Catholic

Church to the imposition of martial law, or the opposition dissident meetings held in East Germany's Protestant churches. These developments were not lost on the Chinese Communists who explicitly sought to forestall religion playing a similar role in their own country when they were discussing new religious laws in the 1990s. The events in Eastern Europe are also one reason that Beijing has been so skittish about establishing diplomatic relations with the Vatican. In the case of Romania, a plausible connection can be made between Graham's visit and the overthrow of the Ceausescu regime chiefly because only four years had elapsed between Graham's visit and the revolution and because of the overwhelming response to him in Timisoara, where the Romanian revolt began. Romanian Christians themselves credit Graham with playing a decisive role in the regime change, and said so to Billy's eldest daughter, Anne Graham Lotz, during her two visits to their country.[36]

The situation with the Soviet Union, however, is much less clear. Graham's imprudent public statements about the degree of freedom in the country no doubt angered rather than encouraged many Soviet Christians. On the other hand, his integrity in his dealings both with Soviet officials and with leaders of the Orthodox Church clearly made an impression on his Soviet hosts. When Graham was in Moscow again in 1991, just weeks before an abortive military coup that led to the eclipse of Gorbachev's power and the rise of Boris Yeltsin, Gorbachev was cordial but neutral on religious issues. Yeltsin, however, gave Graham the impression that he was sympathetic toward Christianity and that he was pleased that all three of his granddaughters wore crosses,[37] a point Yeltsin reiterated when he spoke to the National Press Club when he visited the United States in 1992.

That openness to Christianity meant that when Yeltsin came to power in 1991, Billy Graham was at long last able to fulfill his 1959 prayer: to preach openly to large numbers of Russians in Moscow. In October 1992, Graham filled Moscow's Olympic Stadium (built for the 1980 Olympics, which America and most NATO member nations boycotted) for *Vozrozhdenie* 92 or Renewal 92, the first-ever public evangelistic crusade in Russia. Over the course of three days, it attracted a total of 155,000 people, of whom 42,000 went forward in response to Graham's call for a decision. A touching high point of the crusade was a performance the final Saturday afternoon by the famous

Red Army Choir, traditionally a global touring company performing at the behest of Soviet propaganda. On this day, however, they not only sang Russian religious songs and choruses never performed in Soviet times, but they also sang in carefully learned English the "Battle Hymn of the Republic," which starts with the words, "Mine eyes have seen the glory of the coming of the Lord." In some ways, Graham's Moscow crusade was a fitting epitaph to the entire Cold War.

Earlier in 1992, Graham had embarked on possibly his most ambitious foray to date into the Communist world, a visit to North Korea. Held in the grip of the world's longest-ruling dictator, Kim Il Sung, North Korea had the dubious distinction of being one of only two countries in the world that claimed to have eliminated religion — the other being Albania before its Communist regime, the world's last surviving example of Maoism, fell in 1991. Despite official claims of universal atheism, the North Korean government had authorized the building and operation of two churches in Pyongyang, one Catholic and one Protestant. Graham used the connections of Dr. Stephen Linton, the son of Presbyterian missionaries to Korea who spoke fluent

Korean and who had carefully cultivated relationships with Korean diplomats at the United Nations, to arrange his trip. From the Korean perspective Graham had a legitimate family connection with the peninsula; his wife, Ruth, had studied at Asia's premier Christian boarding school in the 1930s, the Pyeng Yang Foreign School. Pyongyang, now the North Korean capital, was at the time often called the "Jerusalem of Asia" because of its large Christian population.

On his first visit, in April 1992, Graham lectured to four hundred carefully selected students at Kim Il Sung University, spoke at both of Pyongyang's churches, Bongsu (Protestant) and Changchung (Catholic), and, of course, met with Kim Il Sung, to whom he brought a brief, friendly greeting from President George H. W. Bush and a longer, more elaborate greeting from the pope. According to Graham's account in his memoirs, when he returned for his second visit in 1994, Kim Il Sung expressed interest in continuing the friendship he had started with Graham. Graham commented, "I agreed to do so because over the years I had developed a deep conviction that personal relationships sometimes do far more to overcome misunderstandings than formal diplomatic efforts do."[38] Billy adds that it was in this spirit that he encouraged President Jimmy Carter to visit North Korea in the summer of 1994 during a crisis period in US–North Korean relations.

In January 1994, when it was clear bilateral relations were deteriorating because of Pyongyang's refusal to cooperate with international inspections of its nuclear program, Graham visited North Korea a second time. The trip had originally been planned for the summer of 1994, but he accepted an invitation to go in January, following a crusade in Tokyo, because of the bilateral tensions, which had escalated to the point of near war. This time, Graham stopped in Beijing en route to Pyongyang, where the US ambassador to China, J. Stapleton Roy, gave him a message to convey on behalf of President Bill Clinton.

The message Graham carried was Clinton's first contact with the North Korean leader, and in it Clinton insisted that Pyongyang had to open up its nuclear facilities to international inspection. It was precisely what Kim Il Sung was not willing to contemplate, and he received the message conveyed by Graham frostily. Linton said that after he translated Clinton's message, Kim "gestured dramatically," presumably expressing annoyance. "It was not the way you initiate a relationship," said Linton, recalling the meeting. "It was not hostile, but it was not friendly. I was very concerned when I found out what it was." To smooth Kim's ruffled feathers, Graham now deployed his considerable gifts of charm and persuasion, essentially depicting Clinton in warm, friendly terms that enabled Kim to interpret the president's message as less confrontational than it had at first seemed. After Graham's explanation, "the mood changed into a much more positive one," according to Linton.[39]

Linton says that Graham accomplished three things in meeting with the North Koreans; he showed that a visiting American could behave with dignity without being obsequious to his North Korean hosts, that a visitor could be received courteously in North Korea without trashing the United States, and that American citizens who are not part of the government could have a powerful impact on the US government. According to Linton, Graham may have been the first foreign visitor to refuse to participate in North Korea's civic religion rituals, such as laying flowers in front of the statue of the "Great Leader" Kim Il Sung. Graham made an even bigger impression, Linton said, when he invited North Korean Christian leaders to the United States in 1993. They were invited to an informal White House reception where they met President Clinton, the first time any North Korean had ever met a sitting president. The occasion was not a formal meeting but was more of a reception line for a variety of visitors. According to Linton, Graham tapped President Clinton on the shoulder and told him he wanted to introduce him to his North Korean guests. "I was doing the interpreting," Linton recalled, "and these North Koreans almost fainted. Because in their society nobody taps the boss on the back. And here was a guy who clearly had a kind of charisma they had never seen before who could, in a sense, treat his own president in a familiar way without getting shot. I think it's even more than that. I think it's showing them what a real religious person is and could be. One of the North Koreans in that room, where Dr. Graham tapped Clinton on the shoulder, said to me, if there was a religion called Billy Graham, [he] would join it."[40]

Looked at in that light, Graham's impact on both Kim and the North Koreans in general may have been more profound than anyone realizes. Billy, however, made public statements about Kim after his visit, and then again after Kim's death in 1994, that might be compared with a person who visited Hitler and praised him for liking German shepherd dogs. No doubt out of a desire to be kind and complimentary to his hosts, Graham described Kim as "a gentle man and a logical thinker," noting in somewhat wide-eyed fashion, "There are statues of him all over the place. The people there really do love him. This is not a leader the people are ever going to overthrow, in my judgment." The fact that refusing to display public obeisance to the "Great Leader" might result in an instant death sentence appears to have eluded Graham.

The reality was that Kim Il Sung had created one of the most repressive Stalinist dictatorships the world has ever seen, a tyrannical society of servile leader-worship and hatred for much of the outside world that has not improved an iota since Kim Il Sung died in 1994 and his son, Kim Jong Il, took over. It is a society, moreover, with one of the most brutal labor-camp systems of repressing suspected dissidents that any Communist leader, including Josef Stalin, Mao Tse-tung, and Fidel Castro, has ever created. Thousands of North Korean Christians are believed to be held even today in that gulag, and untold numbers in the past have perished there. Such is the society that this "gentle" leader created and from which Billy Graham returned full of praise in 1994.

Graham in the 1990s did not travel to any other foreign countries ruled by oppressive regimes. He never, for example, preached in Castro's Cuba. His overall success as a peace advocate is debatable. He had certainly made a major impact on the Russian Orthodox Church in the Soviet Union, and his preaching in Romania in 1989 was viewed by some Romanians as the tipping moment in their nation's history. But interestingly, Graham's preoccupation with advocating "peace" does not seem to have survived his visits to these oppressive regimes, however earnest he was in the pursuit of peace at the time. The reason might be that to become a "peace" advocate wielding major global impact, he would have had to doff his evangelist cloak and don that of a prophet. And for Billy Graham, being an evangelist has always been his first and greatest calling, one to which he early in life had dedicated himself.

Furthermore, being an evangelist for Graham was inseparable from being a pastor, and he has counseled untold numbers of prominent Americans and foreign leaders in ways that in most instances will likely never be told. In fact, Graham's greatest impact on world affairs, as well as American history, was probably through his complex and long-lived relationship with American presidents.

Eight:
The Presidents
(Part One)

In 1986, on the opening night of a crusade in the nation's capital, George H.W. Bush, then the vice president, introduced Billy Graham as "America's pastor."[1] An even more apt appellation, however, might be the "White House pastor." Graham himself has energetically tried to shake this label, probably because he is uncomfortable with all that it implies. Yet "White House pastor" is valid, not only because Graham has been on close terms with every president since Dwight D. Eisenhower, but also because his relationship with five of them was unquestionably that of a pastor — to some, he was a spiritual confidant, and to most, he was someone they turned to at critical moments for encouragement and prayer. Less than six months into the Nixon presidency, in June 1969, the *New York Times* ran a long, thoughtful feature on Graham with the headline, "The Closest Thing to a White

House Chaplain."[2]

Billy Graham liked this proximity to high political power, and he clearly enjoyed not just the friendship he had with several American presidents, but his familiarity with them. On occasion, he made use of this access either to try to ensure that the president was introduced to people Graham thought the nation's leader ought to meet, or to bypass government bureaucracy when it was giving his family or friends particular problems.[3] But it is surely also true that the presidents used the aura of piety and decency that Graham projected to gain popular political leverage. Lyndon Johnson and Richard Nixon certainly fell into this category, and Graham clearly was aware at least some of the time that he was being used in this way. He has been ambivalent about this, remarking of his relationship to the Nixon White House, "I wasn't used most times, I think. I'm sure there were a few times when I was."[4]

What is striking is how open to him these American presidents were. To a remarkable degree, especially in light of the pressures on the president and the very real risk of information leakage from the White House, Graham succeeded in winning the deep trust of virtually every single chief executive since the 1950s. Though prominent American Protestant religious figures before Graham had been invited to the White House — Billy Sunday was one example — none had ever captured the trust of American presidents to the extent that Graham did. Undoubtedly, his national fame and popularity were major reasons for some of the presidents wanting to be associated with him. But the relationships with Eisenhower, Johnson, Nixon, Reagan, and the first President Bush, for example, went far beyond presidential objectives and were truly caring spiritual associations.

Graham's friendships with every US president in the past half-century varied depending on each particular president's need and desire for and level of comfort with the kind of close relationship and spiritual support that Billy was willing to offer. Some, like Eisenhower, turned to Graham for basic spiritual advice and guidance, in the manner of any ordinary Christian with his pastor. Others, including Reagan and Nixon, seemed to enjoy the intellectual give-and-take with Graham, whether that was over biblical interpretation or national and world affairs. Still others, Bush Sr., for example, welcomed Graham into the bosom of their family. Whatever the specific character of each presidential friendship, in each instance, the Leader of the Free World knew that in Graham he would find a sympathetic, caring, and safe confidant, someone who had no great personal or political agenda, someone who could be trusted with confidences and questions and doubts, and someone who was prepared to help him tackle not only the difficult political questions of the day but the great questions of life. In establishing these close relationships in spite of the presidents' political differences with each other, their wide variety of religious backgrounds, and their hugely varied personalities, Billy Graham occupied an absolutely unique place in the history of the American presidency. Such an accomplishment says a great deal of Graham's unique ability to relate meaningfully to all manner of men, a quality that in turn made Billy uniquely placed to impact the United States and the world over the course of more than five decades.

In 1950, though, when Graham made his first visit to the White House to meet Harry Truman, few would have predicted this crucial role for Billy. As recounted earlier, Graham got off to a rocky start in his relations with American presidents. In fact, Graham himself opens his autobiography with the story of his meeting with Truman, which he bungled by talking to reporters about it afterwards. "It was July 4, 1950," he writes in the first sentence of *Just as I Am,* "and I was about to make a fool of myself."[5] Truman, though, may have been wary of Billy for reasons other than a White House *faux pas.* Graham had been openly and publicly critical of Truman's conduct of the Korean War, saying at one point, "How many of you voted to go into the Korean War? I never did." In May 1952, possibly still smarting from Truman's refusal to pay any attention to his Washington crusade, Graham told a Texas audience, "The Korean War is being fought because the nation's leaders blundered on foreign policy in the Far East. I do not think the men in Washington have any grasp of the Oriental mind. Alger Hiss shaped our foreign policy and some of the men who formulate it [now] have never been to the East."[6] In fairness to Graham, the encounter with Truman took place at the very beginning of his national career as an evangelist. Any thirty-one year old, catapulted suddenly into a national prominence for which little in his education and background had hitherto prepared him, could be forgiven a certain gaucherie at the beginning of things. He did much better with Eisenhower.

DWIGHT D. EISENHOWER

Billy Graham's association with Dwight D. Eisenhower predated the thirty-fourth president's occupancy of the Oval Office. The popular general and war hero was encouraged by many to seek office, and when Eisenhower finally began to seriously consider the idea, Graham appears to have played some role in his decision to run. In December 1951, he wrote to Eisenhower, then Supreme Commander of Allied Powers in Europe, saying that a US district judge had confided to him that "if Washington were not cleared out in the next two or three years, we were going to enter a period of chaos that could bring about our downfall." The letter went on, "Sometimes, I wonder who is going to win the battle first — the barbarians beating at our gates from without, or the termites of immorality from within." Graham wrote that he would be praying for the general, "that God would guide you in the greatest decision of your life. Upon this decision could well rest the destiny of the Western World."[7] Eisenhower told Sid Richardson, a politically connected friend, that it was "the damnedest letter" he had ever received. "Who is this young fellow?" he asked. "I'd like to meet him sometime."[8]

Ike had that opportunity in March 1952, when Graham called on him at his headquarters at Supreme Headquarters Allied Powers Europe in Paris. During a two-hour conversation, the two men compared notes on their upbringing. Eisenhower revealed that his parents had belonged to the River Brethren, a devoutly pious group in the Mennonite tradition, that they had read the Bible in the original Greek, and that as a young boy, he had memorized Bible verses in English. This, of course, resonated with Graham, who had experienced similar pietistic exhortations in his own childhood. The conversation covered the forthcoming US presidential election and Graham's conviction that moral issues were going to be foremost in it. Graham affirmed his strong support of Ike and his desire that the general run, but Eisenhower gave no indication whether he would. "Still, I left feeling that I had met the next president of the United States," Billy wrote in his memoirs.[9]

Eisenhower appears to have been deeply impressed by Graham, either because of his heartfelt support and encouragement to run or simply because of his personal qualities, his combination of humility and outspokenness. He met with Graham briefly after the 1952 Republican Convention in Chicago, and in a more deliberate move invited Billy to meet again a month later in Denver's Brown Palace Hotel. There the conversation became more pointedly personal, with Graham telling Eisenhower that the American people would feel more comfortable if Eisenhower as president were seen to be a churchgoer. Ike, who frankly admitted to Billy that he had strayed from the pietism of his childhood, indicated a preference for the Presbyterian church, and Graham suggested two possibilities in the Washington area. He also presented Ike with a red-covered Bible that the president later often told others he kept by his bedside for many years. Billy had inscribed a greeting to Eisenhower on the flyleaf.

During the Christmas season in 1952, Graham spent two weeks visiting US troops fighting in Korea and made several visits to hazardous locations near the front. He toured hospitals, orphanages, and first-aid stations and prayed with soldiers and preached evangelistic messages to them. One of the officers Billy met was the president-elect's son, Major John Eisenhower, with whom Graham had photos taken. Seeking to keep the lines to Ike open now that the general was soon to occupy the White House, Graham cabled Eisenhower, expressing a desire to meet him. The president-elect invited him to visit him at year's end in the Commodore Hotel in New York. After Billy conveyed the greetings from Eisenhower's son and showed him the photographs of the major, Eisenhower revealed the reason that he had agreed to meet Graham. "I'd like to quote one or two passages from the Bible in my inaugural speech," he said. "I think one of the reasons I was elected was to help lead this country spiritually. We *need* a spiritual renewal," Graham quoted Eisenhower as saying.[10]

Graham suggested he use 2 Chronicles 7:14: *If my people, which are called by my name, shall humble themselves, and pray, and seek my face, and turn from their wicked ways; then I will hear from heaven, and will forgive their sin, and will heal their land.* It is of historical interest that President Reagan also cited this verse at his inauguration twenty-eight years later, in 1981. Eisenhower used this passage, as well as Psalm 127:1: *Except the LORD build the house, they labour in vain that built it.* Graham had earlier suggested, even before the election, that if Eisenhower became president, he proclaim a National Day of Prayer. On the day of his inauguration and shortly afterward, the new president did not disappoint. He quoted the Scripture verses suggested by Graham, added his own prayer at the inauguration ceremony, which, contrary to some reports, Billy had not even suggested, much less written for Ike,[11] and proclaimed the day of prayer. About two weeks later, after a few sessions of instruction from Edward Elson, the pastor of the National Presbyterian Church, one of the churches Graham had suggested, Eisenhower was baptized and joined that church.

Eisenhower's relationship with Billy Graham was respectful and warm, but not close. Graham makes the point that he was never invited to the private quarters of the White House while Ike occupied it, and he seems to have had most of his direct contact with the president over games of golf. Eisenhower's advisors appear not to have wanted Graham to give the impression of being a White House insider. For one thing, Billy in the 1950s was still something of a loose canon with his rhetoric, an enthusiastic advocate of the sometimes noisy and shotgun national crusade against communism, and at times, he was a little too close to the radical end of the anti-communist movement. Speaking in 1953, at the height of the

McCarthy witch hunts against alleged Communists and communist sympathizers, Graham said of Senator Joseph McCarthy, then chairman of the Senate Permanent Subcommittee on Investigations, "While nobody likes a watchdog, and for that reason many investigation committees are unpopular, I thank God for many who, in the face of public denouncement and ridicule, go loyally on in their work of exposing the pinks, the lavenders, and the reds who have sought refuge beneath the wings of the American eagle and from that vantage point try in every subtle, undercover way to bring comfort to the greatest enemy we have ever known — communism."[12]

Eisenhower was angry with McCarthy for his often unsupported allegations against supposed communists in the US government, especially when McCarthy targeted American military icons and friends of the president, such as former Secretary of State and fellow World War II general George C. Marshall. Nonetheless, he was willing to ride the national wave of anti-communism and publicly link it to Billy Graham's brand of Christianity. He told editors of the *New York Times,* "It is only through religion that we can lick this thing called communism."[13] With that in mind, in June 1955, Ike signed

Public Law 140, making it mandatory for all coinage to bear the words "In God we trust," and the following year, he signed Public Law 851 that replaced the national motto "E pluribus unum" with "In God we trust."

Ike was concerned, however, not just with the health of the nation but with his own rather fragile health. The nation caught its breath in September 1955 when the president suffered a heart attack while visiting relatives in Denver. It was the first time Americans had been faced with the possibility that Ike, a popular president, could meet his demise while still in office. It is possible that Eisenhower had intimations of his own mortality when he unexpectedly invited Graham to his farm at Gettysburg, Pennsylvania, just a month before the myocardial infarction. The president took Billy on a tour of the Gettysburg battlefield in a golf cart, and then brought him home for what clearly was on his mind to discuss with Graham: heaven. Did the evangelist believe in it, Ike asked. If so, why? Graham responded by reviewing the New Testament passages that speak of heaven.

The president still was not entirely satisfied. How could a person be sure he was going to heaven, he wanted to know. Graham patiently went over the familiar ground of salvation by faith and heaven and hell, topics he had already on previous occasions discussed with Eisenhower. Although the president did not respond visibly, Billy said he sensed that Ike had been "reassured" by his words.[14]

Graham's friendship with Eisenhower, though not nearly as close as with Johnson and Nixon, set a pattern that was to characterize all his relations with subsequent presidents. Once a man became president, Graham — a lifelong Democrat — appeared to regard it as unthinkable to do anything but support him both publicly and privately, whether the chief executive was Republican or Democrat. Graham's enthusiastic, even gushing, support for the man who happened to be in the White House both authenticated his role as one to whom sitting presidents could confidently turn and ensured his continuing access to the White House itself. This is not to suggest that Graham was calculating or manipulative in his presidential friendships. Rather he simply seemed to feel that he could not be effective in getting spiritual truths across to any president unless he expressed almost euphoric sympathy with him. Thus, in a 1955 letter to Eisenhower that might have caused the president to feel that Graham could be trusted to give wholly sympathetic spiritual advice, Billy signed off with, "You are the greatest president in American history," comparing Eisenhower favorably with Abraham Lincoln, and offering his unqualified support for the president's upcoming reelection bid in 1956.[15]

Eisenhower never had the soulful, almost introspective, conversations with Graham on national policy that were to characterize the Graham–Johnson relationship or, to a lesser extent, the Graham–Nixon friendship. Eisenhower did, however, count on Billy for moral backing whenever he faced highly controversial decisions on domestic matters. In particular, he seemed to value Graham's counsel in giving a Southerner's perspective on how best to implement racial integration in the South. As the civil rights movement gathered momentum in the 1950s, they traded ideas on how to respond. In March 1956, the two men exchanged letters in which Graham promised "to urge Southern ministers to call upon the people for moderation, charity, compassion and progress towards compliance" with Supreme Court decisions.[16] In his turn, Graham was not above some partisan political advice of his own for the president, suggesting that in handling racial matters, "it might be well to let the Democratic Party bear the brunt of the debate. Your deeds are speaking for you. You have so wonderfully kept above the controversies that necessarily rage from time to time."[17]

The following year, though, Eisenhower faced a much bigger challenge to presidential authority and to the approach he appeared to favor, of gradual rather than dramatically swift progress toward integration. On September 4, 1957, in defiance of the Supreme Court ruling ending segregation, Arkansas Governor Orville Faubus deployed 250 Arkansas National Guardsmen to prevent African American students from entering the hitherto all-white Central High School in Little Rock. Under pressure from Eisenhower, Faubus subsequently withdrew the guardsmen from the school, and on September 24, the president federalized the Arkansas National Guard. White segregationist mobs, however, continued to pose a serious danger to the black students trying to integrate the school, and Eisenhower deemed the only response possible was to send in one thousand paratroopers from the US Army's crack 101st Airborne to enforce school desegregation. He telephoned Graham, who was in the middle of his New York City crusade, and asked his counsel. "Mr. President," Billy replied, "I think that is the only thing you can do. It is out of hand, and the time has come to stop it."[18]

Graham kept up intermittently with Eisenhower, briefing him, for example, after trips to India and other parts of the world. When they played golf, Billy used the relaxed environment of the open-air sport to share some spiritual thoughts with the president. But it was not until 1968, eight years after Ike left office, that the Eisenhower–Graham relationship became most intimate. By then, the former president's heart condition had worsened dramatically, and between April and August, he suffered four heart attacks and fourteen cardiac arrests. In November, after Richard Nixon had won the presidential election, Graham visited Eisenhower in Walter Reed Army Hospital. The former president, perhaps more conscious of his mortality than ever, wanted to repair relations with Nixon, some of whose supporters blamed Ike for Nixon's presidential defeat in 1960 because Eisenhower had been conspicuously lukewarm in his support for Nixon. Fortuitously, Graham had been invited to Nixon's apartment for dinner that very evening, and he passed on to his host

Eisenhower's expressed desire for a reconciliation. Nixon, now president-elect, promised to see his old boss the next day.

The next month, Eisenhower, still in Walter Reed, summoned Graham again, this time because he wanted to make things right with his Maker. "Billy, you've told me how to be sure my sins are forgiven and that I am going to heaven. Would you tell me again?" he asked. Graham once more went over all the scriptural assurances of eternal life and reassured him that he had indeed been forgiven by God. He held the president's hand as he prayed for Eisenhower. "Thank you. I'm ready," he said.[19] Three months later, Eisenhower died.

JOHN F. KENNEDY

Billy Graham's relationship with Eisenhower's successor, John F. Kennedy was not at all close, but it was punctuated with pastoral moments that had the potential to change history. Kennedy, or JFK, as he was familiarly called by most Americans, was the first Roman Catholic to occupy the White House. Graham narrowly avoided two dangerous stumbles that might have ensured his exclusion from the White House on all future occasions. One was when the publisher of *Life* magazine, Henry Luce, under pressure from Democrats, at the last minute pulled from publication a column Graham had written in the fall of 1960, essentially endorsing JFK's opponent in the presidential race, Richard Nixon. Another was when Billy decided to remain aloof from a concerted effort by some Protestant ministers — for the most part not fundamentalists — to try to rally American Protestants against a Roman Catholic presidential candidate. Prominent New York minister Norman Vincent Peale, whose wife had been active in preparations for the 1957 New York City crusade, led the charge with an organization called National Conference of Citizens for Religious Freedom. The organization believed that if Kennedy became president, the Vatican would have a hand-hold on American politics.

Kennedy turned this movement to his own political advantage by successfully meeting some of his Protestant critics head-on in Houston in September 1960 and very adroitly insisting that, in a conflict between his loyalty to the United States and his loyalty to the Vatican, his American patriotism would prevail. The news reports and editorials about Peale's abortive attempt to undermine JFK's presidential bid overwhelmingly depicted Peale as a religious bigot for even questioning where Kennedy's loyalties lay. Though pressed hard to lend his support to Peale's movement, Graham astutely realized that any hint of political bigotry from him would help JFK's campaign rather than hurt it. Privately, though, he desperately wanted Nixon to win and tried to advise the Nixon campaign behind-the-scenes to do things that might help his bid. In the end, however, he did nothing that might have sabotaged a relationship with Kennedy as president.

Kennedy did emerge the victor, though by one of the narrowest margins in American history. With an intuitively brilliant political sense of how to patch up relations with a constituency that had viewed him with deep suspicion during the campaign, he invited Graham to Palm Beach about ten days before his 1961 inauguration. Meeting first with JFK's father, Joseph Kennedy, who had been ambassador to Britain during World War II, Billy learned why he had been invited to meet with the president-elect. Joseph Kennedy told Graham that he had been impressed when he happened to see Billy preach in Stuttgart, Germany, in 1955 and told his son he thought Graham could bind up some of the partisan religious wounds that had been opened up by Peale and others during the campaign. After lunch — at which Jacqueline Kennedy was also present — followed by a game of golf, JFK drove Billy from the golf club back to his father's house in his Lincoln Continental. Along the way, he stopped the car, turned to Graham, and asked him if he believed in the second coming of Christ. Billy said he did. Kennedy asked Graham whether his own church, the Roman Catholic Church, believed in the same thing. Billy said it was in the Roman Catholic creeds, but Kennedy said he had never heard any sermon on the subject. Graham then explained his own views, starting with Jesus' crucifixion and resurrection, and indicating that he thought world peace would only come upon Jesus Christ's return. "Very interesting," commented JFK. "We'll have to talk more about that someday."[20]

Sadly, there was never to be that "someday." Graham visited the White House a few times, and once was summoned to the Oval Office to offer Kennedy advice on speaking through an interpreter. He was never, however, invited to any personal meeting with JFK, nor ever entered the private quarters of the White House during the Kennedy presidency. Each year of his presidency, Kennedy attended the annual Presidential Prayer Breakfast, held in late January or early February, to which Graham, each of the years 1961–1963, was also invited. In 1963, Graham was the featured speaker, and when the two men were exiting the hotel toward the presidential limousine, Kennedy invited Billy to come back to the White House with him, giving the impression that he wanted to talk with the evangelist. But Graham, shivering without a coat in Washington's January cold and already suffering from the flu, politely begged off. Rather poignantly in his memoirs, he posed the question: "His hesitation at the car door, and his request, haunt me still. What was on his mind? Should I have gone with him? It was an irrecoverable moment."[21]

The poignancy obviously derived from the fact that Graham never had the chance of close conversations with JFK again and that Kennedy's life ended tragically ten months later, on November 22, 1963, when he was assassinated in Dallas. It may also have sprung from one of the extremely rare occasions in Billy Graham's life when the evangelist reported having a premonition of something terrible. Toward the second week in November 1963, Graham began to feel what he called "a terrible burden" — in evangelical Christian terminology meaning a sense of something really serious and bad about to happen in someone's life — about the president's already announced upcoming visit to Texas. Not having any private phone number for contacting the president in the White House, Graham tried to communicate his misgivings about the visit to Senator George Smathers, the friend who had arranged the Palm Beach meeting nearly three years earlier, just before Kennedy's inauguration. Graham did not get hold of Smathers, whose secretary told him that the senator was then on the Senate floor. Smathers thought the call was about a Kennedy invitation to play golf in Florida that weekend. But it wasn't. In Graham's own words, "All I wanted to tell him and the president was one thing: 'Don't go to Texas!' "[22]

What if Graham had ignored his flu and accepted that invitation to ride in the presidential limousine at the end of January in 1963? Might a friendship have been established with JFK that would have enabled Billy to contact the president directly before his fateful Dallas trip, perhaps even to warn him away from going? It is an impossible question to answer. But if the answer is yes, history would indeed have taken a different course.

Kennedy may have indicated to his family how much he liked Billy, for at the funeral Graham was seated in the section for friends of the family. Graham later learned that JFK had said that Billy was the only Protestant minister with whom he felt comfortable. Months after the funeral, Kennedy matriarch Rose Kennedy complimented Graham on his preaching, mentioning that she often listened to him.[23]

LYNDON B. JOHNSON

When Vice President Lyndon B. Johnson assumed the presidency on Kennedy's death, many Americans had misgivings. Johnson was a clever and aggressive politician — many people were convinced he had first gained office by ballot stuffing — but an earthy Texan and a far cry from JFK's polished New England aristocracy. He was sometimes coarse, was not well traveled, and was known to be a ruthless political arm-twister when he felt such tactics were needed to push legislation through the Senate. But of all the presidents, Graham was closest to LBJ. They genuinely liked each other and enjoyed each other's company. Billy, sometimes accompanied by Ruth, was LBJ's overnight guest at the White House on at least twenty separate occasions during the Johnson presidency and spent numerous nights at LBJ's ranch on the Pedernales River in Texas during and after Johnson's time in office. "I love to be around him, because I love Texas, and he's all Texas," Graham told the *New York Times* in 1969, just after Johnson left office. "And I think you have to be in that Pedernales River valley to understand President Johnson. I understand a little bit of the background of where he came from and where his roots were and what made him tick. And the things people thought of as crude were not crude to me, because I had been there, and I knew that that is the part of Texas he came from."[24] In his memoirs, Graham writes, "Although many have commented on his complex character, perhaps I saw a side of that complexity that others did not see, for LBJ had a sincere and deeply felt, if simple, spiritual dimension." Billy wryly adds, "But while he was serious about it, I could hardly call him pious." He also said of Johnson, "He could be coarse and charming at the same time, and even profanely poignant."[25]

LBJ reciprocated this affection, once writing to Graham about "those lonely occasions at the White House when your prayers and your friendship helped to sustain a president in an hour of trial . . . No one will ever know how you helped to lighten my load or how much warmth you brought into our house. But I know."[26]

Graham's first encounter with LBJ as president — for they had met previously when Johnson was in Congress — was three weeks after JFK's funeral, on December 16, 1963. Billy and Grady Wilson spent the night in the White House and swam in the swimming pool with Johnson and a congressman. Both visitors were astonished that no one wore swimming trunks. LBJ evidently thought such attire unnecessary if women were not present. Later, he and Graham spent several hours in conversation, and Billy prayed for the new president. At this meeting, LBJ proudly showed him a letter from the great Texas hero Sam Houston (1793–1863) to Johnson's great-grandfather, George Washington Baines (1809–1882), a preacher who was close friends with the beloved architect of Texas's independence from Mexico and had influenced him deeply in his faith convictions. Johnson belonged to the mainline Disciples of Christ denomination, though he was no great churchgoer, but he seemed drawn to Graham's frequent references to his direct ancestor Baines.

Thereafter, LBJ would call on Graham again and again for companionship and spiritual solace. Graham told biographer Frady, "I almost used the White House as a hotel when Johnson was president. He was always trying to keep me there. He just wouldn't let me leave."[27] In striking contrast to his more limited access with Truman, Eisenhower, and Kennedy, Graham not only visited the private quarters of the Johnson White House, but he at times also knelt on the floor with LBJ in the presidential bedroom and prayed with him, at Johnson's request. "I never had very many people do that," Graham once observed.[28] He visited LBJ at Camp David, and also occasionally when the president retreated to his ranch on the Pedernales. He frequently read the Bible to LBJ while the president was getting a massage, exchanged gifts and notes with the president, and gave him assurances of intercessory prayer over matters great and small. Graham says that though he tried to be a spiritual counselor to Johnson, he had not been "his confessor."[29]

That is debatable, however. More than any other president, LBJ opened his soul to Graham, and during very private moments, especially near the end of his life, when he was contemplating his own mortality, Johnson may have revealed things to Billy that he had told no one else. But LBJ did not just take from Billy Graham; he very much gave in return. Graham clearly enjoyed the familiarity with presidential power that friendship with Johnson offered, and LBJ became the first sitting president to attend a Graham crusade, in Houston in 1965.

Johnson was curiously possessive of Graham. Conscious at all times of Billy's close relationship with Nixon during the Eisenhower presidency and of the continuing friendship between the two men, LBJ became particularly nervous when supporters of Republican candidate Barry Goldwater in 1964 deluged Billy's hometown in Montreat, North Carolina, with two million telegrams seeking Graham's endorsement of Goldwater's candidacy. Johnson got wind of the campaign of telegrams and called Graham up. "Now, Billy," the powerful Texan drawled, "you stay out of politics."[30] Graham realized that if he endorsed Goldwater, LBJ would probably drop him like a hot brick, and thus declined to back Goldwater. When Johnson won the 1964 election by a landslide, Graham fell easily into his role as chief clerical booster for the president of the moment. Graham wrote to LBJ after the election victory that he was convinced that Johnson was "not only the choice of the American people — but of God." He added, "You are as truly a servant of God as was your great-grandfather Baines when he preached the gospel."[31]

According to biographer Frady, during one of Graham's overnight visits to Camp David, Johnson suddenly got it into his head that Billy himself ought to run for president. "He said to me all of a sudden," Frady quotes Graham as saying, " 'Billy, you know, *you're* the man to become President of the United States. You're the only one who could bring 'em all together. If you ever decide to run, I'll be your manager.' " Frady says that Graham took the whole thing as a "half-joke," but LBJ at other times also thought Billy should have a cabinet position in the administration, or at least an ambassadorship.[32] Graham has often told the story of Johnson suggesting that Billy be ambassador to Israel, to which Graham jokingly retorted, "The Middle East would blow up if I went over there." Later, sitting next to Golda Meir at a White House dinner, Graham assured the Israeli prime minister that, "I am not the man. God called me to preach." Meir responded by reaching over to grab his hand, presumably in relief.[33]

Johnson was not alone in thinking Graham would make a good president. In fact, Texan oil billionaire H. L. Hunt offered to deposit $6 million in Billy's personal bank account if he would agree, in 1964, to run against LBJ. Clearly trying to pressure Graham into taking the offer, Hunt leaked the story to the media, resulting in CBS newsman Walter Cronkite reporting that Graham was considering a run for the presidency. Billy had publicly entertained thoughts of running for political office in the early 1950s, when communism appeared to be an apocalyptic adversary of the United States, and Graham himself was often talking up the need for a Christian response to it. By the 1960s, though, he appeared to have permanently rejected political ambitions, and he called a press conference to refute the CBS report and to say that he definitely would not accept Hunt's offer. He was fortified in his decision by a brusque call from his wife, Ruth, who dryly told him she did not think the American people would elect a divorced man, which is what he'd be if he left the ministry to go into politics (though in 1980 Americans did elect a divorced man in the person of Ronald Reagan). That marked the definitive end of any Graham flirtation with politics.[34]

Meanwhile, Johnson, in his musings with Billy in the White House and at Camp David, returned again and again to the constant burden of what to do about Vietnam. He had inherited Kennedy's commitment to send over American military advisors, but by the mid-1960s, the US presence in Vietnam was escalating rapidly. At the time of LBJ's election in 1964, US troops in Vietnam numbered only about 23,000. Less than two years later, they had spiraled up to 429,000, and protests against the war had escalated far beyond occasional outbursts of dissatisfaction on college campuses into protest meetings in public venues drawing scores of thousands of participants. At his overseas crusades, Graham encountered anti-American protests against the Vietnam War, and fielded increasingly sharp questions about the war at press conferences. The domestic political chaos, which was morphing from mere war protest into a tectonic shift in the nation's youth culture, seemed to alarm him more than the destruction wrought by the war itself. Graham even seemed to think that within ten years the United States might encounter "internal chaos and a political tyranny in the form of some sort of left-wing or right-wing dictatorship, even if there is no war."[35]

During the Christmas period of 1966, Graham visited Vietnam at the invitation of General William Westmoreland, the US commander on the ground. He traveled extensively around South Vietnam, preaching to troops and taking risky, harrowing flights in small planes to difficult and remote airfields, sometimes in dangerously low-visibility weather. In his first public statements at the end of his visit, Graham was downbeat and unusually gloomy with reporters. "I leave with more pessimism about an early end to the war than when I arrived," he said. "How can we have peace? I don't know. I don't have any answers. I had hoped there would be some formula, but I don't see it. I don't know how it could end."[36]

At the end of January 1967, Graham was summoned to the White House together with Cardinal Francis Joseph Spellman, who had also visited Vietnam over Christmas. Spellman said in his report to LBJ that the United States should push hard for a military victory. Graham, while agreeing with Spellman that the morale of American troops was high, was not sure what the US policy should be. Nor, apparently, was Johnson. "Now what do you think?" he asked both Christian leaders rhetorically.

"We can't go on with this thing. The American people are not going to take it. We've got to get out of it. How do we do it?"[37]

In the next two years, the American troop presence in Vietnam continued to rise inexorably, peaking at 543,000 in 1969. Graham visited Vietnam again at Christmastime 1968 as the guest of the new commander, General Creighton Abrams Jr. As before, he traveled around the country extensively, preaching, visiting wounded servicemen in hospitals, and even going to remote firebases. This time, Graham returned much more bullish on the war's outcome than two years earlier. He even declared, "There is no question: the war is won militarily."[38] Johnson, presumably, was delighted to hear this analysis from the nation's leading evangelist.

Graham publicly echoed the administration line on Vietnam while LBJ was in the White House, but he apparently felt comfortable enough with the president to publicly contradict him at times on other issues. One occasion occurred in September 1967, when Graham attended a meeting of police chiefs in Kansas City, at which LBJ spoke. That evening, speaking at a crusade meeting in the city's Municipal Stadium, Graham publicly distanced himself from some of the things Johnson had said, though he does not say in his autobiography what he disagreed with LBJ about. "What's the matter with you?" asked the ever-possessive president in a phone call after reading news reports of Graham's dissent. "I thought you were my friend."

"I am," Billy replied, "but I can't always agree with everything you say."[39]

Graham's close friendship with Johnson continued well after LBJ left office following his March 1968 announcement that he would not run for re-election. The news touched off a storm of political speculation and rivalries among Democratic aspirants to the White House. For Graham, though, the announcement came as no surprise; LBJ had confided to him almost a year earlier that the physical toll of the office was so heavy that he feared he would not survive a second term, even if he were re-elected. Johnson, by this account, was driven from office more by concern over his own mortality than by the national furor over his Vietnam policy. Graham, ever the faithful sounding board, was invited by LBJ to the White House one last time the weekend before Richard Nixon's inauguration in January 1969. Graham has not revealed what Johnson said on that no doubt somber occasion, but he did not abandon LBJ once the Texan left office. He made a few more visits to the LBJ ranch on the Pedernales and heard him out when Johnson seemed melancholic and wanted, as had Eisenhower before him, to be reassured that he would go to heaven when he died. Often LBJ himself would drive Billy around his ranch for several minutes before talking. Graham recalls one such occasion:

> We were sitting in his convertible Lincoln, where he'd been chasing some of the deer right across the fields. We were stopped, looking out, and the sun was sinking. We had a very emotional time because I just told him straight out that if he had any doubts about his relationship with God, that he'd better get it settled. I said, "Mr. President" — I still called him "Mr. President" then; before he became President I called him Lyndon — "according to what you say you don't have much longer to live. You'd better be sure you're right with God and have made your peace with him." He bowed his head over the steering wheel and said, "Billy, would you pray for me." I said, "Yessir," and I did. He was very reflective after that. We must have sat

there for another hour, hardly talking at all, just looking at the sunset.[40]

During that same visit, Johnson showed Graham where he wanted to be buried on his ranch. He said he definitely wanted Billy to preach at his funeral. "You'll stand right here under this tree. I'll be buried right there. You'll read the Bible, of course, and preach the gospel. I want you to. But I hope you'll also tell the folks some of the things I tried to do."[41] In fact, when Johnson died in 1973, the eulogy was delivered by former Texas Governor John Connally. Graham's job was to preach a sermon, and, true to LBJ's instructions, he did indeed preach the gospel. In his memoirs, Billy speaks of Johnson with genuine warmth, "He wanted to harness the wealth and knowledge and greatness of this nation to help the poor and oppressed here and around the world." Defending himself from any possible charges of partisanship or uncritical admiration for LBJ, Graham qualified his comments with the disclaimer that Johnson "will get mixed reviews from historians."[42] As for Billy, he was a true pastor to the end to the thirty-sixth president of the United States.

RICHARD M. NIXON

Billy Graham may have been closer to Johnson than to any other American president, but it is with LBJ's successor, Richard Milhous Nixon, that he is most closely associated in the public mind. Politically, he was closer to Nixon than to Johnson. Personally, because of Nixon's downfall in the Watergate scandal, Graham took a significant blow to his reputation for his close friendship with Nixon. And professionally, Billy paid a heavy price when White House tape recordings of a 1970s-era Oval Office conversation, in which Graham apparently agreed with Nixon's deeply prejudiced comments about American Jews, were made public in 2002.

Graham the evangelist is unlikely to be seriously tarnished by these associations. Nor is Graham the pastor to the presidents. But Graham's astuteness as a political mind and a judge of human character can be — and has been — called into question because of his apparent failure to detect in Nixon the character flaws that ultimately led to his fall from power. To his credit, Graham remained loyal to a fault to Nixon, but, in one of the few instances in his life when personal loyalty seems to have blunted his spiritual and political acumen, Billy simply misread his presidential friend. He remained to his declining years unable to reconcile the picture of Nixon revealed by the Watergate tapes on the one hand, and on the other, the personable, modest, patriotic, highly intelligent, and, indeed, at times, brilliant man he had come to know over many years. In his memoirs, published two years after Nixon's death, he writes with an unmistakable note of puzzlement, "The whole library of literature that has been written detailing the Watergate break-in and the subsequent cover-up has not explained for me what came over President Richard Nixon at that time. I deliberately chose the words *came over* because I cannot accept in my heart that his conduct and conversation during that crisis sprang from the deep wells of his character."[43]

Graham's puzzlement may be understandable given the very long association between the two men. Billy had heard of Nixon, may even have met him, shortly after he burst upon the national scene in 1949 at the Christ for Greater Los Angeles revival. There is no question that he met Nixon's mother, Hannah Nixon, an evangelical Christian belonging to the Quaker denomination, just after the Los Angeles crusade, when he was preaching in the California town of Whittier, Nixon's hometown. Hannah Nixon told Graham how her husband had taken their sons, including Richard, to hear the evangelist Paul Rader (1879–1938) when the latter was preaching at a revival meeting in Los Angeles, a story Nixon himself later confirmed.[44] It was the summer of 1926, and Nixon was thirteen. When Rader commanded his listeners, "Come forward for Christ!" Nixon got up from his seat and dedicated his life to God. It was apparently more than a passing whimsy, because Nixon went on to teach a Bible class and sing in the choir at Whittier Friends Church.

The first time the two men met socially was when Graham was having lunch with North Carolina Senator Clyde Hoey in the Senate dining room in 1950 or 1951 and the senator invited Nixon, then a freshman senator, to join them. That afternoon, they played a game of golf together, and their subsequent friendship was built around their shared love of the game. From 1962 on, when Nixon was vice president, they kept up a regular exchange of birthday gifts and greetings. Graham deeply admired Nixon's outspoken anti-communism, his brilliance at analyzing international affairs, and his tendency to frame complex issues of world power politics in moral terms. He badly wanted Nixon to win the 1960 election, and he only avoided the potential political fallout from publicly endorsing the Republican candidate because *Life* magazine publisher Henry Luce pulled Graham's piece days before the election. To Nixon's credit, he did not object to Graham accepting an invitation from his political opponent, President-elect Kennedy, to meet socially with him in Florida shortly before JFK's inauguration.

Graham and Nixon would meet at least four times each year after the 1960 election, sometimes in the Grahams' Montreat home. In 1962, Billy was photographed with Nixon shortly before the former vice president's unsuccessful bid for the governorship of California. Nixon went through a period of deep discouragement after his California defeat and confided to friends that he thought his political career was finished. On one occasion, Graham told him he thought otherwise. "Dick," he said as they golfed, "I believe you'll have another chance at the presidency. The world situation is getting worse. There'll come a time when the American people will call on you. You have the ability and the training to be president of the United States. Don't give up."[45] How much Graham's encouragement influenced Nixon's later political decisions is not known, but he and Graham shared a common interest in American and international politics. Graham, whose own knowledge of international affairs had been deepened by his contact with several foreign leaders in the 1950s, obviously enjoyed talking about his overseas experiences with Nixon.

The recollections of the two men of their friendship — Graham's accounts being far more extensive than Nixon's — suggest that this was one of the least "spiritual" of all Billy's presidential friendships. Nixon was reserved and reticent about his religious views, and when he did talk about Christian things, his comments did not reveal a deep Christian "walk." Graham certainly read the Bible with Nixon and prayed with him, as well as with Nixon's family on occasion, and appears not to have had any serious doubts about the fervor of Nixon's beliefs. There was, however, one rather curious characteristic of their friendship. When the two men prayed together privately, Nixon was unwilling to pray aloud, and it was always Graham who spoke the words of their prayers.

Over the years, Billy had maintained a

distant but affectionate relationship with Nixon's mother, Hannah, whom he had met before he came to know Nixon. When Hannah died in September 1967, Graham officiated at the funeral and gave the eulogy. Nixon, who was almost always successful at keeping his feelings under control, broke down completely as he was about to leave the church and sobbed on Billy's shoulder. He later said it was only the second time in his life he had wept in public.[46] That he did so on Graham's shoulder suggests a deep level of trust in and closeness to Billy.

That trust displayed itself in the last few days of December 1967, when the two men met again. By this time, Nixon had largely returned to the good graces of the Republican Party after the twin losses of the 1960 presidential race and the 1962 California governorship bid, largely through genuinely selfless campaigning for Republican candidates during his years in the political wilderness. He was clearly in a favored position to be considered for the Republican presidential nomination. But should he put himself in the running? That December, Graham was felled by pneumonia and turned down an invitation to go to Vietnam again and speak to the troops, but when Nixon phoned him after Christmas and invited him to join him in balmy Key Biscayne, Florida, and even sent a private plane for him, Billy agreed, arriving on December 28, 1967. The two friends spent the next three days talking, walking on the beach, and, of course, praying. Nixon opened up his heart about the big decision hanging over him: should he run for president in 1968? Graham was reticent about giving counsel; for one thing, he was heavily overshadowed by his long-term pastoral relationship with LBJ, whose vice president, Hubert Humphrey, would be Nixon's opponent if Nixon were the Republican candidate.

Nixon had invited his close friend Bebe Rebozo to spend New Year's Eve with him as well. Graham, unwell from his pneumonia and the exertion of walking on the beach, retired for the night early. The following day, January 1, 1968, Nixon still felt that he had not heard from Graham whether he thought Nixon should run. He went to Graham's room in the Key Biscayne Hotel and talked to him while Billy packed for his flight out.

"Well, what is your conclusion?" Nixon asked. "What should I do?" According to Nixon, Billy turned to him and said, "Dick, I think you should run. If you don't, you will always wonder whether you should have run and whether you could have won or not. You are the best prepared man in the United States to be president." They talked about the problems facing America, and then, according to Nixon, Graham said simply, "I think it is your destiny to be president."[47] In Billy's version of the same conversation, he recalls having said, "You will always wonder whether you should have," but not "I think you should" nor "It is your destiny to be president." It may be selective memory at work, perhaps on both sides. Nixon obviously wanted his clergyman friend's "anointing" of him as presidential candidate, but Graham may not, in retrospect, have wanted to be held accountable for Nixon's becoming the president at all. Nixon, however, often told friends later that Graham had encouraged him to run and that his encouragement had been more influential than anyone else's input. Nixon wrote to biographer Pollock that Graham had even gone so far as to say he had an obligation to run. Whatever was really said, Richard Nixon certainly had the impression that Billy Graham was urging him into the race.[48]

Once Nixon threw his hat in the ring and began campaigning in earnest for the Republican nomination, Graham made no effort to conceal his desire that Nixon should win. At a crusade in Portland, Oregon, where he acknowledged the presence of Nixon's daughters Julie and Tricia, he declared, "There is no American I admire more than Richard Nixon."[49] He hinted strongly that he might be willing to endorse Nixon, though in the end he did not actually do that. At the Republican convention in August 1972 in Miami, Graham gave the closing prayer. To his surprise, at the same convention, Nixon invited him to a meeting with senior Republican leaders to canvass suggestions for the position of vice president. In response to Nixon's point-blank query, Graham suggested Senator Mark Hatfield, a well-known evangelical politician. Nixon did not take this advice, and Billy shared the disappointment of many Republicans when Nixon selected the governor of Maryland, Spiro Agnew, whom they regarded as less than qualified.

As the presidential campaign gathered momentum, Graham missed few opportunities to not-so-subtly promote Nixon's candidacy. In a crusade in Pittsburgh in September, he seated Nixon in the VIP section and publicly praised him from the platform. Not long afterward, Nixon made a well-publicized visit to see Morrow Graham, Billy's mother, still living in Charlotte, North Carolina, to highlight his close association with America's beloved evangelist. When Nixon was sharply criticized during the campaign for being "tricky" and generally of shifty character, Graham lashed out at the critics, though he did not mention them by name. "He has a great sense of moral integrity," Billy said of Nixon. "I have never seen any indication of, or agreed with the label that his enemies have given him of, being 'Tricky Dick.' In the years I've known him, he's never given any indication of being tricky."[50] Four days before the actual vote, he revealed in an interview that he had cast an absentee ballot for Nixon. That information was instantly exploited by the Republicans in the final days of the campaign, but Graham was such a close friend of Nixon's that he probably did not object to being so used. It was not until the Nixon presidency was in its second term that real problems developed in Nixon's career, and in their friendship.

NINE:
THE PRESIDENTS
(PART TWO)

RICHARD M. NIXON

When the 1968 presidential election returns came in, Richard Nixon was watching in a New York City hotel. Billy Graham had been invited but declined to join him — a sign, perhaps, of a last-minute twinge of his nonpartisan conscience. When Nixon's victory was confirmed, though, Graham did go to the hotel suite, where the president-elect asked everyone to hold hands while Billy prayed. "We want to rededicate our lives," he told Graham. At the inauguration two months later, Billy led the prayer, which *Time* magazine caustically called "Billy Graham's mini-inaugural address."[1]

From the outset, Nixon made it clear he wanted Graham associated with as much of his administration's doings as was reasonable. To forestall security issues and logistical problems that would be associated with regular presidential attendance at a

Washington-area church, Nixon initiated weekly worship services in the White House, ordering his staff throughout his presidency to take great political care to invite clergy who not only represented a broad swath of different denominations — including Roman Catholics — but who could be considered reliably Republican. At the first such White House service, on January 26, 1969, Graham preached the sermon, and he was later invited back three more times. Biographer Martin observed, no president "ever made such a conscious, calculating use of religion as a political instrument as did Richard Nixon."[2]

It is hard to imagine that Graham did not suspect that Nixon was quite politically calculating in his use of religious associations, particularly those connected with such a popular American religious icon as Graham. It is clear, however, that he saw himself not merely as Nixon's longtime close friend but as something of a peer, though not entirely an equal. "I think I always thought a great deal more of [Nixon] than he thought of me," he told biographer Frady within four years of Nixon's resignation.[3] The comment is revealing, because it suggests both that Graham almost idolized his friend even in the face of abundant evidence of Nixon's ethical problems, and that Graham was somewhat subordinate in the relationship. In contrast to the pastoral relationship he had with Johnson, Graham's association with Nixon was first and foremost a genuine friendship, and then a conviction that, behind Nixon's rather ruthless, not to say calculating, political façade, was a spiritual nature struggling to express itself. "He always had that spiritual side to him," Graham said of Nixon's desire for prayer on the morning of his election victory. "It was always coming out."[4] During his presidency, according to Graham, Nixon would often telephone him at his Montreat home, sometimes very late at night. Billy's view was that the "essential bond" between them was "personal and spiritual" rather than "political or intellectual."[5]

When the Watergate scandal cascaded down upon Nixon, why did Graham, almost alone among America's public figures, seem to be taken completely by surprise by the president's behavior? The first reason, probably, was that he regarded Nixon as a friend and was genuinely fond of him; therefore, he simply could not imagine that someone with whom he had been on such affectionate terms over the years could have major, undetected flaws in his character. Graham thus was tripped up by the common weakness of people who fall naturally into liking others: he allowed his affection to eclipse his character judgment. Furthermore, his desire to see Nixon's supposedly "spiritual" nature emerge like a proverbial butterfly from the chrysalis of that famously complex character no doubt blinded him to the president's seriously "unspiritual" side.

Nixon aide Charles Colson, for example, saw the situation with far greater clarity and was not convinced that Nixon was nearly as devout as Graham obviously believed and hoped him to be. Colson, who went to jail for his own role in Watergate but who later rose to prominence and enhanced national respect as a Christian leader through the organization he founded, Prison Fellowship, said, "The things he'd believed as a young man, he said he no longer believed. He didn't believe in the resurrection, or in Jonah being swallowed by the whale. He believed those were symbols."[6] In fact, Nixon had written of his doubts about Christian doctrines while at Whittier College in California for a course entitled, "The Philosophy of Christian Reconstruction" that examined issues such as the theory of evolution and whether the Bible could be believed literally. Students were required to write an essay at the beginning, middle, and end of the course, answering the question, "What can I believe?" In October 1933, at the start of the course, Nixon wrote a composition that concluded that "the literal accuracy of the story of the resurrection was not as important as its profound symbolism."[7] It is revealing that Graham apparently never knew of such doubts, suggesting either that Nixon concealed them from the evangelist or that Billy believed that the inchoate spiritual yearnings he claimed to discern in the president were the "real" Nixon. According to Graham, Nixon told him, "I believe the Bible from cover to cover."[8]

With Nixon as president, Graham could easily have been appointed an ambassador or perhaps a cabinet secretary, but Billy had told Nixon that he would not accept any position within his administration. He did, however, try to help Nixon out unofficially. In March 1969, for example, he convened a conference in Bangkok, Thailand, of missionaries who had lived many years in South Vietnam to try to ascertain what they thought was happening in the war. They told him that the South Vietnamese overwhelmingly did not want Communist rule and were indeed fearful that the Paris peace talks with Hanoi might saddle South Vietnam with a coalition government that would eventually bring a Communist regime to power. Graham reported all this in a thirteen-page report to Nixon, which, a few months later, he also made available to National Security Advisor Henry Kissinger.

Graham also continued to be overwhelmingly publicly supportive of Nixon at a time when the nation was deeply divided over the Vietnam War and many Americans actually hated Nixon. In May 1970 — the same month that four students were shot dead by National Guardsmen called in to control an antiwar demonstration at Kent State University in Ohio — Billy invited Nixon to make a few remarks at a crusade at the University of Tennessee at Knoxville. A crowd of student demonstrators was determined to show their opposition to Nixon and shouted "Bullshit! Bullshit!" and "Stop the crap, and end the war!" as the president spoke. They were drowned out by the overwhelmingly pro-Nixon crowd who cheered the president wildly. Nixon's appearance at a religious event like this was a much more political act than, for example, had been Lyndon Johnson's attendance of Graham's Houston crusade five years earlier. Johnson had merely been seated on the platform, whereas Graham had invited Nixon to address the gathering.

In private, Billy continued to be Nixon's cheerleader well into 1971. "My expectations were high when you took office nearly two years ago, but you have exceeded [them] in every way!" he wrote Nixon late that year. "You have given moral and spiritual leadership to the nation at a time when we desperately needed it — in addition to courageous political leadership! Thank you!"[9] In retrospect, and in light of the Watergate scandal that unraveled the following year, such sentiments might appear today to be vastly exaggerated. In the context of the Nixon White House in 1971, however, they were not. Henry Kissinger had returned triumphantly in July from his secret trip to China, opening up an entirely new direction in American diplomacy. *Time* magazine named Nixon its Man of the Year for 1971, and the magazine was scarcely less laudatory than Graham. "He reached for a place in history," *Time* rhapsodized, "by opening a dialogue with China, ending a quarter-century of vitriolic estrangement between two of the world's major powers. He embarked upon a dazzling round of summitry that will culminate in odysseys to Peking and Moscow. He doggedly pursued his own slow timetable in withdrawing the nation's combat troops from their longest and most humiliating war, largely damping domestic discord unparalleled in the US in more than a century."[10]

In fact, by mid-1972, Nixon seemed set to coast to an overwhelming victory in November's presidential election. When police, alerted by a security guard, interrupted a burglary of the Democratic Party offices in the Watergate building complex on June 17, 1972, few people paid much attention, and the White House initially dismissed it as "a third-rate burglary." The Democrats selected as their candidate a pronouncedly liberal candidate, George McGovern, and Nixon's reelection seemed assured.

Graham himself certainly wanted it to be, offering his services to aid the campaign in every way compatible with IRS restrictions on political partisanship. He also did not stint on making admiring comments about Nixon in media interviews. Speaking to the *Saturday Evening Post,* he described Nixon as "a true intellectual." He said, "We haven't had an intellectual in the White House in a long time . . . But Nixon is a true intellectual, and he is a student, particularly a student of history. In that respect, he is a de Gaulle type."[11] He told the *Charlotte Observer* that Nixon would "go down in history as the greatest president because he studied, prepared himself, disciplined himself for the presidency, and the effects now show."[12]

The Watergate scandal did not really begin to gather momentum until April 1973, two months into Nixon's second term. Then, under the combined pressure of federal grand jury investigations, hearings at a Senate committee investigating the break-in, and the investigative reporting of *Washington Post* reporters Bob Woodward and Carl Bernstein, it unfolded rapidly. What became increasingly evident was that the White House was deeply involved both in the initial burglary and in the cover-up of its connection to the deed, and that perhaps Nixon himself was implicated. Graham stoutly defended the president. "His moral and ethical principles wouldn't allow him to do anything illegal like that," he said.[13] Ignoring the gathering evidence that was beginning to point directly at Nixon, Billy spoke at the White House Christmas service in December 1973 and followed up with a note to Nixon. "I am sure that this coming year will be far better than 1973," he wrote.[14]

If the remark demonstrated anything, it was that Billy Graham was a better pastor than he was an astute predictor of events. In this, Graham acted entirely consistently with his character. As with the civil rights movement, Billy did not view his role as that of a prophetic voice calling for change, but that of evangelist and pastor leading lost souls to Jesus Christ. Hence, in his presidential friendships, Graham repeatedly regarded as more important the need to offer pastoral support and encouragement rather than to point out moral lapses.

After the existence of secretly recorded tapes of White House conversations was revealed, Nixon tried fiercely but unsuccessfully to fend off legal efforts to obtain the recordings. When the contents of the tapes were made known to Congress, legislators set in motion impeachment proceedings. Deserted by his Republican colleagues and with no safe legal course, Nixon on August 8, 1974, announced his resignation, effective the following day. Most Americans were either gleeful or sorrowful over Watergate and Nixon's demise. Those who were gleeful had simply not liked Nixon from the start, had mistrusted him, and had attributed all kinds of nefarious motives to him. The ones who were sorrowful had admired him as a genuinely talented man — "brilliant" in Graham's view — who had somehow become entangled in a mishap that, at its core, they believed, had not been of his personal devising.

Graham's reaction, however, was neither glee nor sorrow; he just wanted to throw up. What seemed to grieve him more than anything else was the coarse and profane language recorded in the transcripts of the White House conversations made public in the spring of 1974, generally indicated in the text simply by: "(expletive deleted)." Graham said, "Never in all the times I was with him, did he use language even close to that. I felt physically sick and went to the seclusion of my study at the back of the house. Inwardly, I felt torn apart."[15] Ruth said that reading the Watergate transcripts was one of the hardest personal things Billy had ever had to deal with in his career, and one biographer describes Graham weeping as he read the transcripts. In them, he encountered a Nixon he had never even seen hinted at in the two decades they had been close friends. "He was just suddenly someone else," Graham said.[16]

Billy had progressively distanced himself from Watergate in interviews he gave in the months before Nixon's resignation. Many

Christians — as well as many just plain critics of Nixon — hoped that Graham would assume the role of an Old Testament prophet to Nixon, a Nathan rebuking King David for his adultery with Bathsheba. To do so, however, would have gone against the norm of his presidential friendships, and indeed would have gone against the norm of Graham's personality. Even before Nixon's resignation in August 1974, he had issued a statement calling Nixon his "friend" and saying that he had "no intention of forsaking him now."[17] When the disgraced president was hospitalized with the potentially life-threatening condition of phlebitis within weeks of flying on *Air Force One* from the White House to his San Clemente home, Ruth Graham hired a small plane to fly over his hospital, trailing a banner that read, "Nixon, God Loves You and So Do We."

Graham has often said that the White House kept him at arm's length during the final months of Watergate, out of kindness in not wanting to involve the evangelist, but there is some dispute about this. According to Graham, he was unable during those months to get through to Nixon by phone to offer him encouragement or solace. In any event, Billy did not see Nixon after his resignation until the spring of 1975, when he was invited to dinner at San Clemente. By then, according to Graham, Nixon had deepened in his religious faith and was without bitterness toward those who had engineered his removal from office. Billy remained in touch with Nixon periodically, visiting him on the East Coast whenever he was within range of Nixon's Park Ridge, New Jersey, home, and never ceased to speak well of his former close friend. "I never thought of him for who he was," Graham told biographer Martin in 1989. "I just thought a great deal of him as a friend. He is one of the great people I have ever known personally, who was a real gentleman. He's always courteous, always thoughtful."[18]

When Nixon died of a stroke in April 1994, Graham was equally generous. "I think he was one of the most misunderstood men, and I think he was one of the greatest men of the century," he was quoted by the *Washington Post* as saying.[19] Graham officiated at the funeral and began an eloquent, conciliatory address with these words: "The great king of ancient Israel, David, said on the death of Saul, who had been a bitter enemy: 'Know ye not that there is a prince and a great man fallen this day in Israel.' Today, we remember that with the death of

Richard Nixon, a great man has fallen. We have heard that the world has lost a great citizen, and America has lost a great statesman. And those of us that knew him have lost a personal friend."[20]

Nixon deeply appreciated Graham's loyalty to him in and out of office. In a 1990 book, *In the Arena,* Nixon summed up his friendship with Graham this way: "I treasure the friendship and wise counsel Billy Graham has extended to me over the years." The president, however, did not view the relationship as one-sided; he had also given the evangelist counsel of his own. "On a few occasions, however, I have been in the position of advising him. In 1960, 1968, and 1972, I advised him not to endorse me, or for that matter any other candidate for office," Nixon wrote, adding that he had also warned him against becoming associated with the Moral Majority, the conservative Christian political pressure group formed by the late Rev. Jerry Falwell in 1979. Nixon said he wanted Graham to stay away from the Christian right because, "I believe a minister cannot carry out his major mission in life as effectively if he dabbles in politics."[21] In fact, with his highly sensitive political antennae, Nixon must have realized that, whereas Graham represented the comforting, unthreatening face of Protestant evangelicalism to most Americans, Christian conservatives — who were not yet nationally organized when Nixon was president — had the potential to alienate other conservative voters.

Graham may have stuck to the letter of Nixon's advice by not publicly advocating political support of Nixon during *most* of the 1968 and 1972 presidential campaigns, but he never left any doubt where his political affections lay. In this sense, Americans were not mistaken in regarding him as a close and loyal friend of Richard Nixon. Nor was it unreasonable when Nixon's involvement in the Watergate affair had become glaringly obvious that they looked to Graham to respond to an apparent inconsistency in his positions. After all, his oft-repeated refrain was that America was morally backsliding. Meanwhile, one of his closest friends had resigned from the highest elected office in the land to avoid probable impeachment for lying and conspiracy.

As the Nixon presidency was collapsing from the Watergate revelations, Graham was unable satisfactorily to reconcile his frequent calls for national moral renewal with his close friendship with a president whose integrity seemed to be in tatters. In early

1974, he was as forthright as he ever was to be in public about Watergate when he told *Christianity Today* in an interview, "I can make no excuses for Watergate. I condemn it and deplore it. It has hurt America." The original break-in in June 1972 and the subsequent cover-up, he insisted, had been "not only unethical, but criminal."[22] This annoyed some Nixon supporters who were even more fervent in their loyalty to the disgraced president than Graham, but it failed to satisfy many Americans who were expecting a much stronger thunder peal of condemnation from the famous evangelist. In the spring of 1973, he said, "The time is overdue for Americans to engage in some deep soul-searching about the underpinnings of our society and our goals as a nation."[23] It was a statement that might have been lifted from any number of his sermons to Americans in the early 1950s.

To the end, Nixon remained a moral conundrum to Graham. Musing aloud to biographer Frady, he said: "I love him, yes, to this very day. If Christ didn't love us when he saw our sins, none of us would have any hope, would we? I loved him as I love Grady, as I love Cliff, and I still do. Maybe I was naive and was used by some others. I can't think that of Nixon. I just can't believe that he exploited me or took advantage of me . . . Some have said there was just a split personality thing, but I don't know. It's still a mystery to me."[24] At other times, Graham likened Watergate to "a nightmare," and in his autobiography, wrote this of Nixon, "I wanted to believe the best about him for as long as I could. When the worst came out, it was nearly unbearable to me."[25]

The problems of Billy Graham's friendship with Nixon did not end with the president's death. Like an unexorcised specter, it rose up to haunt him again early in February 2002 when the National Archives released 426 hours of thirty-year-old Nixon White House tapes, recorded in the first six months of 1972. One of those White House conversations proved to be a huge embarrassment to Graham. In it, he is heard agreeing with Nixon when the president made egregiously prejudicial comments about American Jews. Nixon then lists several American news organizations, mentioning the *New York Times, Newsweek,* the *Los Angeles Times,* among others, as well as prominent TV journalists such as Walter Cronkite and Dan Rather, and claiming that the American media that was so critical of him was dominated and even controlled by

Jewish journalists, especially writers. Graham appears to agree, as the transcript shows:

> GRAHAM: This stranglehold has got to be broken or the country's going down the drain.
> NIXON: You believe that?
> GRAHAM: Yes, sir.
> NIXON: Oh, boy. So do I. I can't ever say that but I believe it.
> GRAHAM: No, but if you get elected a second time, then we might be able to do something.

Later in the conversation, Billy says that he has many Jewish friends and "they swarm around me and are friendly to me. Because they know I am friendly to Israel and so forth." But, he adds to Nixon, "They don't know what I feel about them and what they are doing to this country."[26]

Anti-Defamation League Chairman Abraham Foxman reacted immediately, calling Graham's comments "chilling and frightening."[27] Contacted by several media outlets for his comment on the revelations of such three-decade-old prejudice, Graham responded that he had "scores of conversations" with Nixon on many topics and obviously could not recall them all. "However," he said, "I cannot imagine what caused me to make those comments, which I totally repudiate. Whatever the reason, I was wrong for not disagreeing with the President, and I sincerely apologize to anyone I have offended. I don't recall ever having those feelings about any group, especially the Jews, and I certainly do not have them now. My remarks did not reflect my love for the Jewish people."[28]

The negative reactions did not last long. Foxman accepted Graham's apology, and the widow of the American Jewish Committee's Rabbi Marc Tannenbaum wrote a letter to the *New York Times* saying that Graham had always phoned her husband before a visit to a Soviet-bloc country to see if there was anything he could do for the Jews there and that he had worked behind the scenes to extricate some Jews from the Soviet Union. She was referring to Graham's pointed insistence whenever he preached in Eastern European countries in the late 1970s and 1980s on meeting with leaders of the Jewish community. Significantly, the mini-uproar over the Nixon–Graham conversation about American Jews also brought to light an interesting element of their friendship and its influence over White

House policy. In her *New York Times* letter, Rabbi Tannenbaum's widow said that a Graham phone call to Nixon at the height of the Yom Kippur War had been instrumental in the president's decision to lend military airlift support to Israel during the 1973 war with Egypt and Syria.[29] While this has not been independently confirmed, it is revealing in itself. If true, it suggests that Graham's relationship with Nixon, at a very crucial point in Israel's history, was of decisive and beneficial importance for the Jewish people as a whole.

GERALD FORD

When Vice President Gerald Ford assumed the presidency after Nixon's resignation, the nation seemed to breathe a collective sigh of relief. The quality most commonly attributed to Ford was "decency." He was broadly liked by Americans, and he was untainted by Watergate, having become vice president only because Vice President Spiro Agnew resigned in October 1973 after charges of tax evasion while governor of Maryland surfaced, and Nixon tapped Ford to replace the disgraced Agnew.

Graham had met Ford when he was still a congressman, but he did not know him well. Their friendship during Ford's brief time in office, from August 1974 until January 1977, seems not to have been a close one, but Graham may have played some role in Ford's controversial decision to pardon Nixon. In his autobiography, Graham writes, "I wanted Ford to initiate the healing by pardoning Richard Nixon. Although I had personal reasons as well, I believed that a pardon would be good for the office of the presidency."[30] Graham — and others — feared that if Nixon had to go through the trauma of criminal indictments, he literally might not survive because of his potentially fatal phlebitis. Through friends, Billy called the White House and got through to Chief of Staff Alexander Haig, expressing his concerns for Nixon's health and advocating a pardon for the ex-president. President Ford called Graham the following day and heard out Billy's arguments for a Nixon pardon. Ford did not make any commitment in response, simply noting what everybody knew, namely that whether to pardon Nixon or not was "a tough call."

In the end, Ford decided to pardon Nixon primarily to help the nation heal from the long trauma of the Watergate affair. The terms were painstakingly negotiated by Benton Becker, a member of the Ford administration's legal staff, whom the president had charged with ensuring that Nixon make some sort of public statement showing contrition for what he had brought upon the country through the Watergate scandal. Ford announced the pardon on September 8, 1974, less than one month after he took office, and the decision cost him an immediate drop of more than twenty polling points in his popularity ratings. Some felt that it was because of the pardon that he lost the election to Jimmy Carter in November 1976. Ford to his dying day did not publicly reveal what role, if any, the phone conversation with Graham played in his decision.

Ford was friendly on a personal level toward Billy and Ruth, but Graham seems to have been still nursing wounds from the Nixon friendship. When Ford made discreet inquiries in the summer of 1976, after Carter's selection as the Democratic presidential candidate, about attending a Graham crusade in Pontiac, Michigan, Ford's home state, Billy rather forcefully responded that the president could not make any statement to the audience if he came. "I think the backlash would not only hurt our ministry, but hurt you, as people would think you were 'using' me," Graham said.[31] Rather like closing the barn door after the horse had bolted, Billy piously continued, saying that if the president showed up, Graham would certainly recognize him from the platform, but that in the interest of political neutrality, he would have to extend an invitation to Jimmy Carter as well. Billy explained, "I am maintaining a neutral position, as I always try to do in politics."[32] Hubert Humphrey in 1968 might have disagreed with that claim.

Graham nevertheless writes about Ford with great admiration in his autobiography, calling him "decent and caring." The rather brief chapter on Ford is tellingly titled "The Healer from Michigan," and at the end of it, he credits Ford with having tried to follow God's leading during his presidency; no doubt he had in mind the Nixon pardon in saying that.[33] After he left office, Ford was nevertheless critical of Graham's forays into Eastern Europe, but changed his mind when he saw how warmly — even rapturously — the evangelist was received in Romania in 1985. "When I first read that Billy Graham was going to a Communist-dominated country, I had reservations," he told an interviewer a few years after leaving office. But, he added, "There is no doubt . . . [Graham] reignited the flame of religious belief and conviction. And that in turn has unquestionably had a political impact on what is taking place."[34]

JIMMY CARTER

It is thus one of the great ironies of Ford's 1976 loss to Jimmy Carter that some people attributed it to the incumbent's befuddled response to a question in a presidential debate precisely about the status of Communist-dominated countries in Eastern Europe. It was during the second of the presidential debates in the 1976 campaign, held on October 6, 1976, in San Francisco's Palace of Fine Arts. In answer to a question from Max Frankel of the *New York Times* about the Soviet control of Eastern Europe, Ford said, "There is no Soviet domination of Eastern Europe, and there never will be under a Ford administration." A startled Frankel followed up, saying, "I'm sorry . . . did I understand you to say, sir, that the Soviets are not using Eastern Europe as their own sphere of influence in occupying most of the countries there?" Ford responded, "I don't believe . . . that the Yugoslavians consider themselves dominated by the Soviet Union. I don't believe that the Romanians consider themselves dominated by the Soviet Union. I don't believe that the Poles consider themselves dominated by the Soviet Union." Most observers considered the comment a major blooper that influenced voters decisively against Ford, and Carter pounced on it. The Georgia governor said he would like to see Ford "convince the Polish-Americans and the Czech-Americans and the Hungarian-Americans in this country that those countries don't live under the domination and supervision of the Soviet Union behind the Iron Curtain."[35]

Carter, of course, won the 1976 election and became the thirty-ninth president of the United States. It is one of the paradoxes of Billy Graham's close relationships with ten presidents over five decades that Carter was the one with whom he seemed to have been least close. The paradox lies in the similarity of their backgrounds: both were Southerners, both were Southern Baptists, and both became famous in part due to their very public acknowledgment of their faith. Carter was the first politician in modern times to make a point of his convictions as an evangelical when he forthrightly declared himself a "born-again Christian" in the 1976 presidential campaign. His connection with Graham went as far back as 1966, when he chaired a film crusade in his home state of Georgia associated with the

BGEA evangelistic movie about a teenager's life called, *The Restless Ones.* In 1973, as governor of Georgia, he also chaired Graham's Atlanta crusade and hosted him overnight in the governor's mansion. The doctrinal solidarity was there; the political concurrence of views and the personal chemistry were not. "He doesn't inspire love or loyalty in the way that Reagan does," Graham said with unusual candor in a 1986 interview. "At the same time, you know he would struggle [for] you and do anything in the world you asked him to, if he felt like he could."[36]

There were obvious reasons for Graham's decision after 1974 to keep a visible distance from the presidency thereafter; the scars of the friendship with Nixon through the Watergate period still had not entirely healed. He had liked Ford and his wife, Betty, and the affection was mutual. He was, however, still skittish about the White House in general, and he was not a regular visitor during Ford's time there. Furthermore, Ford was in office only two years before another presidential campaign rolled around. Perhaps bending over too far backwards to avoid the assumption that, as a Southern Baptist, he would automatically favor Jimmy Carter, Graham told a *Los*

Angeles Times reporter, with surely unintentional tartness, "I would rather have a man in office who is highly qualified to be president who didn't make much of a religious profession than to have a man who had no qualifications who made a religious profession."

Carter appears to have viewed the comment as a slap directed at him personally since he had indeed made "religious profession" part of his campaign — and quite successfully, because evangelical Protestants in 1976 voted in greater numbers for Democratic Carter than for Republican Ford. Did Graham mean to suggest that because Carter made a "religious profession" he had "no qualifications"? According to biographer Martin, the Carter camp concluded that Billy was publicly "giving permission" to evangelicals to support Ford and not vote for Carter. Carter immediately lashed back, saying, "I think what people should look out for is people like Billy Graham, who go round telling people how to live their lives."[37] Jimmy Carter's son, Jeff, sniffed — incorrectly — that Graham's doctorate had been acquired by "mail order."

In 1977, for the first time in nearly a quarter century, Graham did not attend the presidential inauguration, although he and

Ruth did overnight a few days later at the White House. In a telling indication that Graham was by then more familiar with the White House than its new occupants, he responded to Rosalyn Carter's question of whether he would like to sleep in the Lincoln Bedroom by saying that he would not because, having slept there in the Johnson and Nixon administrations, he knew the bed to have a lump in the middle of it,[38] something of which Rosalyn was unaware.

Graham describes his relations with the First Family during the 1977–1981 Carter presidency as "cordial though infrequent."[39] Billy, to put it bluntly, just did not find Carter much fun to be around. He certainly didn't dislike him, and it's clear that in many ways he greatly admired him. But he didn't *enjoy* Carter, as he had obviously enjoyed Johnson and Nixon and was to enjoy Ronald Reagan. In his autobiography, he concludes the chapter on Carter in his autobiography, which is titled "The Sunday School Teacher from Georgia," with this observation: "Historians will, I suspect, be kinder to President Carter than some of his contemporaries were. A man of faith and sterling integrity, he was undoubtedly one of our most diligent presidents, persistent and painstaking in his attention to his responsibilities"[40] — an excellent example of damning with faint praise. Yet Carter, interviewed on CNN in 2005 around the time of Graham's last crusade, was more forthrightly complimentary of Billy than might have been expected, considering the relatively cautious, mutually respectful tone of the relationship between the two men. "Billy Graham," said Carter, "always believed in the basic separation of church and state, or keeping a sharp dividing line between religion and politics. And that didn't mean any prohibition against a religious leader like Billy Graham being a friend and a counselor to a president."[41]

RONALD REAGAN

The contrast with Billy Graham's attitude toward Ronald Reagan, and even his wife, Nancy, could not be greater. The chapter on Reagan in Graham's autobiography is revealingly titled "Leading with Wit and Conviction." It fairly brims over with affection for America's fortieth president, whom he cheerfully refers to throughout the chapter as "Ron." Graham even admits that once, during the Reagan presidency, he slipped and addressed Reagan not as "Mr. President" but as "Ron." When he had made the same mistake with LBJ, calling him "Lyndon," he had gotten a "funny look" from the disapproving president. But not from Reagan, whom he describes in the very first sentence of the chapter as "one of the most winsome men I have ever known."[42]

The interesting facet of Graham's relationship with the Reagans was that it was genuinely warm and close but almost completely lacking in pastoral attributes. Cheerful and "winsome" as Reagan was, he allowed no one but his wife, Nancy, to get close to him emotionally. The Reagan–Graham friendship, nevertheless, had an unmistakable theological facet to it. Reagan was fascinated by the Bible and often liked to talk to Graham about it, particularly the passages dealing with end times prophecy.

Though it was largely overlooked by reporters when he was president, Reagan had a profound evangelical Christian faith. In Dixon, Illinois, where he grew up, his mother, Nelle, was a devout Protestant evangelical and insisted her son go to church, which he willingly did. At the age of eleven, he read a Christian novel, *That Printer of Udell's: A Story of the Middle West,* by Harold Bell Wright,[43] and was so struck by the parallels between the hero, Dick Falkner, and himself — impoverished childhood, alcoholic father, saintly mother, heroic civic career — that he announced to his mother upon finishing it that he wanted to be like Dick Falkner, wanted to go to her church with her (the Christian Church in Dixon), and wanted to be baptized, which he was a few days after joining the church. Later he wrote, "I realize I found a role model in that traveling printer whom Harold Bell Wright had brought to life. He set me on a course I've tried to follow even unto this day. I shall always be grateful."[44] Later still, another major influence was the outspoken anti-communist and journalist Whittaker Chambers, whose 1952 book *Witness* describes his involvement in the espionage activities for which State Department official Alger Hiss was convicted. Chambers had been an atheist for many years and converted to Christianity in the course of his disillusionment with communism.

Graham's association with Reagan actually predated their first meeting and goes back to 1953 when he met Reagan's mother-in-law, Mrs. Loyal Davis, on a golf course in Phoenix, Arizona. The first Graham–Reagan meeting occurred later that year, when the two teamed up at a speaking engagement for a benefit to raise money for retired film stars. Graham was profoundly impressed by Reagan's persuasive abilities and charm.[45] As Reagan transitioned from movie actor to political activist, Billy often saw him on his trips to California, and they continued to meet after Reagan was elected governor of California in 1968. In 1971, while in California to address a joint session of the Democratic-controlled state legislature, Graham had lunch with Reagan and his state cabinet. According to biographer Martin, as soon as they sat down, Reagan said, "Billy, tell us what the Bible teaches about things that are happening today, and where you think we stand in the prophetic scriptures."[46]

Reagan, in fact, was himself "prophesied over" in October 1970, during his governorship, in the couple's Tudor-style home in Sacramento, when he and Nancy met with five prominent Californian Christians, one of whom was the singer Pat Boone. As the seven gathered to pray at the end of the social gathering, one of the visitors, Boone's friend George Otis Sr., transitioned from normal, spoken prayer to the style of someone delivering a "prophecy" in the manner of Pentecostal or Charismatic Christianity, in which the speaker sounds as if God is communicating directly through him, often to someone present in the room. In this case, Otis used the term "my son" in referring to Reagan and then dropped the bombshell, "If you walk uprightly before me, you will reside at 1600 Pennsylvania Avenue." This declaration was made six years before Reagan was to challenge Gerald Ford in 1976 for the Republican presidential nomination, and a decade before his actual election to the White House.[47]

During the 1980 presidential campaign, Graham was asked by Reagan aide Ed Meese to endorse the candidate, but he declined. He did agree, however, to appear at a breakfast Reagan was holding in Indianapolis, because he happened to be in the same city, conducting a crusade. That appearance was interpreted as a boost for Reagan's campaign.

On Reagan's election, Graham led prayers at the inauguration in 1981, and also at the inauguration for his second term in 1985. He also participated in the first official Inauguration Day event in 1981, a prayer service in St. John's (Episcopal) Church in Lafayette Square, opposite the White House. Subsequently, he and Ruth were guests at the White House more often than Graham had been during all the years that Johnson and Nixon were president. Most occasions seemed to have been entirely social, with

Reagan happily reminiscing about events earlier in his life — especially in his Hollywood period — and eager to converse with someone who had known him for many years and who was a contemporary — Billy was seven years younger — and therefore familiar with many of the people and events he was discussing. Graham was frequently invited to White House state dinners and private banquets in honor of everyone from visiting Soviet leader Mikhail Gorbachev to Reagan's good friend, the British premier Margaret Thatcher.[48] On one occasion, when Billy and Ruth happened to be in Washington, attending a function, Nancy Reagan phoned them at the Madison Hotel after they had already prepared for bed and asked if they would come to the White House even at that late hour of the night. A car was sent, and the Grahams, now dressed, spent two hours socializing in the White House with a pajama-clad President of the United States and the First Lady.

Although Graham's relationship with Reagan lacked the strong pastoral element of some of his other presidential friendships, Reagan nevertheless recalled Billy's spiritual influence on him during his presidency. "It was through Billy Graham that I found myself praying even more than on a daily basis . . . and that in the position I held [of president] that my prayers more and more were to give me the wisdom to make decisions that would serve God and be pleasing to him," Reagan said.[49] During one of the Grahams' overnight stays at the White House, the issue of Christian salvation came up. Reagan propounded the classical evangelical position that it is only through faith in Jesus Christ that people can be saved, but Nancy questioned his response. She turned to Billy, who confirmed the orthodoxy of the leader of the free world.[50]

Nancy Reagan, however, was no orthodox Protestant evangelical, for she dabbled in astrology, a fact that became known while Reagan was still in office, to his obvious embarrassment. According to the reports, she tried to ensure that major domestic political events or international meetings were scheduled only on astrologically favorable dates. Graham read the newspaper accounts and called her up to ask — he says "bluntly" in his autobiography — if the stories were true. She replied that they were "ninety percent untrue." Graham sternly urged her to seek guidance from the Lord rather than from the stars.[51] Nancy has subsequently spoken of Graham as though he were a constant Christian pastoral presence to the Reagan family. Interviewed by CNN's Larry King in December 2000, when Ronald Reagan was still alive but was severely diminished by Alzheimer's disease, she all but gushed with enthusiasm for Graham. "He's always — he's always there for us," she told King. "He has been by here to see us now, and I mean I really — I really depend on Billy a lot."[52]

The one occasion when Graham assumed his more customary pastoral role with the White House occupants was after the attempt on Ronald Reagan's life on March 30, 1981, when a would-be assassin's bullet narrowly missed his heart by less than an inch. As soon as it became apparent that the president might not survive, the White House placed an emergency call to Graham at his home in Montreat. He dropped what he was doing and flew to Washington by private plane. Upon arrival at the White House, he spent some time with Nancy and, together with other close friends of the family, led prayers for the president's recovery. Later, he phoned the parents of the gunman, John Hinckley Jr., and tried to comfort them in their considerable distress.

Two years later, on February 23, 1983, President Reagan conferred on Billy Graham the Medal of Freedom, the highest civilian honor that a US president can grant a private citizen. Personally reading the citation, Reagan spoke of Graham's "untiring evangelism" which had "spread the word of God to every corner of the globe, and made him one of the most inspirational spiritual leaders of the twentieth-century." Unable to resist a quip at the expense of the Soviet Union, Reagan also told a joke about Graham's visit to Moscow the previous year. Over a sumptuous luncheon with a Soviet bureaucrat, Reagan cracked, Graham had asked, "But how can you live this way, do this, when there are so many people out there in your country that don't have enough to eat, that are hungry?" Reagan then told the punch line, "And the man said, 'I worked hard for this.' And, God bless him, Billy Graham said, 'That's what the capitalists say.' "[53]

When Reagan died in June 2004, Billy and Ruth were the first people to speak to Nancy after the Gipper's passing.[54] Billy was hospitalized and unable to attend the funeral, but Reagan's vice president, former President George H. W. Bush, nevertheless referred to him as "the nation's pastor" and said that he had phoned Graham for a Scripture verse for the occasion. Graham suggested Psalm 37:23–24: *The Lord delights in the way of the man whose steps he has made firm. Though he stumble, he will not fall for the Lord upholds him with his hand.*[55] If Reagan had been able to hear these Scriptures, and had he known that they had been suggested by his old friend Billy Graham, he surely would have tilted his head and grinned in that characteristic, winsome way.

Ten:
The Presidents
(Part Three)

GEORGE H. W. BUSH

Billy Graham's friendship with the forty-first president of the United States, George H. W. Bush, not only predated his election to the highest office in the land but it actually extended back to Bush's own parents. Graham had met and gotten to know his father, Senator Prescott Bush of Connecticut, through friends of the senator who had been converted during the 1957 New York crusade. After Senator Bush's retirement to Florida, the two men became even more closely acquainted over games of golf, a sport for which Graham has had a lifelong passion. Graham greatly admired George Bush's mother, the saintly matriarch of the clan, Dorothy Walker Bush, whom he described as "one of the most remarkable Christian women I had ever known."[1] She had responded to the phenomenal success of Graham's 1957 New York crusade by starting a Bible study group in their Hobe Sound, Florida, community.

When George Bush was vice president, Graham stayed at the family's Kennebunkport summer retreat in Maine for several weekends, during which he conducted informal Bible studies for the extended Bush family. The two couples also traveled and vacationed together on several occasions, including a visit to Acapulco, Mexico, when Graham and Bush both were invited to address the annual meeting of the Young Presidents' Organization in 1979. Graham deeply respected what he called "the devout Episcopalian Christianity" of the entire Bush clan. During one of Graham's 1988 visits to Kennebunkport, Dorothy gathered twenty-five of her friends to hear him give an evangelistic message. On Inauguration Day 1989, the by-now frail old lady of ninety was staying at the White House, and the newly inaugurated President Bush asked Graham to go and spend some time with her. He did, and they prayed together. When Graham finished his prayer, in which he had "asked the Lord to lead, guide, and protect George in the years ahead," Dorothy said softly with tears in her eyes, "He'll need it."[2]

The long family association, however, did

not mean seeing eye-to-eye on everything. As vice president, Bush had read over the phone to Graham in 1982 a letter from a US diplomat highly critical of Billy's plans to attend a Soviet-sponsored peace conference. But to his credit, Bush later applauded Graham's approach to the Communist regimes of Eastern Europe. He said at an ecumenical Christian service in Houston in 1992, "I remember when ten years ago one of God's great soldiers went to Eastern Europe and the Soviet Union. Returning to America, Billy Graham predicted that freedom would outlast tyranny. He felt that religion was alive way back then, and the doubters said that he'd been tricked. But Dr. Graham knew something they didn't. He knew the chains of oppression forged by men were no match for the keys to salvation forged by God."[3]

In an interview with me in Montreat in 1990, Graham positively gushed about the senior President Bush. "He says straight-out that he has received Christ as his Savior, that he is a born-again believer, and that he reads the Bible daily," Billy said. "He has the highest moral standards of almost anyone whom I have known. He and his wife have such a relationship, it is just unbelievable. If you are with them in private, you know, they are just like lovers. When I would go and spend the night, as I did many times when he was vice president, the room that I stayed in was right across the hall from theirs, and they always kept the door open. And there they were, you know, in bed, holding hands, or reading a newspaper or reading a book."[4]

There was nothing informal, however, about an urgent phone call to Graham on January 16, 1991, asking him to have lunch or dinner with the Bushes in the White House. Not having enough time to get there for lunch, Graham arrived for dinner. As he settled into the White House Blue Room to watch television with Bush's wife, Barbara, and Susan Baker, wife of Secretary of State James Baker, it became clear what was happening: CNN was reporting from Baghdad that a major air raid was in progress on the Iraqi capital. "Is this the beginning of the war?" Graham asked. Neither woman replied, but the expression on Barbara Bush's face was answer enough. Five months earlier, Iraqi dictator Saddam Hussein had invaded Kuwait, and now Bush was about to unleash the vast military machine that had assembled on the northern border of Saudi Arabia to expel the Iraqis.

A few minutes later, Bush himself arrived

and confirmed that the war had already started. Graham immediately suggested prayer, and he prayed among other things that the war would be short and casualties as few as possible. Later that same night, Bush left the private quarters of the White House to make a televised announcement to the country from the Oval Office, which Graham also watched on TV in the White House. The following day, Bush asked Billy to lead a prayer service for the cabinet, key members of Congress, and several hundred Marines at the Fort Myer Army base in Virginia, just a few miles south of Washington. Graham again prayed for a minimum of casualties on all sides, for a short war, and for a long peace in the Middle East.[5] A few years later, after he had left office, Bush recounted at a Graham crusade the importance of Billy's presence in the White House on the night the Operation Desert Storm military initiative began.

Bush apparently had a deep need for spiritual comfort that night and in the days following, and he trusted Graham enough to ask him to provide it. Of course, opponents of the 1991 Gulf War could argue that Bush used Graham as some kind of spiritual talisman to theologically legitimize what some thought was a wrong-headed and even immoral military action by the administration. Indeed, key leaders of the Episcopal Church, USA, the denomination to which Bush belonged, had visited the White House in the months leading up to the Gulf War to make clear their opposition to the US military action. But in contrast to his unusual relationship with Lyndon Johnson, Graham was not asked for his opinion on American policy, nor did he offer any. Bush at no point confided his inmost thoughts to Graham, who said he had gone to the White House "as a friend and a pastor, not as a political advisor."[6] Bush's own comments on Graham's role confirm that. "It is my firm belief that no one can be President without a belief in God, without understanding the power of prayer, without faith, and Billy Graham helped me understand that," he once said.[7]

The friendship between the two men actually extended beyond Graham and Bush to their wives. Ruth Graham and Barbara Bush, Billy later wrote, "were two of a kind in many ways." They both were devoted to their husbands and their families, both had what Graham called a "stylish" approach to the atmosphere of their homes, both could be witty at the expense of their husbands, and both were fiercely independent despite their traditional roles and not afraid to speak their minds. Ruth Graham probably had a closer relationship with Barbara Bush than with any of the other presidential wives.[8] According to Billy, "Ruth has often said that it's worth having George Bush as President to get Barbara as First Lady."[9] In a published collection of Ruth Graham's poems and journal excerpts, several of her close friends, including Barbara Bush, contributed memories and anecdotes. Barbara Bush wrote: "I think of Ruth Graham as almost the perfect woman. Perfect because she's got a sense of humor and such family loyalty. And I love her because she says what she thinks. I've enjoyed our friendship . . . I love her support of Billy . . . And Ruth has been very supportive to us."[10] Billy describes Ruth's going to Barbara's bedroom when the Grahams were visiting at Kennebunkport and being greatly amused to see the wife of the former director of the CIA, current vice president, and future president, vigorously exercising on the floor, in time with a TV workout program.[11] It is hard to imagine Lady Bird Johnson or Patricia Nixon in a similar scene.

Billy Graham was often invited to state dinners during the Bush presidency. When Mikhail Gorbachev visited in 1990, Graham was seated next to the Soviet leader's wife, Raisa. Bush likely was thinking that there was no better person to melt Raisa's well-known frostiness than Billy Graham, with his amazing capacity for making everyone feel comfortable. Furthermore, Graham had been briefed by Anatoly Dobrynin, Soviet ambassador to the United States from 1962 to 1986, and knew that Raisa liked to talk about religion and philosophy. Indeed, her interest in these subjects went far beyond "like." She had studied philosophy at Moscow State University, where she met her husband, and had also been an instructor of Marxism-Leninism there. Her thesis for the degree of candidate in the philosophical sciences, approximately the equivalent of a doctorate degree, had been based on research among the collective farm peasantry of the Stavropol region, where her husband had begun his fast-moving political career. Raisa, who died of leukemia in 1999, was often described as haughty and aloof, and she was definitely a more doctrinaire Marxist than her husband. In the thesis, according to an American who read it, she seemed especially irritated that the collective farm peasants insisted on observing the Christian feasts of Christmas, Easter, and the Day of the Trinity. It is not surprising, therefore, that Gorbachev sometimes referred to her as "the atheist of the two" of them.[12] By 1990, when Graham sat beside her at the White House discussing philosophy and the gospel, she seemed to have softened somewhat, admitting to him "her belief that there had to be something higher than ourselves."[13]

As had his predecessors, Bush Sr. continued his friendship with Graham after leaving office. He sat on stage in the Texas Stadium at the opening service of Billy's 2002 Metroplex Mission in the Dallas–Fort Worth area. Invited to say a few words before the crusade started, Bush spoke effusively about Graham as "a genuine American hero and a man the entire Bush family is proud to call a very dear friend." He went on, "Billy Graham has been a personal pastor to America's first family since as long as I can remember. And all of us who have been privileged to call the White House home have gained strength and a greater sense of purpose from his healing ministry . . . And so I'm afraid I can't remain impartial when it comes to Billy Graham. In this case, we Bushes plead a willing bias. We respect him, we cherish him, and we love him."[14]

In April 2006, Graham was being honored

at a ceremony in College Station, Texas, to recognize his years of public service, and the man chosen to present the award was Bush Sr. News reports described Bush as being "nearly in tears" as he did so. Recalling the role that Graham had played, Bush said, "No matter how deep one's faith is, sometimes you need the guidance and comfort of a living, breathing human being. For me, and for so many occupants of the Oval Office, that person was Billy Graham. When my soul was troubled, it was Billy I reached out to, for advice, for comfort, for prayer." At the end of the ceremony, according to one reporter's description of the event, Bush "threw his arms in the air and hollered (there is no other word for it): 'Go in peace, and thank you!' "[15]

BILL CLINTON

Bush's successor, Bill Clinton, was equally effusive about Billy Graham. On the occasion of Billy and Ruth's receiving the Congressional Gold Medal, Clinton observed that "I hardly ever go anywhere as President that Billy Graham hasn't been there first — preaching."[16] In an appearance on CNN's *Larry King Live* talk show, he said, "I adore Billy Graham. I've known him a long time." In fact, in a revealing episode recounted in his autobiography, Clinton describes being taken by a Sunday school teacher from his Baptist church in Hot Springs, Arkansas, to hear Graham preach during his 1959 crusade in Little Rock's Memorial Stadium. What impressed the thirteen-year-old Clinton even then was that Graham had refused a request by Little Rock's White Citizens' Council to preach to a segregated crowd of whites only. "The Reverend Graham delivered a powerful message in his trademark twenty minutes. When he gave the invitation for people to come down onto the football field to become Christians or to rededicate their lives to Christ, hundreds of blacks and whites came down the stadium aisles together, stood together, and prayed together," Clinton recalled. "It was a powerful counterpoint to the racist politics sweeping across the South. I loved Billy Graham for doing that."[17] Clinton, however, has never indicated whether he was among those who "went forward" at the crusade after hearing Graham's salvation message.

For months after that, according to Clinton, he regularly sent part of his small allowance to support the BGEA, keeping that fact secret even from his own family. The first direct contact between the two men, however, had to wait twenty-five years, until 1985, when Graham was a speaker at the National Governors' Conference in Boise, Idaho. According to Billy, Arkansas Governor Clinton sought him out that day and talked to him for a couple of hours, but Graham's autobiography does not give any details. When Graham returned to Little Rock in 1989, three decades after his first visit, Clinton was still the governor and sat on the platform with him one night of the crusade. On the occasion of that visit, Graham went to see Clinton's Little Rock pastor, W. O. Vaught, who was dying of cancer. Clinton recalled, "It was amazing to listen to these two men of God discussing death, their fears, and their faith. When Billy got up to leave, he held Dr. Vaught's hand in his and said, 'W. O. it won't be long now for both of us. I'll see you soon, just outside the Eastern Gate,' the entrance to the Holy City."[18]

Also during the September 1989 Little Rock crusade, Clinton's wife, Hillary, asked to see the evangelist, suggesting they have lunch together. At first, in keeping with the Modesto Manifesto of 1949, in which Graham pledged never to be in a room alone with a woman who was not his wife, he declined, saying he did not have private lunches "with beautiful ladies." Hillary suggested that a table in the center of the dining room at Little Rock's Capital Hotel would be public enough while also allowing the two of them to converse privately. Graham agreed. They discussed Hillary's Methodist upbringing in Park Ridge, Illinois, and her career as a lawyer. Whether Hillary brought up any of her private concerns about Bill's extramarital flirtations is not known. "I left our luncheon greatly impressed by her," is Billy's only comment in his autobiography.[19]

When Bill Clinton won the presidential election in 1992, Graham was invited to lead prayers at the inauguration the following January, as he had done at almost every inauguration since 1952. Many evangelicals criticized him for doing so, on the grounds that Clinton was a liberal on moral issues and that he and his wife were pro-choice on the divisive abortion issue. Graham responded that he felt an obligation to pray for Clinton, even if he did not agree with everything the president said. Some two weeks later, on the night before the annual National Prayer Breakfast, Billy and Ruth stayed overnight at the White House. Dinner at the White House that night, Graham reported, was "a delightful and informal time, almost like a family gathering."[20] It was, he said, "very moving" to hear Clinton and Vice President Gore the following morning acknowledge their need for God's guidance. Like so many others, Graham was won over by Clinton's famed charisma, which led him to comment in a 1993 interview with *US News & World Report,* "President Bill Clinton would make a great evangelist." He added that he was impressed "with some of the things he believes . . . From a biblical point of view, we should be headed in the direction of goodness and righteousness, away from crime and immorality and towards one's neighbors who are in need. I'm encouraged by the emphasis President Clinton and Hillary are putting on that."[21]

Graham saw a pastoral side to Clinton after the memorial service for the victims of the Oklahoma City bombing in 1995. The president spent time expressing his condolences privately to relatives of the victims of the bombing, and Graham was impressed that it was all done without any regard for publicity. "I felt that he, not I, was the real pastor that day," Billy writes in his autobiography. "I couldn't help but wonder if his own years of hardship and pain as a child had given him an understanding of the heartache and pain of those who suffer, whatever the cause."[22]

In May 1996, Billy and Ruth were invited to the Capitol Rotunda to receive jointly the Congressional Gold Medal, only the one hundred fourteenth to be awarded since 1776. Clinton himself was not present, and the senior administration figure on hand was Vice President Al Gore, president of the senate. It was thirteen years after Ronald Reagan had presented Graham with the Presidential Medal of Freedom. Clinton had invited Billy to the White House on the day before the ceremony, and they spent much of the afternoon talking about the world, the Bible, and God's role in individual lives. "It was a time of warm fellowship with a man who has not always won the approval of his fellow Christians but who has in his heart a desire to serve God and do His will," Graham said of their hours together.[23] After a dinner in Washington following the award ceremony, Clinton presented Graham with a framed copy of the legislative bill that he had signed approving the commendation. The two men, according to Graham, then had a long hug.[24] When Clinton was elected to a second term in 1996, Billy once again was on hand for the inaugural ceremonies.

By the middle of Clinton's second term, however, one of the most mesmerizing — some would say, vulgar — episodes in American presidential history had occurred: President Clinton's brief romantic, and, at times, sexual liaison with White House intern Monica Lewinsky. Clinton allegedly began meeting with Lewinsky at the end of 1995, but the affair did not become public until the following summer. The nation was riveted by the unfolding scandal that led to a Congressional impeachment vote in 1999 against President Clinton, approved by the House of Representatives, but rejected by a vote of the Senate. Because Graham had traditionally had a pastoral relationship with every president, he was asked to comment on the affair on national television. It led to one of his most embarrassing statements about matters to do with the White House. "I forgive him [President Clinton]," Graham told *The Today Show* host Katie Couric, "because I know the frailty of human nature and I know how hard it is — especially a strong, vigorous man like he is. He has such a tremendous personality that I think the ladies just go wild over him."[25] Many commentators wondered what theological authority gave Billy Graham the right to forgive an act of presidential wrongdoing. Others could not believe that Graham seemed essentially to be excusing Clinton for his actions because the president was so attractive that women simply were unable to resist him.

What followed were some of the cruelest media jokes ever made at Graham's expense, the worst of which (not repeatable here) were on the ABC show *Politically Incorrect with Bill Maher.* Perhaps the most cogent (and printable) remark on that program was made by commentator Arianna Huffington, who noted logically enough, "Here you have absolution before you have repentance."[26] On Worldnet Daily, a Christian news Web site, a critic commented, "It is not my business, or, with all due respect, Dr. Graham's, to forgive Bill Clinton for his sexual trespasses. It would be up to Hillary Clinton, Gennifer Flowers, Paula Jones, Monica Lewinsky, and an untold list of other women he has violated to make any meaningful offer of forgiveness to the president."[27] The BGEA was acutely discomfited by the embarrassment caused by Graham's amiable but clearly unreflective observations about Bill Clinton and issued a statement essentially saying Billy had been misquoted.

Eventually, this "ladies go wild" comment was forgotten, and people, sensibly enough, realized that one *faux pas* on national TV did not undermine the credibility of an entire career and close friendship with American presidents. But Graham's propensity to allow his natural friendliness to eclipse his sense of prudence was to occur one more time with Bill Clinton. At his last American crusade, in New York City's Flushing Meadow in late June and early July 2005, Bill and Hillary Clinton were on stage with Graham on the second night of the crusade. Clinton once again harked back to the Little Rock Crusade of 1959 and Graham's refusal to speak to a segregated audience there. "I was just a little boy, and I never forgot it, and I've loved him ever since," he said. "He's about the only person I know who I've never seen fail to live his faith." As New York Mayor Michael Bloomberg and New York's senior senator, Democrat Charles Schumer, sat in the crusade audience beaming with pleasure, Graham made another friendly comment that, unfortunately, was immediately pounced upon by people offended at its apparent political partisanship. "They're a great couple," Graham said, referring to the Clintons with obviously genuine affection for the former president and his wife, the junior Democrat senator from New York.

Billy went on, "I told an audience that I felt when he left the presidency he should be an evangelist because he has all the gifts and he'd leave his wife to run the country."[28]

I was present that night when Graham made these remarks, and it never occurred to me that the comments would be taken as a serious endorsement of Hillary Clinton. The warm remarks made about the former president seemed entirely in line with the effusive comments Graham has made about every single occupant of the White House, past and present. It seemed to me not unreasonable that an eighty-six-year-old man, in the gloaming of a six-decade career as an evangelist, might be permitted some humorous verbal repartee about political figures with whom he was sharing the stage, regardless of their political affiliation. But perhaps one should never assume that everyone is uniformly generous-spirited. Within hours, e-mails were dashed off to the BGEA protesting the supposedly wholesale endorsement by a Christian conservative leader — America's most famous evangelical, no less — of a president whose immorality had resulted in his near-impeachment and of his politically ambitious wife. The BGEA received more than one hundred protest e-mails and phone calls, forcing its CEO, Graham's son Franklin, to issue a formal statement denying that the comments were meant to endorse Hillary Clinton. "For a long time," he said, "my father has refrained from endorsing political candidates and he certainly did not intend for his comments to be an endorsement for Senator Hillary Clinton. My father, of course, was joking."[29]

That's certainly how it seemed to me, and, I think, to most of those around me in the press section of the very last Billy Graham crusade, on a hot June night in Queens, New York.

GEORGE W. BUSH

Surely there is something rather fitting in the fact that, at the very end of Billy Graham's career, the man occupying the White House should have owed his evangelical Protestant faith indirectly to the friendship between his father, who had also occupied the Oval Office, and the world-famous evangelist. George W. Bush is not unique among American presidents to embrace religious faith in adulthood; Abraham Lincoln, though certainly a theist, by his own testimony did not become a committed Christian until 1863, when he was already president. Arriving in Gettysburg, where later that day he would deliver his famous Gettysburg Address, Lincoln, upon seeing the graves of the nearly six thousand killed in action during the famous Civil War battle there four months earlier, realized to his horror how great the carnage had been. "I then and there consecrated myself to Christ," he was reported to have later said.[30] George W. Bush's coming to faith was far less dramatic and occurred openly and explicitly long before anyone even considered that he might be White House material. In fact, it happened a full fifteen years before Bush even ran for the office, which contradicts assertions that his espousal of conservative Christian positions was carefully and cynically calculated to advance his political ambitions.

George W. Bush's conversion to a personal Protestant faith was not a sudden event, but developed over a two-year period. The first stage seems to have been a time of prayer with evangelist Arthur Blessitt in early April 1984, when Blessitt was conducting a week of evangelistic meetings in Midland, Texas, then Bush's hometown. The culminating stage of it appears to have been a sudden decision Bush took to stop drinking after a bibulous evening celebrating a friend's birthday at a hotel in Colorado Springs,

Colorado, in July 1986.[31] But by Bush's own reckoning, repeated to many close to him, the most decisive stage of that process appears to have been an encounter with Billy Graham in the summer of 1985 at the Bush family summer vacation home when his father was still vice president.

Graham had become close friends with Vice President Bush's family over many years, and during two or three summers in the 1980s, according to Barbara Bush, would spend a few days at a time at the family enclave at Kennebunkport, Maine. His visits often included informal Bible study sessions for the vice president's grandchildren, with Billy sitting in the living room and answering questions posed by the children on such weighty moral issues as prenatal death, good and evil, and suffering. "It made a huge experience," Barbara said. "I think that was a great opportunity for our children."[32]

Graham's 1985 visit turned out to be a huge opportunity for George W. Bush in particular. The thiry-nine-year-old had prayed with Arthur Blessitt about asking Jesus Christ to be Lord of his life a year earlier, but there had been little evidence of any dramatic change in his life. Now apparently more serious about the important things in his life than he had been during Graham's previous visits, George W. Bush and the evangelist went for a long walk on the beach at Walker Point, close to the family compound. Graham has never written about the conversation the two of them had on that walk, but Bush spoke to a few close friends about it afterwards. According to former Secretary of Commerce Don Evans, a close friend of Bush since the 1970s, at least one of the issues apparently troubling Bush was whether some sins were worse than others. "Well, sin is sin," Graham replied in the Evans account. "You can't place one sin as higher than another sin."[33] More powerful than Graham's words, however, was the evangelist's demeanor. "He was like a magnet," Bush later wrote. "I felt drawn to seek something different. He didn't lecture or admonish; he shared warmth and concern. Billy Graham didn't make you feel guilty; he made you feel loved." Bush said he felt he had been "in the presence of a great man," adding, "the Lord was so clearly reflected in his gentle and loving demeanor."[34] Bush elaborated, "Over the course of that weekend, Reverend Graham planted a mustard seed in my soul, a seed that grew over the next year. He led me to the path, and I began walking. And it was a beginning of a change in my life. I had always been a religious person, had attended church, even taught Sunday school and served as an altar boy. But that weekend, my faith took on new meaning. It was the beginning of a new walk where I would recommit my heart to Jesus Christ."[35]

The meeting with Graham in 1985 seems to have been the most decisive spiritual encounter of George W. Bush's life up to that point. That fall, he joined a weekly men's Bible study group in Midland, and it became apparent to other members of the group that the Bush family was indeed well acquainted with the great evangelist. In one anecdote, one member recalled hearing that Bush, newly re-committed to his faith, had gotten into a discussion with his mother on the meaning of "born again," a term which Barbara Bush had not grown up hearing but which was now commonly used by evangelical Christians. In this account of the conversation, Bush had insisted that the term *born again* comes from the New Testament (it does: John 3:8), but his mother had not been convinced. "Let's call Billy Graham," was her response. The evangelist set the record straight, "Yes, Barbara, it's true."[36]

This story, as journalists say, had legs. At least two different versions of it surfaced, one when Bush was running for the governor of Texas for the first time in 1993. Asked at a news conference whether he thought only Christians could go to heaven, Bush, according to one version, replied, "I believe that people who do not accept Jesus cannot go to heaven." In another version he is said to have responded, "Heaven is only open to those who accept Jesus Christ." According to Ken Herman, at the time a reporter for the *Houston Chronicle,* when he interviewed George W. on the day he announced his decision to run for governor, the candidate reported the anecdote of his conversation with his mother and of the phone call to Billy Graham. According to the version Bush told Herman, Graham had said to Barbara Bush, "Just don't worry about it. Just live your life the way you're supposed to. Love everybody and move on."[37] Bush's definition of the requisites to heaven in his 1993 conversation came back to haunt him in late 1998 after he had been re-elected governor of Texas and had just returned from his first visit to Israel. Many in the Jewish community objected to the fact that he seemed to have been saying, some six years earlier, that Jews were not going to heaven. At a press conference back in Texas on his return from Israel, Bush backpedaled furiously on his earlier comment, making the point that it was up to God alone to decide whether a person goes to heaven or not.

In the case of George W. Bush's inaugurations, Graham was on hand for his two installments as governor of Texas, but could not make it either time when Bush took office as president. At Bush's first gubernatorial inauguration in 1995, Graham gave the invocation and referred to "the moral and spiritual example [George W.'s] Mother and Father set for us all." Then, in a move that may have reminded Graham of his friendship with Johnson, on taking the oath of office, George W. Bush laid his hand on a Bible that once belonged to the Texas hero Sam Houston, whom LBJ's great-grandfather, George Washington Baines, had helped turn away from the bottle to a more sober life.

Once installed as governor in Austin, Bush had several phone conversations with Graham, but age had slowed Billy down, so they did not have much face-to-face contact. This remained true when George W. Bush became the forty-third president in January 2001. It was Graham's son, Franklin, who delivered the invocation at the inauguration in his father's stead. The only other public event during the Bush presidency at which Graham was present was the memorial service in Washington's National Cathedral on September 14, 2001, after the September 11 terrorist attacks. By then, the great evangelist had become too frail and aged to engage in the lively pastoral functions he had performed for Eisenhower, Johnson, Nixon, and Reagan. President Bush, though, had not forgotten the aging Graham, and phoned him "out of the blue" one day to ask how he was doing.[38]

Graham's legacy as a pastor to the presidents is incalculable. Many, perhaps most, of the confidences he was privy to will never be known by any others. Enough is known, though, to suggest that, even if his role as an international evangelist is disregarded, Billy Graham's unique access to several presidents actually had specific policy consequences in national life and in international affairs, even if only indirectly. He steadied Eisenhower's hand during crucial periods of America's racial desegregation crisis in the 1950s. He listened to and tried to strengthen LBJ's spirits as Johnson coped first with further consequences of racial change in the 1960s and later with how to disentangle the nation from the Vietnam quagmire. He boosted his friend Richard

Nixon through diplomatic and political challenges. He failed, however, to challenge Nixon's prejudicial comments about Jews, and more significantly failed to perceive until the very end of things how deeply Nixon had been morally compromised by Watergate.

The Watergate crisis caused Graham to alter substantively his relationship with the White House. From the mid-1970s on, he tried to avoid being too closely identified with any administration. Yet his old friendship with the Reagans was transformed in some measure into a pastoral relationship, especially after the 1981 assassination attempt on Reagan. Bush Sr. leaned on him during the tense moments leading up to the 1991 Gulf War, and in many ways the friendship with the Bush family was the most uncomplicated and affectionate of that with any president. That, in turn, led to the decisive influence Billy Graham had on the life of yet another future president, George W. Bush. The nadir of Graham's White House influence may have been the presidency of Bill Clinton. This was not because Clinton did not admire Billy immensely — he did — but because Clinton's admiration for Graham did not translate into personal ethical standards that might have kept this president out of the scandals that nearly engulfed his presidency.

By the time of George W. Bush, in the ebbing years of Graham's ministry, the evangelist was not physically strong enough to maintain a pastoral relationship, even by phone, with the president. But in an interesting transition in his life, Graham had by then taken on yet another role in American public life, that of the national consoler in America's times of sorrow.

ELEVEN:
NATIONAL CONSOLER

Billy Graham did not grow into his role as a close confidant of American presidents in a theological vacuum. The presidents he knew arrived in the Oval Office with widely varying theological viewpoints, and to be close friends with them, let alone pastoral, Graham had to be open to Christian perspectives that often were different from the fundamentalist and later the Southern Baptist viewpoints with which he had first become famous as an evangelist. That openness was a critical factor in his later assuming the role of the national consoler, which required broad acceptance across American society.

Moreover, the great evangelist's own Protestant theology had been evolving too. In the mid-1950s, Graham parted company with the fundamentalists, as recounted in Chapter Six, and endorsed a theology that many have since dubbed "neo-evangelical."

Critics have not relented even in the closing years of his life in attacking Graham for his alleged betrayal of the very truths of the gospel that he proclaimed at the start of his career, and the Internet now brims with Web sites devoted to bromides against him. In the larger sense, Graham never for a moment in his six decades as a preacher changed his message of the need for those in the crowds he addressed to "come forward" and make a decision for Christ. The fundamentalists who have criticized Graham for his evolving theology, however, do have a point: Billy Graham's views, as demonstrated by his own words, *did* change, often in substantial ways, as his long life proceeded.

The accusation most frequently hurled at Graham is that he is *ecumenical,* a charge to which he freely pleads guilty. The core of the complaint is twofold: the Protestant liberals he befriended are apostate Christians because they deny key doctrines of the Bible, such as the inerrancy of Scripture, the virgin birth, the divinity of Christ, and the physical resurrection of Jesus Christ; and the Roman Catholics are not even true Christians because they believe that Christian salvation is dependent on *both* faith in Jesus Christ *and* submission to the doctrines of the Roman Catholic magisterium. For many fundamentalists — especially those who lambaste him on myriad Internet sites[1] for his alleged compromises on core Protestant doctrine — it is Graham's willingness over many years to be associated both with Protestant liberals and with Roman Catholics that they regard as a betrayal of his original (i.e. "true") version of the gospel. They often quote Billy speaking in the early 1950s against Protestant liberals and Roman Catholics to prove their point.

Not only has Graham never denied his friendship with Roman Catholic prelates, including in particular American bishops and the pope, he has expressed pride in these relationships. "I am far more tolerant of other kinds of Christians than I once was," he told *McCall's* magazine in January 1978. "My contact with Catholic, Lutheran, and other leaders — people far removed from my own Southern Baptist tradition — has helped me, hopefully, to move in the right direction. I've found that my beliefs are essentially the same as those of orthodox Roman Catholics, for instance. They believe in the virgin birth, and so do I. They believe in the resurrection of Jesus and the coming judgment of God, and so do I. We only differ on some matters of later church tradition."[2] Describing his first meeting, in 1981, with Pope John Paul II, Graham told *USA Today* in an interview published on June 8, 1989, "There was a pause in the conversation; suddenly the Pope's arm shot out and he grabbed the lapels of my coat, he pulled me forward within inches of his own face. He fixed his eyes on me and said, 'Listen Graham, we are brothers.' " Ruth Graham once told me that neither she nor Billy had "ever had a nasty letter from a Roman Catholic." The implication was that they *had* received over the years bagfuls of dyspeptic letters from disgruntled Protestants.[3]

In fact, though, the evolution of Graham's theology over the years had many features not connected at all with his ecumenicism. Take the question of heaven and hell and how a person winds up in one place or the other. The classic Protestant fundamentalist position, to which probably most neo-evangelicals adhere, is that a person must come to a personal knowledge of Jesus Christ by a process of conversion, or being "born again," to be "saved" and thence to gain admission to heaven. But in the same *McCall's* interview, Graham expressed a different view on this subject, "I used to think that pagans in far-off countries were lost — were going to hell — if they did not have the gospel of Jesus Christ preached to them. I no longer believe that . . . I believe there are other ways of recognizing the existence of God — through nature, for instance — and plenty of other opportunities, therefore, of saying yes to God." At some point in his ministry, Graham also abandoned the traditional view that hell is a place of burning fire. In an interview with *Time* magazine in 1993, he said, "The only thing I could say for sure is that hell means separation from God. We are separated from His light, from His fellowship. That is going to hell. When it comes to a literal fire, I don't preach it because I'm not sure about it. When the Scripture uses fire concerning hell, that is possibly an illustration of how terrible it's going to be — not fire but something worse, a thirst for God that cannot be quenched."[4]

In a May 1997 interview with Rev. Robert H. Schuller, senior pastor of the Crystal Cathedral in Garden Grove, California, Graham had the following thoughts on God's relationship with people of other faiths: "He's calling people out of the world for His name, whether they come from the Muslim world, or the Buddhist world, or the Christian world, or the non-believing world, they are members of the Body of Christ because they've been called by God.

They may not even know the name of Jesus, but they know in their hearts that they need something that they don't have, and they turn to the only light that they have, and I think that they are saved, and that they're going to be with us in heaven."

Schuller seemed pleased with this answer, and followed up with this question: "What I hear you saying is that it's possible for Jesus Christ to come into hearts and soul and life, even if they've been born in darkness and have never had exposure to the Bible. Is that a correct interpretation of what you're saying?"

"Yes, it is," Graham replied, "because I believe that. I've met people in various parts of the world in tribal situations, that they have never seen a Bible or heard about a Bible, and never heard of Jesus, but they've believed in their hearts that there was a god, and they tried to live a life that was quite apart from the surrounding community in which they lived."[5]

Newsweek magazine in 2006 asked him whether "good Jews, Muslims, Buddhists, Hindus, or secular people" would be denied entry to heaven. Graham's reply was, "Those are decisions only the Lord will make. It would be foolish for me to speculate on who will be there and who won't . . .

I don't want to speculate about all that. I believe the love of God is absolute. He said he gave his son for the whole world, and I think he loves everybody regardless of what label they have."[6]

In 1994, Graham said in an interview with British television journalist Sir David Frost, "And I think there is that hunger for God, and people are living as best they know how, according to the light that they have. Well, I think they're in a separate category than people like Hitler and people who have just defied God, and shaken their fists at God . . . I would say that God, being a God of mercy, we have to rest it right there, and say that God is a God of mercy and love, and how it happens, we don't know."[7]

Graham conspicuously distanced himself from evangelical Protestant efforts to proselytize Jews, and has never gone on record saying that the Jews need a personal knowledge of Jesus Christ just as much as any other ethnic group to gain entrance to heaven. Indeed, he has leaned distinctly toward a version of the gospel which, if it excluded the Hitlers and Pol Pots of the world, seems to be entirely accessible to just about everyone else. He has refrained from speaking out against homosexual behavior, and indeed even on the question of abortion has sometimes sounded distinctly equivocal. When asked on ABC's *Good Morning America* show in September 1991 about his views on abortion, he responded, "There is a Christian position, I think. But I'm not prepared to say what it is."[8]

While Graham was raising eyebrows among Protestant evangelicals over his views on hell, the commonality of world religions, and, indeed, how to get into heaven, the Billy Graham Evangelistic Association hummed along with its cottage industry of Graham's newspaper column "My Answer," where no hints of theological universalism were evident. The columns were written not by Graham himself but by a series of trusted subordinates within the organization. They offered safe, winsome responses to a garden-variety of general questions. For example, when an eight-year-old asked in November 2003 why people did not all believe in Jesus if doing so would guarantee entrance to heaven, the reply attributed to Billy Graham was simple: he also did not understand why people chose not to accept Jesus Christ as Savior. "It doesn't make sense for anyone to turn his or her back on God and deliberately choose hell instead of heaven," the writer of the "My Answer" column replied, "and yet people do it all the time."[9] In this reply, heaven and hell were clear concepts, and no reference was made to people trying "to live a life that was quite apart from the surrounding community in which they lived," whatever that meant.

Graham, continuing to be a sort of Rorschach test of American Protestant Christianity, seemed to have smoothed down some of the sharper edges of his earlier theology. Undoubtedly, as he explained many times, this was in part the result of his meeting over the years not only many Christians from faith traditions very different from the fundamentalism of his early years, but simply of meeting many fine, noble people who were not Christians at all. Would all these noble people end up in hell just because they had not accepted Christ? Perhaps not: the God whom Billy Graham had come to know over the years was indeed a God of infinite mercy, as well as infinite justice. And what about evil? Why did bad things so frequently happen not just to innocent people but to good people? Hurricanes, earthquakes, and floods took a toll of human lives every year in America and all over the world. How was that to be explained within the sovereignty of the Christian God of love? And what about terrorism? Why did God allow that to happen?

Some American Protestant evangelicals declaimed that natural and man-made disasters were the result of God's judgment on sinful communities. Some have even proclaimed that AIDS was God's way of punishing homosexual behavior. In a remarkable instance of an almost instantaneous about-face as a result of public pressure, Graham asked rhetorically during a 1993 crusade in Columbus, Ohio, "Is AIDS a judgment of God? I could not say for sure, but I think so." After his organization received many protest letters, however, he reversed himself and contacted a local newspaper, Cleveland's *The Plain Dealer,* by phone to express a different view on the issue. "I remember saying it," he told the newspaper, "and I immediately regretted it and almost went back and clarified the statement." Graham added that he never intended to make the remark, explaining that he was tired during the sermon and forgot to retract or clarify his statement. "I do believe God stands in judgment of all sins," he explained to the paper, "but AIDS is a disease that affects people and is not part of that judgment. To say God has judged people with AIDS would be very wrong and very cruel."[10] He probably meant to say, "AIDS is a disease that affects *all* people," that is, not just sexually active homosexuals.

Some Protestant fundamentalist Internet Web sites immediately accused Graham of having reversed himself merely to please the crowd.[11] It was certainly an understandable conclusion. But saying that AIDS was a judgment from God would have actually run counter to the lifelong evolution of Graham's own theology and his sense that, after years of preaching a hard-hitting gospel, he had fundamentally morphed into a new role, that of spokesman for God's love. Christians often say that the Christian life is a balance of truth and grace — the "truth" component being God's convicting people of the sin that Christians believe every single human being on earth has been born with, and the "grace" component is God's payment of the penalty of death required for that sin and His forgiveness of it through Jesus Christ. There is little doubt that Graham's early Christian faith was deeply sympathetic to the "truth" component, both in the experience of his conversion under Mordecai Ham and his sense, early in his career, that he needed to warn Americans about a possible impending judgment on the nation. The "sleek Russian bombers" he mentioned in his early sermons were undoubtedly his perception of God's impending wrath.

By the late 1970s, which was when Graham began to cooperate with Eastern European Communist governments in conducting evangelistic meetings in their countries, not only had his political views changed but his theological perceptions had clearly broadened. In short, Billy had mellowed. In fact, Graham himself has publicly and openly acknowledged this transformation in his thinking. In a 1997 interview, he was asked how his message had changed over time. He responded: "I think there's a greater emphasis on social issues. A greater emphasis on the love of God. D. L. Moody put a tremendous emphasis on the love of God and some evangelists put it on the judgments of God. Certainly God is a God of judgments and I believe there is a hell, so people are going [there] if they reject Christ. But at the same time, the overwhelming message is the grace and the love and the mercy of God. And that's what I emphasize now a lot more than I did in the earlier years."[12] A decade later, at the age of eighty-seven, Graham explained, "I think the Lord led me in that decision, and that's where I am now. I spend more time on the love of

God than I used to."[13] Asked how that change had occurred, he said, "I think the Lord has just gradually changed me. As I began to study the Scriptures I began to see much love and mercy and grace, because I'm not going to heaven because I'm good. I'm not going to heaven because I preach to a lot of people. I'm going to heaven because of God's grace and mercy in Christ at the cross . . . I haven't worked for it. It's a free gift from God for me."[14]

Fundamentalist critics, who often emphasize the "truth" component of Christianity more than the "grace" element, certainly believe that Graham has betrayed the Christian principles of his early evangelism. Most ordinary Americans, however, probably think that Billy Graham has come closer to their own thinking in his retreat from doctrinal dogmatism, in his growing openness to people of different faith convictions, and in his desire to present God as a supernatural source of love and compassion rather than as a vengeful judge waiting to catch people out. So when America was rocked by two great terrorist catastrophes in just over six years, Billy Graham was uniquely qualified to express a Christian message of inclusion. He had become America's most beloved Christian voice, the most comforting and the least threatening. Thus it was that Billy Graham transitioned quite naturally into a new role, that of national consoler.

When five thousand pounds of ammonium nitrate and nitromethane loaded onto a truck parked outside Oklahoma City's Alfred P. Murrah Federal Building were detonated by remote control on April 19, 1995, it was the largest domestic-originated terrorist action in American history. The resulting blast, which could be heard thirty miles away, killed 168 people, nineteen of them children in a day-care facility in the building. Some eight hundred people were injured, and three hundred nearby buildings were damaged. The bombing was a wakeup call to millions of Americans about just how vulnerable they were. Because Islamic radicals in 1993 had set off terrorist explosions under New York City's World Trade Center towers, in which mercifully only six people died, many Americans at first assumed the Oklahoma City bombing was of Muslim origin too. The real culprit, though, was American Timothy McVeigh, who was apprehended within ninety minutes of the blast, stopped by a highway patrolman because his getaway car did not have license plates. McVeigh, it turned out, was motivated by a hatred of all symbols of the federal government and had timed his attack to coincide with the second anniversary of a federal assault on a religious compound in Waco, Texas, where it was believed children were being mistreated by members of a cult.

Whether domestic or Islamic, those who planned the Oklahoma City bombing and the September 11 attack on the World Trade Center more than six years later exposed Americans to a streak of evil in the human condition from which, on the whole, they had been blessedly insulated throughout most of US history. They needed someone to tell them that the bombing was indeed a manifestation of some recognizable evil and was not just "dysfunctional" behavior by social misfits. They also needed to hear that, in spite of everything, God somehow was still in his heaven. At a memorial service four days after the Oklahoma blast, with President Bill Clinton and future president George W. Bush, then the visiting governor of Texas, in attendance, Graham responded to this need. By then, Billy Graham had become such a regular fixture at events of national importance that his appearance at the service apparently was considered as naturally American as the singing of the national anthem at ballgames.

Speaking to the more than ten thousand people crowded into the State Fair Arena for the memorial service — another ten thousand had to be turned away because there was not enough room — Graham said he wanted to express "the horror and the shock and the revulsion" everybody felt. "The tragedy," he said, "runs against the grain of every standard, every belief, and every custom we hold as a civilized society in the United States. And the images of devastation and human suffering we have seen here will be indelibly imprinted on each one of our minds and hearts as long as we live. That blast was like a violent explosion ripping at the very heart of America. And long after the rubble is cleared and the rebuilding begins, the scars of this senseless and evil outrage will remain." But Graham added, though it was incumbent on everyone "to pray and forgive and love," the perpetrators — it was not clear at the time exactly who, other than McVeigh, was involved — needed to be convinced that their dastardly act would be met by defeat in Oklahoma. America's most beloved preacher was making it utterly clear that evil was a reality in the modern world. At the same time, he was putting forward the conviction, surely of deep consolation to his audience, that evil would never have the final word.

Then Graham transitioned to the question that he acknowledged many people had asked him since he arrived in Oklahoma for the memorial service: why does God allow evil? "Why does a God of love and mercy that we read about and hear about allow such a terrible thing to happen?" he asked rhetorically. He referred back to the Old Testament figure of Job, who, through no apparent fault of his own, lost seven sons, three daughters, his home, his wealth, and his health. " 'Why did I not perish at birth?' " Graham quoted Job saying. "Perhaps this is the way you feel. And I want to assure you that God understands those feelings. The Bible says in Isaiah 43:2, 'When you pass through the waters I will be with you; and when you walk through the fire, you will not be burned. The flames will not set you ablaze.' And yet, Job found there were lessons to be learned from his suffering, even if he didn't fully understand it."

But still, why this evil? Wasn't God supposed to be in charge of things? Billy Graham the evangelist was challenged to respond to this question, and he did. "First, there's a mystery to it. I've been asked why

God allows it. I don't know. I can't give a direct answer. I have to confess that I never fully understand — even for my own satisfaction. I have to accept by faith that God is a God of love and mercy and compassion — even in the midst of suffering. I can remember, many years ago, lying on a dirt floor in a field hospital in Korea and looking up into the face of a soldier, suspended in a frame, who was horribly wounded. And the doctor said he'll never walk again. And I asked myself, 'Why?' I can recall standing at the bedside of children who were dying, and I've asked myself, 'Lord, why?' . . . There's something about evil we will never fully understand this side of eternity."

Graham was not content, however, to let the question echo in the wind over the plains of Oklahoma, and he kept returning to the troubling question of the existence of evil, as though explaining this was more important than providing consolation for the bombing victims' families and loved ones. "The Bible says," he said, repeating a phrase he had uttered thousands of times in decades of evangelistic crusades, "two other things that we sometimes are tempted to forget. It tells us that there is a devil, that Satan is very real, and he has great power. It also tells us that evil is real, and that the human heart is capable of almost limitless evil when it is cut off from God and from the moral law. The prophet Jeremiah said, 'The heart is deceitful above all things, and desperately wicked; who can know it?' That's your heart and my heart without God. And that's one reason we each need God in our lives. For only He can change our hearts and give us the desire and the power to do what is right and keep us from doing wrong."

Above all, Graham insisted, amid the tragedy, Christians were people who had hope, not just for this life, but for the life to come. He referred to the fact that the bombing had occurred only three days after the Christian holiday of Easter. "Our Lord on that cross asked the question: 'Why?' 'My God, my God why hast thou forsaken me?' And He received his answer. He knew: To redeem the world. To save you and me from our sins. To give us assurance that if we died we're going to heaven. He was saying from the cross, 'I love you!' And I know the heartaches and the sorrows and the pain that you feel. Easter," he summed up, "points us beyond the tragedy of the cross to the hope of the empty tomb. It tells us that there's hope for eternal life, that Christ has conquered death. And it also tells us that God has triumphed over evil and death and hell. This is our hope, and it can be your hope as well."

Graham closed his address with a reference to the former US ambassador to the United Nations, Andrew Young, who had been a speaker at the National Prayer Breakfast in Washington, DC earlier in the year, and who was still grieving over his wife's untimely death from cancer. Young, he said, had testified to his abiding faith in God by quoting the fourth stanza of a famous hymn, "How Firm a Foundation,"

> The soul that on Jesus hath leaned for repose
> I will not, I will not, desert to its foes;
> That soul, though all hell should endeavor to shake,
> I'll never, no never, no never, forsake![15]

"My prayer for you today," Graham said as he closed, "is that you will feel the loving arms of God wrapped around you and will know in your heart that he will never forsake you, as you trust Him. God bless Oklahoma."[16] The great national consoler had addressed the painful, worrying question on everybody's heart, and he had reached out, figuratively, to hug the grieving nation. Blast survivor Brad Nesom recalled that although President Clinton and other "important people" spoke at the service, "nothing seemed to help." Nesom said, "Then Billy Graham got up to speak God's word in a simple, reassuring way that spoke right to me. A deep peace washed over me . . . I knew that everything would be okay. God was still God."[17]

It was a moving and masterly address, incorporating into a national memorial service whole chunks of the gospel message that Graham had been preaching throughout his life to different audiences all over the world. It is unlikely, however, that Billy Graham would have been invited to the Oklahoma City memorial service if people had not by this stage of his career identified him more as the exponent of God's grace than the exponent of God's truth. At Oklahoma, Graham consoled; and he was listened to.

Ten years later, this was confirmed at the service inaugurating the Oklahoma City National Memorial honoring the victims, survivors, and rescuers of the bombing. Looking back to the first memorial service, Oklahoma Governor Brad Henry said, "When the Reverend Billy Graham came to Oklahoma City ten years ago to comfort us in the wake of the Murrah Building bombing, he told us that we could do one of two things. Either we could become hard and embittered and angry at God, or we could let our hearts become tender and open to trust and divine faith. We Oklahomans chose the latter."[18]

Six years after the Oklahoma City bombing, the second great terrorist attack on American soil took place, when Arab terrorists loyal to Osama bin Laden's Al-Qaeda organization on September 11, 2001, crashed two airliners into the twin towers of New York City's World Trade Center, and another into the Pentagon. This time, there was no doubt who the terrorists were or what they wanted to do, which was to bring down with them not only American civilization but global civilization, insofar as it derived its economic life-blood from world trade. At the memorial service three days later in the solemn Gothic surroundings of the National Cathedral in Washington, President George W. Bush, former Presidents Carter, Bush Sr., and Clinton, cabinet members, diplomats, and a veritable Who's Who of American culture were all present. Moreover, Graham was not the only religious figure to be part of the service; a Jewish rabbi gave the Old Testament reading, a

Roman Catholic archbishop gave the gospel reading, and a Muslim imam led the prayer. The latter's inclusion in the service was to underscore the administration's message that the United States did not consider the whole of Islam to be its attackers, despite the fact that an Islamist totalitarian ideology had motivated the suicide terrorists. The challenge now, quite different from that of Oklahoma City, was to label the terrorist action as evil without mentioning the Muslim motivations of the perpetrators.

And Billy Graham did just that, once again characterizing what had happened as evil, as wicked, and once again acknowledging that even he did not understand the existence of evil in a world created by a loving God. "Why does God allow evil like this to take place?" he said, voicing the question on the minds of many. "Perhaps that is what you are asking now. You may even be angry at God. I want to assure you that God understands these feelings that you may have." The lessons to be learned from the wickedness, Graham continued, was that evil remained a mystery, that amid the wickedness there had been heroic examples of courage and selflessness on the part of the firefighters and rescuers, and that there was still great hope for the American people.

The nation needed spiritual revival, he said, adding that the Bible promised it would happen if people repented of their sins.

Graham said that his hope for the future lay in the fact that "as a Christian" he knew that there was hope not just for the present life "but for heaven and the life to come." He continued, "And many of those people who died this past week are in heaven right now. And they wouldn't want to come back. It's so glorious and so wonderful. And that's the hope for all of us who put our faith in God. I pray that you will have this hope in your heart." The senseless deaths ought to remind everyone, he said, of "the brevity and the uncertainty of life . . . And that's why each of us needs to face our own spiritual need and commit ourselves to God and His will now." Essentially, Graham was preaching what is regularly proclaimed from Protestant and Catholic pulpits across America week in and week out. What made his reaffirmation of a commonality of the Christian faith so powerful was that by the eighth decade of the evangelist's life, scarcely an American existed, even if he was an atheist, who was not prepared to listen to such an affirmation from Billy Graham.

With consummate skill, Graham then turned what was an ostensible memorial service for nearly three thousand people of a host of different faiths who had perished in the World Trade towers into a full-scale Christian evangelistic sermon. "Here in this majestic National Cathedral," he said, "we see all around us symbols of the cross. For the Christian — I'm speaking for the Christian now — the cross tells us that God understands our sin and our suffering. For He took upon himself, in the person of Jesus Christ, our sins and our suffering. And from the cross, God declares 'I love you. I know the heartaches, and the sorrows, and the pains that you feel, but I love you.' The story does not end with the cross, for Easter points us beyond the tragedy of the cross to the empty tomb. It tells us that there is hope for eternal life, for Christ has conquered evil, and death, and hell. Yes, there's hope.

"I've become an old man now," Graham said poignantly. "And I've preached all over the world. And the older I get, the more I cling to that hope that I started with many years ago, and proclaimed it in many languages to many parts of the world." Graham repeated the story he had told at Oklahoma of the hymn that had encouraged Ambassador Young after his wife's death, "How Firm A Foundation." "Yes, our nation has been attacked," Graham said.

"Buildings destroyed. Lives lost. But now we have a choice: Whether to implode and disintegrate emotionally and spiritually as a people, and a nation, or, whether we choose to become stronger through all of the struggle to rebuild on a solid foundation. And I believe that we're in the process of starting to rebuild on that foundation. That foundation is our trust in God. That's what this service is all about . . . My prayer today is that we will feel the loving arms of God wrapped around us and will know in our hearts that He will never forsake us as we trust in Him. We also know that God is going to give wisdom, and courage, and strength to the President, and those around him. And this is going to be a day that we will remember as a day of victory. May God bless you all."[19]

The nation had turned expectantly to Billy Graham for solace and for answers in its greatest moment of tragedy. And once again, Billy Graham had comforted and consoled; he had offered no pat answers but had, as always, pointed to a God of hope and renewal.

It would have been the most natural thing for Graham to deliver a message at the next occasion of national mourning in Washington National Cathedral, when former President Ronald Reagan died in June 2004. But Graham had just undergone double hip replacement surgery and could not attend the funeral. His son Franklin went in his stead. His absence on that occasion notwithstanding, the fact that Graham was now widely regarded as the great consoler during times of national stress was underlined by publicity announcing the release in 2006 of a new documentary on the evangelist's life. The online announcement said, "It is impossible to think of a public ceremony of national importance, whether a presidential inauguration or a time of national mourning such as the 9/11 Remembrance or the Oklahoma City bombing memorial service, without his [Graham's] resonant voice offering hope for the future or healing to a grieving nation."[20]

At the time of the September 11 memorial service, Billy Graham was already eighty-three, and as he made his way slowly from his seat to the pulpit that morning, the years showed in the slow pace of his gait and the slight stooping of his shoulders. In his lifetime, though, there was to be at least one more occasion yet for him to take up his final role of the national consoler. When Hurricane Katrina wreaked havoc on New Orleans in August 2005, Graham was not there, nor did he arrive in the months afterward. On the spur of the moment, however, he decided to accompany son Franklin, the CEO of BGEA, for the two-day "A Celebration of Hope" in New Orleans in March 2006. Speaking to an audience of 16,500 in the New Orleans Arena, with 1,500 more watching on large TV screens in the Superdome, which had been the scene of chaos and violence in the days immediately after the hurricane, Graham said that he was probably preaching his last evangelistic sermon. Neither he nor his son Franklin was willing to describe the devastation left by the hurricane as God's judgment on the city. "God has allowed it. I don't believe He sent it, but He allowed it for a reason and a purpose, and it may be to build a new New Orleans," Graham said.

The occasion may or may not have been Billy Graham's last evangelistic sermon, but if it was, it was appropriate that Graham's role in New Orleans, where he had held a crusade in 1954, was of national consoler as much as seeker after souls. Much had changed since that weeks-long New Orleans crusade more than five decades earlier. He now needed the aid of a walker to reach the stage of the New Orleans Arena and had to deliver his twenty-two-minute message sitting down. In contrast to the energy that charged his early sermons and helped propel him to fame, his voice occasionally wavered, and reporters noted that he appeared frail. But the message Graham brought to New Orleans was the same basic one he had been preaching for six decades, delivered as usual with references to the headlines of the day. In a separate address to the city's clergy, he said, "We are living in a very tumultuous period in history. With Katrina's after-effects and the war in Iraq and all these things going on, if ever the country needs to turn to God, it is now." And as always, he concluded his New Orleans Arena sermon with his hallmark altar call, "If you're not sure of your relationship to God, if you're not certain and you'd like to be certain, I'd like you to come."[21] National consoler though he may have become, in what may well have been his last sermon, Billy Graham left no doubt that he still considered his foremost calling to America and the world to be pointing people to Jesus Christ.

Twelve:
Family and Legacy

Billy Graham could not have survived the pressures of his six-decade-long career as an evangelist in the public eye without the companionship, encouragement, and support of his late wife, Ruth Graham, who died on June 14, 2007, just four days after her eighty-seventh birthday. He has often said that their marriage was not "perfect," but it was "great." She had not only taken on the bulk of the job of raising their five children, but she was also an indispensable counselor, prayer-supporter, and basic friend to Billy when there simply was no one else to whom to turn but this wise and dependable wife. She was throughout her life a woman of enormous spiritual strength and depth, exceptional courage, sometimes irrepressible feistiness, deep compassion, simple fun and good humor, and much-needed steadiness not only for Billy but for all of their children. Theirs was a marriage that, though traditional in the roles they took up, was unquestionably a partnership of equals. Ruth was never the retiring "wifey" wife, and Billy has never failed to give her full credit for her invaluable contribution to his phenomenal success.

Ruth McCue Bell was the second of four children born to Dr. L. Nelson and Virginia Bell, Presbyterian medical missionaries to China. She had an older sister, Rosa, and a younger brother and sister. Born on June 10, 1920, in Tsingkiangpu (or Qingjiangpu in the transliteration now in use in China; it is now a district called Huaiyin in the city of Huai'an), coastal Jiangsu Province, she grew up against the backdrop of a China torn apart by decades of war, first by warlords, then by civil war, and finally by World War II. She was exposed early, to a degree unimaginable to her American contemporaries, to some of the great brutalities of life. As Ruth herself described it: "mysterious deaths and kidnappings, bandits in the night, gunfire, air raids, dangers all around."[1] When the Japanese invaded China, she heard the roar of Japanese bombers overhead and the *clump-clump* of artillery as fighting swirled back and forth not far from the medical missionary compound where Dr. Bell was a surgeon.

Lemuel Nelson Bell, a Virginian, grew up in a devoutly Christian family of several generations and felt called at the age of seventeen to be a medical missionary. Just six months after passing his medical boards, at the age of twenty-two, he and his bride, who was his high school sweetheart, were on their way to China, arriving in Shanghai in early December 1916. A few days later, they were at the Presbyterian missionary hospital in Qingjiangpu, which served 3 million people in the surrounding area. During the quarter century that the Bells served at the mission, Dr. Bell's duties, in addition to practicing medicine, included preaching, going on evangelistic missions, and occasionally acting as temporary hospital administrator. His wife, who had trained as a nurse, not only took up nursing duties and homeschooled the children until they were in high school but also led Bible studies and ran the women's clinic. The Bells served in the Renci Hospital (variously translated as Love and Compassion, Love and Mercy, or Benevolence and Compassion Hospital) from 1916 to 1941, returning to the United States only on furlough, for additional medical training and when China's domestic strife forced them to evacuate.

Dr. Bell, whose Chinese name, Zhong Aihua, means "bell loves China," left his mark on that part of the country. The hospital where he labored still functions today as a hospital, and local Communist authorities have in recent years restored its original name. More meaningfully to the Bell family, when Ruth and her siblings returned to their childhood home for the first time in 1980, a Chinese friend came to tell them, "The seed your father sowed is still bearing fruit. Most of the older Christians are dead, but the younger ones are still carrying on."[2]

Ruth was born almost three and a half years to the day after her parents arrived in China and was a tenderhearted, thoughtful child. She was the sort who rescued wounded animals and performed funerals for every dead animal she found. Once she even found a sickly, abandoned baby whom her father tried but failed to revive. Perhaps partly in response to such an early introduction to the harsh realities of life, she started in her childhood to write poems and keep a journal; both became lifelong habits, and several collections of her writings have been published. "I struggled — to find my place, my niche, my own sense of beauty," she later wrote in describing feeling out of place in

431

an alien society and culture.[3] And yet, "China is our home," she wrote.[4]

Ruth carried with her aspects of her childhood in China for the rest of her life, and apparently also conveyed some of it to her children. When her three grown daughters accompanied her on a return trip to China, one of them wrote, "We stepped off the plane and onto Chinese soil for the first time. Yet, in some way, my sisters and I felt as though we'd been there before. Something about it seemed familiar."[5] When Ruth and Billy returned to her childhood home in 1988, he told the local Chinese officials who feted them that he finally understood the reason behind one of Ruth's habits that he had always found curious. All their married life, he had wondered why she always insisted, when their guests were departing from the Graham home, on seeing them not only out the front door but down their long driveway. It was only during the China trip that Graham observed this Chinese practice that is as much a mark of good manners as saying "Thank you" is in American society. At that same banquet with local officials, Ruth apologized that she had forgotten all her Chinese, which she had spoken as a child.[6]

At the age of thirteen, Ruth was packed

off to the Pyeng Yang Foreign School, a Christian boarding school for Western children in Asia, in what is now Pyongyang, North Korea. The night before her departure, her dread of leaving home was so great that she prayed that the Lord would let her die. At the boarding school, Ruth was desperately unhappy, cried herself to sleep night after night, and wrote pleading letters to her parents to withdraw her from the school and bring her home. Her father at one point wrote to the school authorities: "We feel Ruth has a slight tendency to revel in the sad side of things, letting her religion (which is exceedingly real and precious to her) take a slightly morbid turn."[7] Ruth would later say of her time at boarding school, "I didn't realize then that this initial separation from my parents would serve as my 'spiritual boot camp' for the years that lay ahead."[8] This early experience of loneliness and separation from loved ones clearly helped prepare her for coping with the many and often very long separations from Billy, whose preaching tours sometimes lasted as long as six months. Even more importantly, though, it was a foundational experience in her Christian life, when she learned to turn to prayer and the Bible when there seemed no hope and no one to turn to.

After four years in boarding school, Ruth enrolled at Wheaton College in October 1937. Though only seventeen, she brought with her a wealth of life experiences unknown to most American teenagers, some of which caused adjustment problems. She was restricted to campus for violating the Wheaton curfew when her dates kept her out too late. "See, I'd come from a world of air raids, bandits, and Japanese bombers, so this new threat of curfew did not impress me," Ruth wrote in recounting the punishment.[9] Despite the infraction, Ruth impressed her classmates with a disciplined spiritual life that included daily prayer and devotions beginning as early as 3 a.m. Although she had an active social life — Billy says that Ruth had fifty-two boyfriends at Wheaton, based on her sister Rosa's count — she continued to hold firm to her conviction to remain single so that she could be a missionary in Tibet. But when Billy Graham arrived on campus in 1940, that all changed.

Theirs was an awkward, odd courtship, each privately passionate about the other, but sometimes acting hesitant and unsure, and even prickly. Billy's first reaction upon spotting her on campus not long after he arrived was to think, *She is gorgeous.*[10] Yet after he started dating her, he told her, "I haven't tried to win you, Ruth. I haven't asked you to fall in love with me.[11] I haven't sent you candy and flowers and lovely gifts. I have asked the Lord, if you are the one, to win you for me. If not, to keep you from falling in love with me." Ruth was captivated by the intensity of his passion for evangelism, the ardor of his prayer life, and his gangly energy, and prayed after their first date, "Lord, ifYou will let me spend the rest of my life with that man, I will count it the greatest privilege possible."[12] She was still set on going to Tibet, however, and tried but failed to convince Billy to join her. Ruth started to date other men until Graham demanded that "either you date just me or you can date everybody but me." She retorted, "I think being an old-maid missionary is the highest calling there is." He replied, "Woman was created to be a wife and mother," to which she responded, "God has many exceptions, and I believe I am one of them."[13] The Tibet question remained an issue even after they became engaged, and when he told her that "I'll do the leading and you'll do the following," Ruth remembers that "I almost slapped the ring back into his hand."[14]

She wrote in her prayer journal in 1941,

"If I marry Bill I must marry him with my eyes open. He will be increasingly burdened for lost souls and increasingly active in the Lord's work. After the joy and satisfaction of knowing that I am his by rights — and his forever, I will slip into the background . . . In short, be a lost life. Lost in Bill's."[15] Throughout their courtship and marriage, Ruth always called him "Bill," not Billy, because, as she once said, "How in the world can you call a grown man, who is 6'-2", *Billy?*"[16] But no one else did. She wrote to her parents about "this humble, thoughtful, unpretentious, courteous" boy. As to being part of Billy's "background," Ruth — with her good looks and stunning smile, quick wit, and lively and sometimes mischievous sense of humor, which clearly served her well throughout her marriage to Billy — was unlikely to assume the "little wife" role in anyone's life.

Graham's boundless enthusiasm for preaching and his willingness to accept speaking engagements caused some tensions early on. Just days after their honeymoon, for example, he abandoned an ailing Ruth to the care of a local hospital so that he could keep a routine preaching engagement in another state, clearly hurting her feelings. It was not to be the last occasion when the demands of "ministry" eclipsed urgent marital and family demands, but as one biographer observed, growing up in China and Korea, Ruth had "developed a sense of independence and self-assuredness that would prove invaluable as she matured."[17]

When it became apparent, especially after the Los Angeles revival in 1949, that Billy would be absent from home more often than he was present — by his own estimate, he was on the road 60 percent of the time — Ruth set to work on raising their growing brood of children with a vigor and practicality that did much to compensate for Billy's absences. She even selected and bought their one-hundred-fifty-acre mountainside land in Montreat. After looking at the property together, Billy had left for a crusade in California with the words, "I leave it up to you to decide." Nonetheless, he responded with, "You what?" upon his return, when Ruth told him she had borrowed money from the bank and bought the land.[18] She almost single-handedly designed their family home of Little Piney Cove, which was completed in 1956. There the children were able to grow up in relative privacy and security from the incessant demands of their father's growing fame.

Graham leaned upon Ruth for companionship, counsel, and quite often wisdom to a remarkable degree. Asked "Who do you go to for counsel, for spiritual guidance," Billy replied, "My wife, Ruth. She is the only one I completely confide in. She is a great student of the Bible. Her life is ruled by the Bible more than any person I've ever known. That's her rule book, her compass."[19] Though Ruth was sometimes able to travel with Billy during crusades at home and overseas, there were many times when her absence caused him to pine. They would part before one of his trips ordinarily enough — "She just kissed him, said goodbye, and we moved on to the next thing," recalls youngest daughter Ruth Jr. ("Bunny")[20] — but Billy often felt Ruth's absence acutely. Missing her keenly while in Scotland in 1955, he wrote her, "You see what an important place you had on the team. Your letters have been a balm in Gilead. They have given me inspiration, quieted my nerves."[21] Billy was profoundly aware of Ruth's deep-rooted spiritual affections, and he openly acknowledged his debt to her. He often tried to correspond daily when he was on the road, and in a letter to her from Los Angeles in August 1963, he wrote, "One reason that in spite of my own lack of spirituality, discipline and consecration I have found favor of the Lord is because of you. I found a good wife and as a result have found favor with God . . . I did not think that age would bring greater and deeper love but it has and is [sic]."[22] From Billy's own account and the observations of their children, in spite of the inevitable friction created when two energetic and spirited personalities meet, the couple remained deeply in love into old age. Ruth was often quoted saying, "I'd rather a little of Bill than a lot of any other man."[23]

And according to Billy, the romance had actually grown over the years. He told CNN talk show host Larry King in 2005, "I love her more now, and we have more romance now than we did when we were young. We both agree to that, and . . ."

"You have romance?" King, who is on his sixth marriage, interrupted, apparently amazed.

"Yes, we can look each other through the eyes," Graham replied. "We don't have the physical love, but we have eye contact that tells you I love you and there is not a single day, not a single night after [the] 'Larry King' [show] that I don't say 'I love you' and I love her with all my heart."[24]

Daughter Ann said poignantly in a *USA Today* interview in 2001 that she believes that "God in his grace is making up for some of that time" that Billy and Ruth had to spend apart during his six-decade evangelistic career.[25] The very length of Billy's absences created what Ruth sometimes called "the honeymoon effect," the sense of heightened physical desire because of the lack of constant and regular contact. Even the ordinary husband-wife contact assumed a special dimension because of Billy's absences. "Every conversation is important," Ruth once said. "It's more than news about the office or what happened at the grocery store, so I always get a lift in talking with Bill."[26] The children all recall that when they were growing up, their parents were constantly affectionate, hugging, kissing, and holding hands.

That did not mean, however, that Ruth was the silent, conforming wife; she had definite views of her own. She thought Billy's decision to accept the pastorate at Western Springs, Illinois, upon graduation from Wheaton was a serious mistake because she believed he had been called to be an evangelist and not to pastor a church, and Graham had made matters worse because he had not consulted her beforehand. Before they were married, she warned him, "I will not become a Baptist. I have always been and will always remain in the Presbyterian Church!"[27] She disagreed with Billy's decision to accept the presidency of Northwestern Schools in 1947. When an administrator from the school asked when they would be moving into the president's mansion, she curtly replied, "Never."[28] She argued strongly against Billy's decision to attend a Soviet peace conference in Moscow in 1982, and had, in front of outsiders, differed with him on issues such as capital punishment (she favored it strongly; he thinks it is unfair because disproportionate numbers of poor and blacks are executed) and his tendency to be generous-spirited to certain individuals with whom the Grahams have had differences. Early on in Billy's career, newspaper reporters often liked to interview Ruth because she provided them with good and often irreverent copy. When Billy in the 1950 Boston meetings was well into the hamming-up phase of his preaching, Ruth tartly observed to him, "Bill, Jesus didn't act out the gospel. He just preached it. I think that's all He has called you to do!"[29]

In this way, Ruth had a healthy effect on Billy, ensuring that he did not take too seriously the praise heaped upon him by others. When Billy was once explaining with some amazement how the president of Mexico had embraced him, Ruth piped up, "Oh, Bill, don't be flattered. He did that to Castro too."[30] Billy has suffered from a variety of illnesses throughout his career — pneumonia, prostate cancer, thrombophlebitis, pseudomonas, bacterial infection in his lungs, hydrocephalus (water on the brain, which mimics the symptoms of Parkinson's disease) — and he has tended to be something of a hypochondriac in private. On one occasion, when he was in his seventies, he was reciting a litany of his ailments to his family and Ruth cut him off with, "Oh, why don't you just die like a good old Christian." She could get away with it because there was never any doubt in Billy's own mind that Ruth was totally committed to him and his ministry. That commitment, however, did not mean blind support, especially at moments when he might have been carried away by the excessive flattery of others.

Billy has readily admitted how much he owes to Ruth. This is a typical answer when asked the secret of his enduring marriage, "Oh, you'd have to ask Ruth . . . It's her. I mean, she's been a marvelous person to be able to stay here, raise five children, nineteen grandchildren, and eight great-grandchildren. She's been the one that's done the work and kept up with them and talked with them and loved them, taught them the Scriptures and so forth. She let me travel all over the world preaching the gospel. I think if there is any secret in our marriage, it's Ruth. There's very few women that I've ever known like her."[31]

The Grahams' five children are Virginia ("GiGi"), born in 1945; Anne, born in 1948; Ruth Jr. ("Bunny"), born in 1950; Franklin, born in 1952; and Nelson Edman (Ned), born in 1958. Ruth developed a matter-of-fact four-step approach to child rearing that she adapted from dog training: keep commands simple and at a minimum, be consistent, be persistent, and praise the correct response. She monitored their TV watching, supervised their homework, and when necessary, disciplined them, sometimes physically. When Billy was away, she made sure that daily family prayers were said, and she herself spent many hours on her knees, praying both for her husband in his travels and crusades and for the children. Ruth continued to keep a journal and, in entries that she showed to others, could be mercilessly self-critical of what she considered her failings as, essentially, a single mom. One entry read:

The children misbehave. I reprimand them more sharply — more probably, peevishly. The very tone of the voice irritates them. (I know, because if it were used on me it would irritate me.) They answer back, probably in the same tone. I turn on them savagely. (I hate to think how often. And how savage a loving mother can be at times.) And I snap, "Don't speak to your mother like that. It isn't respectful." Nothing about me — actions, tone of voice, etc., — commanded respect. It doesn't mean I am to tolerate sass or back talk. But then I must be very careful not to inspire it either.[32]

Another entry recorded, "I am a weak, lazy, indifferent character; casual where I should be concerned, concerned where I should be carefree; self-indulgent, hypocritical, begging God to help me when I am hardly willing to lift a finger for myself; quarrelsome where I should be silent, silent where I should be outspoken; vacillating, easily distracted and sidetracked."[33] These entries reveal Ruth's clear-eyed self-criticism, even pitiless awareness of her own faults — some might call it overly harsh judgment — that was as much part of her incredible self-confidence and self-reliance as the irreverence and fun she exuded.

Stories abound of some of Ruth's unorthodox ways of dealing with the challenges of parenthood. On a family outing once when Billy was away and Franklin was still quite young, the boy's antics so exasperated Ruth that she ordered him into the trunk of the car until they reached their destination. Had she done the same thing in the twenty-first century, she almost certainly would have been arrested and charged with child abuse. Of the five, Franklin was the most rebellious as a teenager, and both he and others refer to his prodigal son phase. He openly smoked in his room in Little Piney Cove, drank whenever he could, played his stereo loud enough to annoy everyone in the house, even fired his shotgun out of his bedroom window. Ruth once dumped the contents of his ashtray on his head while he was sleeping, and she tried to cure him of smoking early on by forcing him to smoke an entire pack of cigarettes in front of her. But it didn't work; Franklin had already become so inured to smoking that puffing away at twenty cigarettes one after another did not make him ill.

Ruth was not all disciplinarian, however. She had an adventurous side that sometimes got *her* into trouble. She once tried to learn to ride a motorcycle, but careened off the road and down an embankment. In her fifties, she fell fifteen feet from a cord she had suspended between two trees, with the intention of providing a line for her grandchildren to slide down, and was in a coma for a week. Ruth also took care to lavish individual attention on each child when he or she reached the thirteenth birthday. The third daughter, called "Bunny" from the very beginning "because she looked like a rabbit,"[34] recalls with special fondness the gift she received from her mother on her thirteenth birthday: a silver locket that Ruth had been given by a favorite teacher in China. Because Ruth herself sometimes traveled with Billy, Ruth's parents, having retired from missionary life and living across the street in Montreat, played a major role in the child rearing.

There is no question that Billy's frequent and long absences, as well as their mother's occasional absence to be with him, affected the Graham children profoundly, though all have uniformly praised Ruth for her skillful and loving nurturing and none has openly expressed any resentment of their father for his frequent and long absences. Early in his career, in fact, Billy's inner circle of men

446

had invited "Ma Sunday," the widow of the famous fundamentalist preacher of the 1920s, Billy Sunday, to have lunch with them. Her advice to Billy and Ruth was serious and sobering. "Whatever you do, don't neglect your family. I did. I traveled with Pa all over the country, and I sacrificed my children. I saw all four of them go straight to hell," she said.[35]

None of the Grahams' children "went to hell," and all are engaged in highly visible Christian ministries of their own. Franklin is now CEO of the Billy Graham Evangelistic Association, and before that, took over leadership of a large missionary assistance group called The Samaritan's Purse, of which he is still CEO. Firstborn "GiGi" is a speaker and author of inspirational books. Anne Graham Lotz is the founder and president of AnGeL Ministries, a teaching and speaking ministry based in Raleigh, North Carolina, and author of six books. She is widely acknowledged by many people, including Billy, to be the one among the Graham children who has inherited their father's gift for preaching, though Billy — in a nod to conservative Christians who believe that women should not preach to men — calls what she does "teaching." Ruth Jr. has her own speaking ministry and has written or coauthored four books. Ned is the president of East Gates International, a ministry that prints and distributes Bibles within China.

In varying degrees, though, the children have been marked by the weeks and months that their father was away, as well as by the more subtle — and perhaps more painful — fact that, even when their father was at home, his time was often taken over by others. Ruth Jr. has candidly admitted, "I was not as generous in my heart when it came to sharing my father's time. He might not have resented the interruptions, but I must admit that I did. We had him at home with us so little . . . And while I never doubted that my father loved me, often he was simply busy with someone else. I missed my father."[36] She says this of the probable effect on her own emotional life: "It may be that seeing my father give so much to others when I was a child caused me to become reserved in loving. I think I felt he gave away so very much of what was mine — attention, concern, love, and time — and that I became protective of my heart. I was not willing to give everything away."[37] Anne Graham Lotz has commented similarly to Larry King, "We did have an absentee father, and that brings its own hardships and, you know, difficulties. And there were times I wanted my daddy and needed my daddy and he wasn't there."[38] Interestingly — and the credit surely must go to Ruth — none of the children when young seemed to realize that their father was very famous or that it was highly unusual for a father to be gone so much.

All five of the children spent some time away at boarding schools in different parts of the country (and, in Ned's case, for some time in England), and the experience appears to have been painful and perhaps even counterproductive to the overall emotional health of each. Franklin was sent at age thirteen to The Stony Brook, a boarding school in Long Island, New York, which he found rigid and populated by spoiled brats from Northern families. He continued his smoking there, though he was never caught by the staff even though they knew all along what he was doing. He "hated Stony Book with a passion," he said, "because of the structure and confinement."[39] At Christmas in his junior year, he was allowed to return to Montreat to finish high school, but his rebelliousness there and the taunting of a classmate almost got him expelled for fighting. By his own admission, Franklin in his late teenage years was, in Christian terms, "backsliding in high gear," smoking, drinking, and continuing to nurture a hard, rebellious attitude.[40] He was expelled from LeTourneau College, a private Christian school, for being out with a date overnight, and enrolled in another small Christian college nearby, Montreat-Anderson College, a Presbyterian school, where he graduated in the spring of 1974. After being confronted by his parents, Franklin later that year, while in a hotel in Jerusalem, knelt down and made a confession of faith in Christ.

The three girls all married at age eighteen, despite Billy and Ruth's reservations about such early marriages. Ruth Jr. candidly admits again that her father's long absences from home may have been a factor. "I did have a hole in my heart due to the long separations from daddy," she wrote. "My choice to get married at eighteen was probably my way of trying to fill that hole. My father didn't want me to marry so young." She also admitted that she might have resisted her father's caution against the early marriage because she felt he really did not know her.[41] Ruth Jr.'s marriage to Ted Dienert, a man who at one point was producing Billy Graham's syndicated movies, ended in divorce twenty-one years later, and she has subsequently gone through two more divorces. Her youngest daughter, Windsor, had two teenage pregnancies. Ruth Jr., however, has been honest and open about these and other mistakes, and has built a ministry to reach out to others who have had similar experiences.[42] Revealingly, one of her books is called *In Every Pew Sits a Broken Heart.*

GiGi, the Grahams' eldest daughter, after a marriage of some four decades to Stephan Tchividjian, the son of a wealthy Swiss friend of the Grahams, was also divorced and in 2005 married Chad R. Foreman, a Florida private investigator. Youngest son Ned was divorced, too, from his wife, Carol, in 1999 after nineteen years of marriage. The breakup of the marriage and his admission of alcohol abuse and "inappropriate" though nonsexual relationships with two women on his staff rocked his organization, East Gates Ministries International, and resulted in the resignation of most of the board and staff.[43] He has since married one of the women, Tina (Christina) Kuo, whom he had admitted spending an "inappropriate amount of time with." Kuo joined the organization in 1998 and now serves as its director of operations. Anne married, apparently successfully, a college basketball star from North Carolina, Danny Lotz. But her son, Jonathan, walked out on his marriage to wife Alicia and showed no willingness for reconciliation even though his wife expressed hopes that this might take place. Franklin's marriage to Jane Austin Cunningham seems to have been successful, though there is some indication that it took place when it did — later the same year of his Jerusalem prayer — under pressure from his parents. Franklin's first child, Will, was born in 1975, apparently full-term and within seven months of his parents' wedding.

In short, it is hard to avoid drawing the conclusion that there is a connection between Billy's long periods away from home and the broken marriages of three children, the unorthodox beginning of Franklin's marriage, and the troubled domestic circumstances of some of his grandchildren. Certainly, none of the children strayed as far from the gospel as the children of Billy and Ma Sunday. But just as certainly, Billy's family paid a high price for his single-minded commitment to crusade evangelism.

Graham has often paid tribute to the BGEA as a sort of "second family" for him and for Ruth and the children. The organization has been extraordinarily tight-knit, and its senior associates are fiercely loyal to each other and to Billy. The bond created among George Beverley Shea, ninety-eight in 2007, a gospel singer who was singing in Graham crusades into his nineties; Cliff Barrows, crusade musical guru; and T. W. Wilson and his brother Grady Wilson was one of the closest and longest lasting of any group in major public Christian ministry in this country. That cohesion, however, did not always extend to the administrative side of the BGEA, which was led by different corporate executives who sometimes were irked by Graham's impulsive and free-wheeling changes of direction. Within just a few years of Franklin Graham's assumption of the CEO job, it was apparent that there was significant friction between some of the organization's old-timers and their new chief executive, whose somewhat swash-buckling style (motorbikes, private planes, black jeans) did not jibe well with the buttoned-down white-shirt corporate tradi-tions that had always characterized the BGEA under Billy's tenure as CEO. Some longtime BGEA associates have privately indicated that they would leave the organi-zation after Billy Graham died. Long before he retired from being CEO, Graham had privately opined more than once to others that he would like nothing better than to close the institution down before his death.

That, of course, was unlikely. Institutions, no matter how entrepreneurial their founder, have a way of perpetuating themselves and being resistant to radical change or unpredictable reorientations. Employees have mortgages and children in college; few employees want to be uprooted from a settled lifestyle. Had Graham been serious about closing down the BGEA, one of the most effectively run Christian organizations in American history and an enterprise with an operating budget in excess of $100 million, he surely would have encountered stiff resistance. Somewhat nervously, the organization sought to ensure its continuity by crowning the heir to the throne, Franklin Graham.

The controversial decision to put Franklin at the helm created a situation that threatened family harmony as the Grahams aged and pondered the site of their final resting place. A brewing family feud went public with a front-page, in-depth report in the *Washington Post* in December 2006 that disclosed that Franklin and the BGEA wanted Billy and Ruth's burial plot to be at the end of a theme park tour celebrating Billy Graham's life on the BGEA grounds in Charlotte. Franklin and other BGEA officials were quoted as explaining that fund-raising concerns were behind the decision to build the Billy Graham Library, which was designed in part by consultants who once worked for the Disney Co. and which is not a library at all. Billy reportedly had agreed to be buried there, but Ruth had long wished to be laid to rest in the mountains of western North Carolina, in lieu of her first choice of burial spots: China. She was supported in her wish by the Grahams' other son, Ned, with whom she was especially close. As the quarrel intensified, Ned had his mother's wishes preserved in a notarized statement witnessed by six people in which she says, "Under no circumstances am I to be buried in Charlotte, North Carolina."[44] The day before Ruth's death, however, Billy Graham said in a statement that the couple had agreed in the spring to be buried side by side at the memorial library in Charlotte after all. News reports noted that Ruth had, once again, set aside her own desires and deferred to her husband.

As Billy Graham neared his nonagenarian years, health issues have meant a much more circumscribed life. The man who once flew more miles than any other passenger on United Airlines now was spending his days with Ruth in their mountaintop Montreat home, reading his Bible for hours and having long conversations with his bed-bound wife. A 2006 *Newsweek* cover story about the eighty-seven-year-old Graham said he was "increasingly reflective" and no longer as concerned as he once was with the hot political issues of the day. "The older I get, the more important the eternal becomes to me personally," he said.[45]

Newsweek described the evangelist as "a man of unwavering faith who refuses to be judgmental; a steady social conservative in private who actually does hate the sin but loves the sinner; a resolute Christian who declines to render absolute verdicts about who will get into heaven and who will not; a man concerned about traditional morality . . . who will not be dragged into what he calls the 'hot-button issues' of the hour. Graham's tranquil voice, though growing fainter, has rarely been more relevant."

To sum up Billy Graham's entire life and ministry, what can be conclusively said? Few would dispute that he was the greatest Protestant evangelist America and the world have ever seen. Over the course of six decades, he altered the nature of worldwide Protestantism by influencing it decisively toward an evangelical direction, emphasizing the need for a personal relationship with

Jesus Christ as the norm for Christian authenticity. Though he started out as an American flag-waver deeply committed to the worldwide struggle against communism, over the years he evolved to become a global statesman: still an American patriot, but convinced that to proclaim the gospel internationally with fidelity to its original spirit required a broad, internationalist approach.

Billy Graham was statesman as well in his inclusive view of the Christian experience, readily accepting as brothers and sisters in the faith those from the Roman Catholic and Orthodox traditions and unwilling to write out of the kingdom of heaven even those Protestants who had doctrinal doubts about the infallibility of the Bible or about some of the Bible's claims of miraculous events. In time, this very attitude of inclusiveness not only made him America's best-loved preacher, but earned him a special place among Christians the world over. And not just Christians. He was a wholehearted advocate of good Protestant relations with the Jews in general and with the State of Israel in particular, notwithstanding a single incident of appearing to share President Nixon's anti-Jewish bigotry. His attitude toward other global faiths evolved from one of sharp criticism early on to benevolent acceptance in his final years. He did not retreat at all in his writings and his crusade sermons from the position that individuals, in order to have a right relationship with God, needed to ask Jesus Christ into their lives. But as he concluded his public career, he declined to speak critically of any world religion.

Above all else, Billy Graham remained true to the end of his life to the calling to be a Christian evangelist that, at the age of nineteen, on a golf course in Florida in 1938, he felt he had received from God. Torrey Johnson, the Youth for Christ leader who launched Graham's nationwide preaching career in 1944, recalled in a 1984 interview with researchers from the Billy Graham Center at Wheaton College a conversation with Billy in those early years. "He told me one more time, he said, 'Torrey, God's given me one great gift. I have a gift of bringing people to Christ. And that I've got to do,'" Torrey said. "And he's done . . . better at that one thing than most of us put [to] any one thing that we think we do especially good. He has been undeviating. And there's been many distractions and many pressures to get him into the field of education, to get him into the field of politics, to get him into other things which are good and for some people would be primary, but would have turned him aside from the one thing that he believes and I believe with him God's called him to do, to bring people to Christ."[46] So single-mindedly and successfully did he pursue this calling that even secular America took note: in 1989, the nineteen-hundredth star on the landmark Hollywood Walk of Fame was awarded to Graham, in recognition of his radio programs. But when Larry King asked Graham in June 2005 how he wanted to be remembered, the great evangelist said with characteristic simplicity and humility, "That he was faithful to the gospel."[47] On another occasion, Graham said, "I intend to keep on going, preaching the gospel, writing the gospel, as long as I have any breath. I hope my last word as I am dying . . . I hope my dying word will be *Jesus*."[48]

It is true that Graham evolved in his understanding of core evangelical issues, such as heaven and hell and of the unique necessity to know Christ to gain eternal salvation. He appeared, at times, to wander perilously close to universalism. Some of his remarks in his twenty-four appearances on *Larry King Live*, for example, seemed to suggest that all religions had valid messages and the overall theme of love was more important than faith in Christ alone. In the same June 2005 appearance on the show, an obviously perplexed King, who has interviewed virtually all the major American evangelical and fundamentalist leaders many times, posed this question: "How do you feel when you see a lot of these strong Christian leaders go on television and say, you are condemned, you will live in hell if you do not accept Jesus Christ, and they are forceful and judgmental?"

Graham's reply was: "Well, they have a right to say that, and they are true to a certain extent, but I don't — that's not my calling. My calling is to preach the love of God and the forgiveness of God and the fact that he does forgive us. That's what the cross is all about, what the resurrection is all about, that's the gospel. And you can get off on all kinds of different side trends, and in my earlier ministry, I did the same, but as I got older, I guess I became more mellow and more forgiving and more loving. And the Jerry Falwells and people like that, I love them . . . but [they are] at the other end of the extreme . . ."[49]

"The other end of the extreme." Graham does not spell it out, but the implication is clear: those "at the other end of the extreme" emphasize the "truth" component of Christianity, that is, heaven and hell and eternal judgment, whereas he now emphasized the "love" component of it: salvation, forgiveness, redemption, grace, and peace. Despite an impression created in some news interviews that Graham had watered down his core beliefs, in his crusades themselves, right up to his very last one in New York City in the middle of a steamy summer in 2005, he was as consistent in his evangelical message as he had been at the very start of his career six decades earlier: "Come to Jesus" and receive forgiveness, peace, and love. As religion historian Martin Marty told the newspaper *USA Today*, Graham "never left the integrity of the gospel but never needed to be in your face about it."[50] In Graham's newest book, *The Journey*, there is not a hint of theological syncretism, universalism, or of wandering off from the core doctrinal positions of his early evangelism.[51]

There can be a simple explanation for the apparent softening of his theological positions over the years: Billy Graham just does not want to offend anyone. He became America's most beloved evangelist because he was so likable. The criticism that "likability" is not part of the gospel message is

461

valid. Indeed the Bible itself warns in the account of Jesus' Sermon on the Mount in the gospel of Luke against "likability": *Woe to you when all men speak well of you, for that is how their fathers treated the false prophets* (Luke 6:26). On the other hand, Graham most emphatically was not called to be a "speaker of truth to power," as prophets had traditionally been. Indeed, when he did stray into the "prophetic," casting himself as a champion of world peace or speaking well of repressive regimes or even despicable national dictators, he stumbled badly, as in his blundering statements while in the Soviet Union and his almost incomprehensible praise of North Korea's megalomaniac Kim Il Sung. Even in Moscow and in Pyongyang, however, Graham's "likability" became a most effective tool of evangelism. While he may not have converted anyone in the Soviet Politburo in 1982, nor in any Eastern European Politburo later in the same decade, his clear desire to avoid offense opened doors to his preaching that all of the fundamentalist bromides wished upon him by critics at the "truth" extreme of the gospel would never have managed to pry open in a thousand years. Simply put, Billy Graham's very likability was an essential component of his singularly effective worldwide evangelism.

That likability played a central role as well in the pastoral relationship Billy Graham had with America's presidents. Graham certainly never met an American president he did not admire and to whom he did not express that admiration. That was the price for access to their hearts, which he had from Dwight Eisenhower to George W. Bush. And Nixon? Graham was clearly blind to the true complexity of Richard Nixon's character, especially its deep, dark streaks. Even if he had known of that darkness prior to Watergate, though, it is far from certain that he could have influenced Nixon in a different direction. Graham's friendship with America's thirty-sixth president, cemented, in his own memory, during nearly one hundred games of golf played on courses all across the country, was genuine, affectionate, and in many ways, simply innocent. Billy saw — or perhaps chose to see — only the warm, generous, and brilliant sides of Nixon; his desire to see the good and the spiritual in everyone blinded him to any other aspect of this complicated, multifaceted president. Had he even breathed of any doubts about Nixon's behavior to the president while he was in office, in all probability Nixon would have turned his back on Billy forever.

Should Graham have taken that risk anyway? Not if he ever wanted to perform any pastoral service to subsequent residents of the White House.

One final point about Billy Graham's "likability" must be made, one that shows that this core trait of his is more spiritual than most people realize. While it is true that he was born with a pleasing personality, grew up well-liked by almost everyone he met, and could with great ease deploy enormous personal charm, those are natural attributes, whether essentially the product of genes or of a benevolent childhood environment. What Graham showed from the very earliest days of his public life was something not at all "natural," and often something cultivated only at great cost. This was a teachability, a willingness to subject himself to criticism, often of the harshest and most unfair kind. In a word, at the very core of Graham's natural likability was something much more profound: a deep, overarching humility. Virtually everyone, famous or obscure, who has ever met Billy Graham has commented on this quality. From his repeatedly expressed desire not to be "famous," not to be the center of attention because he wanted the gospel message to be the center of attention, to his "Why me?"

amazement at the worldwide success of his ministry, to his genuinely humble demeanor to virtually every human being with whom he has had any personal connection, Billy Graham's overwhelmingly single most prominent moral quality, his supreme virtue, has been his humility.

This was one of the very first things that struck Ruth when she met him at Wheaton. After hearing him preach for the first time, she wrote, "I was surprised. He spoke with such authority . . . and, at the same time, humility."[52] This humility continued to reveal itself even as Graham started to achieve national fame. In the late 1940s, when his wide-ranging preaching all across the country at Youth for Christ evangelistic rallies had already made him such a well-traveled United Airlines frequent flier, Graham would return to Charlotte where he could be found sitting at the feet of a tiny old black man who owned a ramshackle grocery store in the black part of town, listening to him expound the Bible. Graham's brother Melvin recalled, "Billy loved to hear Bill Henderson tell him about the Scriptures . . . In the afternoons Billy would go there and sit on an old crate — I don't think they had a chair in the place — and let Bill teach him . . . And Henderson could pray. He'd pray for Billy and his young ministry." Melvin added, "Billy Frank would interact with just about anybody. It didn't matter who they were, kings or paupers." When Graham visited England in the chill winter of 1946, it was this very humility in the face of an aggressively critical clergy in Birmingham, England, that completely won over his critics. BGEA photograper Russ Busby, who has been photographing Graham since 1956, said that from his unique vantage point he has concluded that the main reason "God has used Billy Graham" is that "first, Billy is truly humble before both God and man."[53] The late Bill Bright (1921–2003), founder of Campus Crusade for Christ, made a similar observation, "He's one of the great men of the century. The key, I think, to his effectiveness is that he really has a heart for God. He seeks first the kingdom. God has honored his humility. With all the great honors and applause and praise that's been heaped upon him, Billy's very humble and gracious."[54] That humility has even been noted by the secular press. The 2006 *Newsweek* profile said, "A unifying theme of Graham's new thinking is humility."

I saw this same humility up close in November 1999 when two documentary filmmaking colleagues and I met with Graham and a few of his associates in a hotel in Los Angeles to discuss a possible documentary on his life. He seemed genuinely alarmed by the prospect of a film project that would focus attention on him personally, and agreed in principle to the production concept only when we emphasized that the documentary was intended not to bring glory to him personally but to focus on his evangelism. Then he turned confessional. "People put me on a pedestal, you know," he said, "but they don't know me. I am a sinner like everyone else. I constantly must go to God and ask forgiveness."[55] Billy Graham, America's most famous evangelist, most famous Protestant Christian, needed to go "constantly" to God to "ask forgiveness"? What kinds of sins could he possibly have been talking about?

Then it became clear to me. Graham's understanding of sin was of anything that disrupts the spiritual harmony of a Christian in union with God: any unkind thought, malicious word, any trembling of impatience or anger. He was obviously not suggesting that he was as wicked as the Boston Strangler or Adolf Eichmann. He was expressing a sentiment that every honest Christian experiences in his or her prayers every day of the week: *Lord, I know that I have displeased you today, so please forgive me.* Or, as expressed by the ancient Eastern Orthodox prayer, "Lord Jesus Christ, Son of God, have mercy on me a sinner," which Graham indeed sometimes uttered publicly from the platform of his crusades. This humility surely has helped keep him out of serious trouble and scandal throughout his career, even as other famous American evangelists in the 1980s fell in disgrace over various financial and moral scandals. Billy Graham's humility, in effect, was a powerful secret weapon, a protective cloak that kept him safe from the pitfalls that have tripped others up when they have become heady with success and fame.

This humility of deportment may turn out to be Billy Graham's most memorable and most important legacy. People will always think of his crusades in terms of the more than 2.1 million people he addressed personally or the more than 3 million who "came forward." They will examine for decades the impact of his presidential friendships and his international travels. Did he help save Israel in 1973? Did he really contribute to the collapse of communism? Did his soothing representation of President Clinton's somewhat forceful objections to

North Korea's development of nuclear weapons in 1994 help defuse a crisis that US officials later admitted came perilously close to war? Did he, in his private conversations with kings, queens, and presidents all over the world bring any of them to a saving knowledge of Jesus Christ?

Some of the answers may become clear in time; others may not be known until — if we believe in its existence — we are in eternity. But we do know that Billy Graham, evangelist, one of the most successful men in America of the second half of the twentieth century in any conceivable endeavor, was also one of the most humble. When speaking of how people would recognize his followers, Jesus taught, "You will know them by their fruits." What fruits? The fruits of moral virtue in their lives, sometimes referred to as "the fruits of the spirit." By that criterion alone, Billy Graham, world-famous evangelist, sometimes called the Protestant Pope, a seven-decades-long servant of the call to preach the gospel, has been singularly and to the end a faithful follower of Jesus Christ.

AFTERWORD

In the last two and a half years, Billy Graham has been confined almost completely to his and Ruth's rural mountaintop home at Piney Cove, near Asheville, North Carolina. Just a few months after the publication of the hardcover edition of this book, Graham experienced a body-blow with the loss of his faithful and loving wife of nearly sixty three years, Ruth Bell Graham. The last years of her life had largely been spent as an invalid. She had contracted spinal meningitis in 1995, a condition that developed out of the osteoarthritis that she had experienced after injuring herself badly in a fall at her home in 1974 while testing a children's slide-line slung between two trees. Much of the time she was in great pain, and after contracting pneumonia in the final months of her life, she was entirely bedridden. At her own request, and with her family's consent, life-support systems were removed on June 11, 2007, and she died in the late afternoon of June 17, 2007. Graham issued a statement about her through the BGEA. "Ruth is my soulmate and best friend," he said, "and I cannot imagine living a single day without her by my side. I am more and more in love with her today than when we first met over 65 years ago as students at Wheaton College."

Graham suffered immensely from the loss of his wife, particularly because they had somehow rediscovered in extreme old age the romance of their first years of courtship and marriage. But rather than descend into a torpor of griping and grunting, Graham, within two months of Ruth's death, proposed to a publisher a book on the process of growing old. "Old age isn't for sissies," he has joked with many visitors to Piney Cove. For years, Graham has struggled with severe physical challenges, barely shuffling about between bedroom and bathroom in his own home. He suffers from hearing loss and the threat of blindness, due to macular degeneration. He has been hospitalized several times over the years for repeated falls, and had to have a shunt inserted into his brain to regulate the flow of blood. Graham, in fact, has been grappling with the physical and mental limitations of extreme old age for a few years. Indeed, with the help of trusted members of the Billy Graham Evangelistic Association, he set about putting together his meditations on coping with the condition of very old age, a book to be called *Nearing Home: Growing Older with Grace.* The book is scheduled to be published sometime after he passes away. "I never thought I would live to be this old," he wrote early in the book. "All my life I have been taught how to die as a Christian," he describes an aged friend telling him not long ago, "but no one ever taught me how I ought to live in the years before I die. I wish they had, because I am an old man now, and believe me, it's not easy."

In February 2010 he had a brief but revealing conversation with his son Franklin, who at that time was fifty-seven.

"My son, my advice to you," Billy Graham almost whispered to his firstborn son and his fourth child.

"Yes, sir?" responded Franklin, with a decorous courtliness that seemed to belong to a different century.

"Don't get old."

The poignancy of these words derive from the fact that, as a young and impassioned evangelist, Billy Graham had told many people close to him that he thought that he would die young. So intense was the work of his evangelistic crusades that he wondered if his body could cope with all the stress. At least once in his early years as an evangelist, he had been attacked by a man with a knife outside his home, and he may have wondered if some crazed critic of his preaching might not break through the various layers of security that surrounded him. Graham was also something of a hypochondriac throughout his life, and wondered aloud to many people if he would survive his various ailments. Yet despite this rather gloomy perception of possible early mortality, Graham nevertheless threw himself into his preaching and traveling schedule as though there would not be enough time in the world to complete the task of preaching the Gospel to all mankind. Perhaps, in a way, his very energy and commitment to the life of an evangelist added strength and length of life to his bones. Instead of succumbing to mortality through the pressures of the work he imposed upon himself, Graham somehow became rejuvenated precisely because of his intensive work. He often used to say that, no matter what physical weakness he might have been experiencing at the beginning of one of his crusades, when it came time for him to speak out the message of Christian salvation, he somehow gained the necessary strength.

Though he is physically limited in his movements at Piney Cove and complains that his memory of people's faces has deteriorated, Graham is still very alert mentally. Franklin describes him as being "sharp as a tack," and able to receive a significant stream of visitors. In keeping with a lifelong habit, Billy Graham remains in touch with major political figures. In November 2009 he played host to former governor of Alaska Sarah Palin, who brought along her Down Syndrome son, Trig. He spoke by phone during 2009 with former president George W. Bush, whom he had significantly influenced to become serious about his own Christian faith while visiting the Bush family compound at Kennebunkport, Maine, in the early 1980s. Billy also had a conversation by phone with President Barack Obama, just before Obama's official visit to China in mid-November 2009. It is not known what the two men talked about, but it was unlikely to have had anything to do with politics. Franklin Graham in February 2010 put it this way: "He will offer spiritual advice to anyone who comes to him."

This commitment to preaching the Gospel

to everyone who will listen willingly to it is the consistent theme of Graham's entire life as a servant of God. Billy Graham put his faith in Jesus Christ as his Savior just days before his sixteenth birthday in 1934. Seventy-seven years later, he is still faithful to that commitment.

February 26 2010
Lincoln, VA

ACKNOWLEDGMENTS

Few books spring up from an author's mind unassisted by the contribution of many different people, often without their being aware of it. This book certainly didn't.

Billy Graham: His Life and Influence quite definitely owes its birth to a conversation with David Moberg, publisher at W Publishing, and Greg Daniel, then an executive assistant to David, and an idea for a book-length evaluation of Billy Graham's life. Throughout the project both David and Greg were encouraging, especially at times when it didn't seem that the book would ever get written.

I am, of course, deeply indebted to Billy Graham and his wife, the late Ruth Bell Graham, for taking me into their confidence when they were preparing in 1987 and 1988 for their visit to China. I had many fascinating meetings with them both, and Ruth Graham also kindly invited me into their home at Little Piney Cove. Franklin Graham was open, honest, and informative during an interview for the TV version (PBS Broadcasting) of my book *Great Souls: Six Who Changed the Century,* which profiled Billy Graham and five other world figures.

The late Stephen Olford (1918–2004) gave me a fascinating telephone interview about his decades-long friendship with Billy Graham, including details of Graham's apparently life-changing prayer meeting with Olford in 1946.

The late Allen Yuan Xiangchen (1914–2005), a prominent leader in China's independent Protestant house church movement, became a good friend during several visits to China between 1998 and 2004 and spoke warmly of his friendship with Graham. So also did another brave Chinese house church leader, Samuel Lamb. Graham personally visited Lamb's church in Guangzhou, in south China, in 1988 and delivered a "greeting" from the pulpit to a congregation who filled every nook and cranny of the cramped little apartment that was then the venue for Lamb's house church.

When I was in Sydney, Australia, in 2005, I had a fascinating and informative conversation with the Most Reverend Peter Jensen,

Archbishop of Sydney, who had been converted in 1959 during Billy Graham's first crusade in Australia. Also in 2005, in Seoul, Korea, Rev. David Yonggi Cho, senior pastor of Yoido Full gospel Church, the largest church in the world with a membership of 800,000, gave me a very helpful interview. Rev. Cho had become well acquainted with Billy Graham during the latter's trips to Korea. Dr. Billy Kim, Graham's interpreter during the 1973 visit and a long-time friend, was extremely helpful and informative during a phone interview from Korea.

I am very grateful to Bob Jones University for making available their own documentation of their correspondence with Billy Graham and his father-in-law Dr. Nelson Bell.

Adi Ignatius, currently the executive editor of *Time* magazine and previously the Beijing bureau chief for *The Wall Street Journal,* provided me with fascinating and little-known reporting details of Billy Graham's 1988 trip to China.

I am very grateful to World Net Daily reporter Art Moore for his notes on a phone interview with Dr. Stephen Linton concerning Billy Graham's visits to North Korea.

Finally, I am indebted to my editor and researcher, Charlene L. Fu, who spent painstaking hours double-checking quotes and facts, uncovering innumerable errors, and at all times improving the fluency of the text of the book. Charlene was herself an Associated Press reporter covering the Grahams' 1988 China visit and had important memories of it.

July 2007
Virginia, USA.

NOTES

Chapter One

1. Jeffrey M. Jones, "George W. Bush, Hillary Clinton Most Admired Again, Billy Graham Finishes in Top 10 for 50th Time," Gallup News Service, 29 December 2006. Available online at http://www.galluppoll.com/content/default.aspx?ci=25996&erefaol (cited May 2007).

2. The top 10 rankings were: Denzel Washington (85%), Oprah Winfrey (83%), Bill Gates (80%), Tim McGraw (72%), Faith Hill (71%), Mel Gibson (69%), Jimmy Carter (68%), George Clooney (67%), Bill Clinton (64%), and Billy Graham (64%). "Billy Graham Tops Religious Leaders," The Barna Update, 19 February 2007. Available online at http://www.barna.org/FlexPage.aspx?Page=BarnaUpdate&BarnaUpdateID=265 (cited May 2007).

3. Jon Meacham, "Billy Graham's New

Thinking on Politics, the Bible," *Newsweek* magazine, 14 August 2006. Available online at http://www.msnbc.msn.com/id/14204483/ (cited 25 May 2007).

4. Dan Rather, interview by author for video *Billy Graham: Ambassador of Salvation,* 2002, Volume 1 in the 6-part PBS Series *Great Souls.* AIM International Television, Vision Video.

5. Richard Ostling, interview by author for video *Billy Graham: Ambassador of Salvation,* 2002, Volume 1 in the 6-part PBS Series, *Great Souls.* AIM International Television, Vision Video.

6. Billy Graham, *Billy Graham: Ambassador of Salvation,* 2002, Volume 1 in the 6-part PBS Series, *Great Souls.* AIM International Television, Vision Video.

7. Uwe Siemonetto. "Faith: Church Year Begins with Perplexity," The Associated Press, 30 November 2001.

8. Billy Graham, *Billy Graham: Ambassador of Salvation.*

Chapter Two

1. The term *flapper,* which became common slang in the 1920s, referred to a "new breed" of young women who wore short skirts, bobbed their hair, and flaunted their disdain for what was then considered

"decent" behavior. The typical flapper was unafraid to wear cosmetics or to be seen smoking or drinking alcoholic beverages in public. Adapted from http://en.wikipedia.org/wiki/Flapper (cited July 2007).

2. Paul Johnson, *A History of the American People* (New York: Harper Perennial, 1999), 761.

3. Nathan Miller, *New World Coming: The 1920s and the making of Modern America* (Cambridge: Da Capo Press, 2003), 204.

4. Charles Finney, *Lectures on Revivals of Religion* (Cambridge: The Belknap Press of Harvard University Press, 1960), 13. Available online at: http://xroads.virginia.edu/~HYPER/DETOC/religion/finney1.html (cited June 2006).

5. William Martin, *A Prophet with Honor* (New York: Harper Perennial, 1992), 60.

6. Miller, *New World Coming,* 283.

7. Ken Garfield, "Ministry to Reclaim Old Home," *Charlotte Observer,* 11 March 2004, 1B Metro.

8. Question 1 of the Westminster Shorter Catechism is: "What is the chief end of man?" and the answer is: "Man's chief end is to glorify God, and to enjoy him forever." Question 107 is: "What doth the conclusion of the Lord's prayer teach us?"

and the answer is: "The conclusion of the Lord's Prayer, which is, *For thine is the kingdom, and the power, and the glory, forever. Amen,* teacheth us to take our encouragement in prayer from God only, and in our prayers to praise him, ascribing kingdom, power, and glory to him; and, in testimony of our desire, and assurance to be heard, we say, Amen."

9. Martin, *A Prophet with Honor*, 57.
10. Ibid., 60.
11. Marshall Frady, *Billy Graham: A Parable of American Righteousness* (London: Little, Brown, 1979), 64.
12. Ibid.
13. Ibid., 52.
14. Sam Wellman, *Billy Graham: The Great Evangelist* (Uhrichsville: Barbour Publishing House, 1996), 19.
15. Martin, *A Prophet with Honor*, 61.
16. Frady, *Billy Graham,* 73.

Chapter Three

1. Billy Graham, *Just as I Am: The Autobiography of Billy Graham* (New York: Harper-Collins Worldwide, 1997), 23.
2. Martin, *A Prophet with Honor,* 62.
3. Frady, *Billy Graham,* 79.
4. See for instance this biography of Mordecai Ham. Available online at Believersweb

.org   http://www.believersweb.org/view
.cfm?id=128&rc=1 (cited June 2006),
and "Measure of Gold Revival Ministries,"
http://www.evanwiggs.com/revival/portrait/
ham2.html (cited June 2006).

5. Billy Graham, *Billy Graham: Ambassador of Salvation.*

6. Frady, *Billy Graham,* 52.

7. Martin, *A Prophet with Honor,* 63.

8. Words of the hymn "Almost Persuaded" are:

Almost persuaded now to believe;
Almost persuaded Christ to receive;
Seems now some soul to say
"Go Spirit, go thy way
Some more convenient day
On thee I'll call . . ."

The hymn "Almost Persuaded" was written by Philip P. Bliss after listening to a sermon given by a Rev. Brundage in which the reverend ended with these closing words: "He who is almost persuaded is almost saved, and to be almost saved is to be entirely lost." Later that same afternoon, Bliss started writing what was to be one of his most popular hymns. One of the most impressive occasions on which this hymn was sung was in the Agricultural

Hall in London in 1874. A deathlike stillness fell over the audience of fifteen thousand when D. L. Moody asked the congregation to bow their heads while the hymn was performed at the close of his sermon. Available online at www.gospel piano.com/articles/hymn-stories-12-almost-persuaded.htm and Ira David Sankey, *My Life and the Story of the Gospel Hymns* (New York: Harper & Brothers, 1906), 112.

9. Martin, *A Prophet with Honor,* 64.
10. Ibid.
11. Ibid.
12. Ibid., 67–68.
13. Ibid., 67.
14. Billy Graham, *Just as I Am,* 39.
15. Martin, *A Prophet with Honor,* 70.
16. Frady, *Billy Graham,* 113.
17. Martin, *A Prophet with Honor,* 74.
18. Ibid., 75.
19. Billy Graham, interview on CNN show *Larry King Live,* "Encore Presentation: Interview with Billy Graham," aired 29 May 2005. Available online at http://transcripts.cnn.com/TRANSCRIPTS/0505/29/lkl.01.html (cited June 2006).
20. Martin, *A Prophet with Honor,* 75–76.
21. Ibid., 78.
22. Ibid., 79.

23. Ibid., 82.

24. Ruth Graham's poem:

Dear God, I prayed, all unafraid
(as we're inclined to do)
I do not need a handsome man
But let him be like You;
I do not need one big and strong nor yet
   so very tall,
Nor need he be some genius,
Or wealthy, Lord, at all;
But let his head be high, dear God,
And let his eye be clear,
His shoulders straight, whate'er his state,
Whate'er his earthly sphere;
And let his face have character,
A ruggedness of soul,
And let his whole life show, dear God,
A singleness of goal;
Then, when he comes,
(as he will come)
with quiet eyes aglow,
I'll understand that he's the man
I prayed for, long ago.

Quoted by permission from Betty Frist,
My Neighbors, The Billy Grahams
(Nashville: Broadman Press, 1983), 3.

25. Billy Graham, *Just as I Am*, 72.

26. Martin, *A Prophet with Honor*, 83.

27. Frady, *Billy Graham,* 146.

28. Martin, *A Prophet with Honor,* 86.

29. Ibid., 90.

30. Ibid., 93.

31. Ibid., 95.

32. Ibid., 96.

33. Ibid., 98.

34. Billy Graham, *Just as I Am,* 111.

35. A sort of "genealogy" of Billy Graham's pathway to Christian conversion is very popular in evangelical circles. This, from a South African Web site, http:// www.nathan.co.za/story.asp? PageID=131 (cited June 2006), and entitled "One Sunday School Teacher," is typical:

"In 1855, a Sunday School teacher named Kimbell led a nineteen-year-old shoe clerk to Jesus Christ. He in turn became a Sunday School teacher leading other youth to Christ.

"Later he became a world renowned evangelist. His name — Dwight L. Moody. He led hundreds of thousands to Christ in the USA and England. Though poorly educated, Moody, in one of his English trips, influenced the well-educated and cultured theologian, Frederick B. Meyer, to change his preaching style and emphasis.

"Later F. B. Meyer came to the USA on

an evangelistic tour. On one occasion, a discouraged preacher, Wilbur Chapman, was in the audience and, through his preaching, influenced him to become an evangelist. As his evangelistic ministry grew, he needed an assistant, so he hired a former baseball player with a high school education to help him. His name — Billy Sunday.

"The latter won over 1 million persons to Christ. In 1924 in Charlotte, NC, a prayer group was formed, which met regularly. When the Depression started, they became convinced it was God's judgment on the nation. They specifically prayed for another revival, and Mordecai Ham responded.

"Later, when Ham became an evangelist and he was preaching, a sixteen-year-old farm lad was converted. His name — Billy Graham."

36. "Dwight Moody — The Empowered Life." Part of an online series of biographies called "Portraits of Great Christians." In Touch Ministries; Available online at http://www.intouch.org/myintouch/mighty/portraits/dwight_moody_213637.html (cited June 2006).

37. Martin, *A Prophet with Honor,* 98.

38. Stephen Olford, telephone conversation

with the author, 15 June 2001.

39. Ibid.
40. Martin, *A Prophet with Honor,* 99.
41. Ibid.

Chapter Four

1. Charles Templeton, *An Anecdotal Memoir* (Toronto: McClelland & Stewart, 1983). Templeton gives the date as 1936, but if he was nineteen, the correct year would have been 1934. Available online at http://www.templetons.com/charles/memoir/ (cited July 2007).
2. Templeton, *An Anecdotal Memoir.*
3. Martin, *A Prophet with Honor,* 92–93.
4. Ibid., 99.
5. Ibid., 110.
6. Templeton, *An Anecdotal Memoir.*
7. Martin, *A Prophet with Honor,* 109; and Frady, *Billy Graham,* 178.
8. Frady, *Billy Graham,* 180–82.
9. Billy Graham, *Just as I Am,* 138.
10. John Pollock, *The Billy Graham Story,* (Grand Rapids: Zondervan, 2003), 44.
11. Frady, *Billy Graham,* 184.
12. Templeton, *An Anecdotal Memoir.*
13. Charles Templeton, *Farewell to God: My Reasons for Rejecting the Christian Faith* (Toronto: McClelland and Stewart, 1996).
14. Lee Strobel, *The Case for Faith: A*

Journalist Investigates the Toughest Objections to Christianity (Grand Rapids: Zondervan, 2000), 18.

15. Tom Harpur, "Templeton's Widow Tells of 'Transcendent' Deathbed Encounter," *The Toronto Star*, 24 June 2001, F3.

16. Sherwood Eliot Wirt, *Billy: A Personal Look at the World's Best-Loved Evangelist* (Wheaton: Crossways, 1997), 100.

17. Sandra Chambers, "A Faithful Witness," *Charisma* magazine, July 2005, 37–38.

18. Billy Graham, *The Evangelist: The Worldwide Impact of Billy Graham*, DVD Newsreel of Los Angeles Crusade Attached to Lewis A. Drummond. (Nashville: Word Publishing, 2001).

19. Frady, *Billy Graham*, 198.

20. Martin, *A Prophet with Honor*, 115.

21. Billy Graham Evangelistic Association, *Billy Graham, God's Ambassador*, (New York: Time-Life Books, 1999), 54.

22. Billy Graham, *Just as I Am*, 161.

23. Martin, *A Prophet with Honor*, 126.

24. Ibid., 125.

25. Ibid.

26. Billy Graham, *Peace with God*, revised and expanded (Nashville: W Publishing, 1984), 78.

27. Martin, *A Prophet With Honor*, 127.

28. Ibid., 131.

29. Merle Miller, *Plain Speaking: An Oral Biography of Harry S. Truman* (New York: Putnam Publishing Group, 1974), 363.

30. According to the National Association of Church Administrators, salaries for senior pastors range from $15,500 to $361,000. Tax documents filed by the Billy Graham Evangelistic Association in 2002 showed Billy Graham's salary as "director and chairman" as $189,385, with $233,979 more listed as "expense account and allowances." A footnote says that $225,255 of that latter amount was spent on "health and support care." Available online at www.prettygoodnews.com/form_990/billy_graham.pdf (cited July 2007). Online sources monitoring charitable giving and top salaries of ministry leaders in more recent years have listed Billy Graham's compensation as topping $400,000. (See for instance, Charity Navigator's entry on the BGEA at www.charitynavigator.org/index.cfm/bay/search.summary/orgid/3367.htm, or this comparison of compensation received by 27 high-profile ministry leaders at http://www.prettygoodnews.com/form_990/hagee_spreadsheet.pdf. cited July 2007.) These much higher figures presumably reflect both Graham's salary and his

expense account and allowances.

31. Martin, *A Prophet with Honor,* 146.
32. Ibid.
33. Billy Graham, *Just as I Am,* 191.
34. Billy Graham Evangelistic Association, *Billy Graham, God's Ambassador,* 157.

Chapter Five

1. Martin, *A Prophet with Honor,* 174.
2. Pollock, *The Billy Graham Story,* 65.
3. Martin, *A Prophet with Honor,* 176.
4. Ibid., 175.
5. Maurice Rowlandson, "50 Years in Christian Work #9," from the 50-year diary of Maurice Rowlandson, ASSIST News Service, 6 November 2001. Available online at http://www.assistnews.net/strategic/s0111009.htm (cited June 2006).
6. Pollock, *The Billy Graham Story,* 66.
7. Ibid.
8. David Frost, interview by author for video *Billy Graham,* volume 1.
9. Wirt, *Billy,* 45.
10. Billy Graham, *Billy Graham: Ambassador of Salvation.*
11. David Winter, *Call Me Early, Call Me Late* (London: Oxford Lion Publishing, 2001), 46.
12. Ibid.
13. Martin, *A Prophet with Honor,* 180.

14. Ibid., 181.
15. Billy Graham, *Just as I Am*, 235–37; Pollock, *The Billy Graham Story*, 73–74; and Martin, *A Prophet with Honor*, 183.
16. Martin, *A Prophet With Honor*, 188.
17. Ibid., 185.
18. Ibid., 186.
19. Billy Graham, *Just as I Am*, 258.
20. Martin, *A Prophet with Honor*, 189.
21. Ibid., 194–95.
22. Ibid., 195.
23. Ibid., 196.
24. Frady, *Billy Graham: A Parable of American Righteousness*, 327.
25. Peter Jensen, archbishop of Sydney, in interview with author, Sydney, Australia, August 2005.
26. Pollock, *The Billy Graham Story*, 103.
27. Billy Graham, *Larry King Live*, "Encore Presentation: Interview with Billy Graham," 29 May 2005.
28. Frady, *Billy Graham*, 247.
29. Billy Graham, *Just as I Am*, 354.
30. Martin, *A Prophet with Honor*, 265.
31. Billy Graham, *Just as I Am*, 354.
32. Frady, *Billy Graham*, 227.
33. Billy Graham, *Just as I Am*, 565.
34. Ibid.
35. Ibid.
36. Martin, *A Prophet with Honor*, 411.

37. William Martin, "Fifty Years, The Impact of Billy Graham's Ministry to the World," *Christianity Today,* November 1995, 20–43.

38. Dr. Billy Kim, telephone conversation with the author, 15 January 2005.

39. Martin, *A Prophet with Honor,* 446–47.

40. Ibid., 449.

41. From Wikipedia online encyclopedia entries on "Major Religious Groups," "Christianity," "Protestantism," and "List of Christian Denominations by Numbers of Members." Available online at http://en.wikipedia.org/wiki/Major_world_reli gions; http://en.wikipedia.org/wiki/Christianity; http://en.wikipedia.org/wiki/Protestantism; http://en.wikipedia.org/wiki/List_of_Christian_denominations_by_number_of_members (cited May 2007).

Chapter Six

1. Web site promoting Bishop Fulton Sheen's audio and video materials, http://www.lcchristiansoftware.com/BishopSheen audios.htm (cited June 2006).

2. Billy Graham, *Just as I Am,* 692–693.

3. Martin, *A Prophet with Honor,* 309.

4. Quoted in *Bookstore Journal,* November 1991; Cited by David W. Cloud in "Billy Graham and Rome," part 2 of a 6-part

series excerpted from *Evangelicals and Rome* (Port Huron: Way of Life Literature, 1999, 2001). Available online at http://www.wayoflife.org/fbns/grahamrome2.htm (cited June 2006).

5. Iain H. Murray, *Evangelicalism Divided: A Record of Crucial Change in the Years 1950 to 2000* (Edinburg: The Banner of Truth Trust, 2000), 29.

6. Ibid., 23.

7. Ibid., 27.

8. Martin, *A Prophet with Honor,* 210–11.

9. Martin, "Fifty Years," 20–34.

10. George Marsden, *Reforming Fundamentalism: Fuller Seminary and the New Evangelicalism,* (Grand Rapids: Wm. B. Eerdmans Publishing Company, 1987), 35.

11. Martin, *A Prophet with Honor,* 220.

12. Ibid., 219.

13. Billy Graham, *Just as I Am,* 253.

14. Martin, *A Prophet with Honor,* 223.

15. Billy Graham, *Just as I Am,* 305.

16. Pollock, *The Billy Graham Story,* 90.

17. Martin, *A Prophet with Honor,* 228.

18. Ibid.

19. Ibid., 229.

20. Pollock, *The Billy Graham Story,* 88.

21. Ibid., 89.

22. Billy Graham, *Just as I Am,* 318.

23. "1st Item on First Day," part of the

"Madison Square Garden 1957 NY Crusade" exhibit, A Billy Graham Archives Exhibit. Available online at http://www.wheaton.edu/bgc/archives/exhibits/NYC57/08sample113-1.htm (cited June 2006).

24. Billy Graham, *Just as I Am,* 251.

25. Martin, *A Prophet with Honor,* 222.

26. Dr. Bob Jones's statement, circa 1957. Source: Correspondence of Dr. Bob Jones during 1957, distributed for several years to incoming students at Bob Jones University. Copies of the correspondence kindly made available to the author by Bob Jones University.

27. Letter from Dr. Bob Jones to Dr. Nelson Bell, 26 March 1957. Source: Correspondence between Dr. Bob Jones and Dr. Nelson Bell and others during 1957, distributed for several years to incoming students at Bob Jones University. Copies of the correspondence kindly made available to the author by Bob Jones University.

28. Ibid., letter of Dr. Bob Jones to Dr. Nelson Bell, 11 May 1957.

29. Ibid., letter of Bob Jones, Jr. to Dr. Nelson Bell, 16 May 1957.

30. Ibid., Text of article sent to Dr. J. H. Hunter by Bob Jones Jr., 12 June 1957.

31. Ibid., Letter by Bob Jones Jr. to Dr. J. H.

Hunter, 12 June 1957.

32. Ibid., Letter by Bob Jones Jr. to Dr. J. H. Hunter, 15 August 1957.

33. Ibid., Dr. Bob Jones's statement, circa 1957.

34. Martin, *A Prophet with Honor,* 240.

35. Bob Jones University, Dr. Bob Jones Jr., 8 February 1965.

36. Martin, *A Prophet with Honor,* 317–18; and Frady, *Billy Graham,* 248.

37. Bob Jones Jr., "Why We Do Not Support Billy Graham," circa 1972 or 1973. Text provided by Bob Jones University.

38. Martin, *A Prophet with Honor,* 240.

39. One Web site typical of the ongoing fundamentalist sallies against Billy Graham is the Way of Life Literature site at www.wayoflife.org (cited June 2006).

40. Martin, *A Prophet with Honor,* 167.

41. Billy Graham, *Just as I Am,* 426.

42. Pollock, *The Billy Graham Story,* 113.

43. Roger Bruns, *Billy Graham: A Biography* (Westport: Greenwood Press, 2004), 88.

44. Martin, *A Prophet with Honor,* 168–169.

45. Ibid., 170.

46. Ibid., 171.

47. Ibid., 172.

48. Bruns, *Billy Graham: A Biography,* 90.

49. Ibid., 92–93.

50. Billy Graham, *Just as I Am,* 426.

51. Martin Luther King Jr.'s 31 August 1957 letter to Billy Graham is part of the "Symbol of the Movement, January 1957 — December 1958" portion of The Papers of Martin Luther King Jr., Volume IV at The King Center, Stanford University. Available online at http://www.stanford.edu/group/King/publications/papers/vol4/570831-002-To_Billy_Graham.htm (cited June 2006).

52. Billy Graham, *Just as I Am*, 360.

53. Rev. Howard Jones's interview with Dr. Lois Ferm of the Billy Graham Evangelical Association, 16 November 1984. It is part of the "Madison Square Garden 1957 NY Crusade" online exhibit as "6th Item on Preaching," A Billy Graham Archives Exhibit. Available online at http://www.wheaton.edu/bgc/archives/exhibits/NYC57/10sample55-1.htm (cited June 2006).

54. Bruns, *Billy Graham: A Biography*, 92.

55. Jesse Jackson, *Billy Graham: Ambassador of Salvation*, Volume 1.

56. Pollock, *The Billy Graham Story*, 116.

Chapter Seven

1. Billy Graham, in an interview with the author in November 1975 in Hong Kong, worried aloud that Christians might have

to face persecution even in the United States.

2. Pollock, *The Billy Graham Story,* 154.
3. Billy Graham, *Just as I Am,* 485.
4. Martin, *A Prophet with Honor,* 476.
5. Ibid., 479.
6. The author, then bureau chief of *Time* magazine in Eastern Europe, recalls hearing anguished complaints from several Europe-based American ministries to Eastern Europe that Graham would be used for propaganda purposes.
7. Martin, *A Prophet with Honor,* 487.
8. Pollock, *The Billy Graham Story,* 151.
9. Ibid., 153.
10. Billy Graham, *Just as I Am,* 485–86.
11. Ibid., 485. See also on this visit, Pollock, *The Billy Graham Story,* 154; and Martin, *A Prophet with Honor,* 490.
12. Billy Graham, *Just as I Am,* 486.
13. Martin, *A Prophet with Honor,* 500.
14. Pollock, *The Billy Graham Story,* 176.
15. Martin, *A Prophet with Honor,* 499.
16. Ibid., 502.
17. Ibid., 499.
18. Ibid., 493.
19. Ibid., 505.
20. Ibid., 506.
21. Ibid., 507–8.
22. Billy Graham, *Just as I Am,* 505.

23. Martin, *A Prophet with Honor,* 515.
24. Ibid., 516.
25. Ibid., 518.
26. Dan Rather, *Billy Graham: Ambassador of Salvation,* Volume 1.
27. Billy Graham, *Just as I Am,* 506.
28. Martin, *A Prophet with Honor,* 524.
29. Billy Graham, *Just as I Am,* 551.
30. Billy Graham Evangelistic Association, *Billy Graham, God's Ambassador,* 141.
31. Pollock, *The Billy Graham Story,* 190.
32. Martin, *A Prophet with Honor,* 525.
33. Billy Graham, *Just as I Am,* 609.
34. Adi Ignatius, in telephone conversation with the author, 15 June 2001.
35. Information supplied to the author by a Chinese who had access to high levels of government administration of religion at the time.
36. Pollock, *The Billy Graham Story,* 231.
37. Billy Graham, *Just as I Am,* 553.
38. Ibid., 628.
39. Art Moore, interview with Dr. Stephen Linton, 16 December 2004.
40. Ibid.

Chapter Eight
1. Martin, *A Prophet with Honor,* 28.
2. Edward Fiske, "The Closest Thing to a White House Chaplain," *New York Times,*

8 June 1969. Available online at http://www.nytimes.com/books/97/07/06/reviews/graham-magazine.html?_r=1&oref=slogin (cited June 2006).

3. Graham once called President Carter at the White House to seek the president's assistance in obtaining US citizenship documentation for the sister of one of his sons-in-law (who was indeed entitled to it, having been born in the United States). Carter took care of the matter immediately, and personally called the young woman to tell her that her US citizenship had been confirmed. Source: Billy Graham, *Just as I Am*, 494–95.

Billy Graham also told the *New York Times* in 1969 that he once went to President Kennedy on behalf of a staff member who feared for his job. Source: Edward Fiske, op. cit.

4. Martin, *A Prophet with Honor*, 399.

5. Billy Graham, *Just as I Am*, xvii.

6. Martin, *A Prophet with Honor*, 147.

7. Billy Graham, *Just as I Am*, 189.

8. Roger Bruns, *Billy Graham: A Biography*, 47; and Martin, *A Prophet with Honor*, 147.

9. Billy Graham, *Just as I Am*, 191.

10. Ibid., 199.

11. Eisenhower's prayer at his first inauguration:

Almighty God, as we stand here at this moment my future associates in the executive branch of government join me in beseeching that Thou will make full and complete our dedication to the service of the people in this throng, and their fellow citizens everywhere.

Give us, we pray, the power to discern clearly right from wrong, and allow all our words and actions to be governed thereby, and by the laws of this land. Especially we pray that our concern shall be for all the people regardless of station, race, or calling.

May cooperation be permitted and be the mutual aim of those who, under the concepts of our Constitution, hold to differing political faiths; so that all may work for the good of our beloved country and Thy glory. Amen.

Available online at http://www.bartleby.com/124/pres54.html (cited June 2006).

12. Bruns, *Billy Graham: A Biography,* 56.

13. "President Sees Editors," *New York Times,* 10 April 1953, cited in Eric Crouse, "Popular Cold Warriors: Conservative Protestant, Communism and Culture in Early Cold War America," *Journal of Religion and Popular Culture,* Vol. II: Fall 2002. Available online at http://www.usask

.ca/relst/jrpc/article-popcold-war.html (cited June 2006).

14. Billy Graham, *Just as I Am*, 204.

15. Martin, *A Prophet with Honor*, 208.

16. Bruns, *Billy Graham: A Biography*, 90.

17. Martin, *A Prophet with Honor*, 201–2.

18. Ibid., 247.

19. Billy Graham, *Just as I Am*, 205; and Frady, *Billy Graham: A Parable of American Righteousness*, 268.

20. Billy Graham, *Just as I Am*, 394–5.

21. Ibid., 399.

22. Ibid., 400.

23. Ibid., 401.

24. Fiske, "The Closest Thing to a White House Chaplain."

25. Billy Graham, *Just as I Am*, 404.

26. Pollock, *The Billy Graham Story*, 125.

27. Frady, *Billy Graham*, 260.

28. Martin, *A Prophet with Honor*, 305.

29. Graham, *Just as I Am*, 414.

30. Martin, *A Prophet with Honor*, 302.

31. Ibid.

32. Frady, *Billy Graham*, 267.

33. BGEA, *Billy Graham, God's Ambassador*, 190.

34. Martin, *A Prophet with Honor*, 301.

35. Ibid., 347.

36. Ibid., 345.

37. Ibid.

38. Ibid., 347.

39. Billy Graham, *Just as I Am,* 406.

40. Martin, *A Prophet with Honor,* 349.

41. Billy Graham, *Just as I Am,* 403.

42. Ibid., 418.

43. Ibid., 456.

44. Richard Nixon, "A Nation's Faith in God," *Decision* magazine, November 1962; Larry Eskridge, "Paul Rader, 1920s Evangelist," biography on Web site, "The Village of Tower Lakes." Available online at http://www.villageoftowerlakes.com/history/Rader/rader.htm (cited June 2006).

45. Billy Graham, *Just as I Am,* 443.

46. Jonathan Aitken, *Nixon: A Life* (Washington, DC: Regnery Publishing, 1993), 339.

47. Richard Nixon, *RN: The Memoirs of Richard Nixon* (New York: Grosset and Dunlap, 1978), 293.

48. Billy Graham, *Just as I Am,* 445.

49. Martin, *A Prophet with Honor,* 352.

50. Ibid. 354.

Chapter Nine

1. Martin, *A Prophet with Honor,* 355.

2. Ibid.

3. Frady, *Billy Graham,* 424.

4. Martin, *A Prophet with Honor,* 355.

5. Billy Graham, *Just as I Am,* 454.

6. Martin, *A Prophet with Honor,* 359.

7. Nixon, *RN: The Memoirs,* 16.

8. Billy Graham, *Just as I Am,* 459.

9. Martin, *A Prophet with Honor,* 371.

10. "Nixon: Determined to Make a Difference," *Time* magazine, 3 January 1972. Available online at http://www.time.com/time/archive/preview/0,10987,879010,00.html (cited June 2006).

11. Martin, *A Prophet with Honor,* 394.

12. Ibid., 397.

13. Ibid., 425.

14. Ibid., 427–28.

15. Billy Graham, *Just as I Am,* 457.

16. Martin, *A Prophet with Honor,* 431.

17. Ibid., 432.

18. Ibid., 434.

19. Martin Weil and Eleanor Randolph, "Richard Nixon, 37th President, Dies," *Washington Post,* 23 April 1994, A01. Available online at http://www.washingtonpost.com/wp-dyn/content/article/2002/06/11/AR2005112200809.html (cited June 2006).

20. Billy Graham, "Remarks by Billy Graham at Richard Nixon's Funeral," 27 April 1994. Available online at http://watergate.info/nixon/94-04-27_funeral-graham.shtml (cited June 2006).

21. Richard Nixon, *In the Arena* (New York: Simon and Schuster, 1990), 90.
22. Martin, *A Prophet with Honor,* 428.
23. Pollock, *The Billy Graham Story,* 124.
24. Frady, *Billy Graham,* 424–25.
25. Billy Graham, *Just as I Am,* 458.
26. James Warren, "Nixon, Billy Graham, Make Derogatory Comments About Jews on Tapes," *Chicago Tribune,* 28 February 2002. Available online at http://www.fpp.co.uk/online/02/02/Graham_Nixon.html (cited May 2006).
27. "Nixon's Ghost," a *Christianity Today* editorial, 22 April 2002, posted online 3 April 2002. Available online at http://www.christianitytoday.com/ct/2002/005/23.24.html (cited June 2006).
28. Bruns, *Billy Graham: A Biography,* 123.
29. Pollock, *The Billy Graham Story,* 129–30.
30. Billy Graham, *Just as I Am,* 467.
31. Martin, *A Prophet with Honor,* 462.
32. Ibid.
33. Billy Graham, *Just as I Am,* 472.
34. Ibid., 470–71.
35. "1976 Presidential Debates; Presidential Debates #2, Highlights," AllPolitics, The Debates '96, CNN-Time. Available online at http://cgi.cnn.com/ALLPOLITICS/1996/debates/history/1976/ (cited June 2006).

36. Martin, *A Prophet with Honor,* 463–64.

37. Ibid., 463.

38. Ibid.

39. Billy Graham, *Just as I Am,* 494.

40. Ibid., 498.

41. Jimmy Carter interview on CNN news show "Live from . . . ," 24 June 2005. Available online at http://transcripts .cnn.com/TRANSCRIPTS/0506/24/ lol.01.html (cited June 2006).

42. Billy Graham, *Just as I Am,* 528.

43. Harold Bell Wright, *That Printer of Udell's: A Story of the Middle West* (New York: A. L. Burt Company Publishers, 1903), reprinted in 1996 (Gretna: Pelican Publishing Company, 1996).

44. Ronald Reagan, letter written to daughter-in-law of Harold Bell Wright, 14 March 1984, in Dixon Public Library. Source of this information: Harold Kengor, "The Intellectual Origins of Ronald Reagan's Faith," The Heritage Society, Heritage Lecture #832, 30 April 2004. Available online at www.heritage.org/ Research/PoliticalPhilosophy/hl832.cfm (cited June 2006).

45. Billy Graham, *Just as I Am,* 529.

46. Martin, *A Prophet with Honor,* 473. See also Ibid.

47. Bob Slosser, *Reagan Inside Out*

(Nashville: Word Books, 1984), 13–15.

48. Billy Graham, *Just as I Am,* 533–534.

49. Billy Graham Evangelistic Association, *Billy Graham, God's Ambassador,* 185.

50. Billy Graham, *Just as I Am,* 534.

51. Ibid., 537.

52. Nancy Reagan, interview on CNN talk show *Larry King Live,* "Is Billy Graham Passing the Torch?" aired 21 December 2000. Available online at http://transcripts.cnn.com/TRANSCRIPTS/0012/21/lkl.00.html (cited June 2006).

53. "Ronald Reagan Memorial Thread," *Free Republic,* 10 June 2004. Available online at www.freerepublic.com/focus/f-news/1151325/posts (cited June 2006).

54. Reagan family spokeswoman Joanne Drake, as quoted by *The Orlando Sentinel,* cited in Ted Olson's "Weblog: Remembering Ronald Reagan," *Christianity Today* magazine, week of 7 June 2004. Available online at http://www.christianitytoday.com/ct/2004/123/12.0.html (cited June 2006).

55. "Reagan's Vice President Remembers His Good Friend," CNN online, 11 June 2004. Available online at http://www.cnn.com/2004/ALLPOLITICS/06/11/bush.sr.transcript/ (cited June 2006).

Chapter Ten

1. William Martin, *A Prophet with Honor,* 614.
2. Billy Graham, *Just as I Am,* 593.
3. Pollock, *The Billy Graham Story,* 259.
4. Billy Graham, in conversation with the author, Montreat, North Carolina, February 1990.
5. Billy Graham, *Just as I Am,* 584–86.
6. Ibid., 586.
7. Billy Graham Evangelistic Association, *Billy Graham, God's Ambassador,* 186.
8. Billy Graham, *Just as I Am,* 587.
9. Billy Graham Evangelistic Association, *Billy Graham, God's Ambassador,* 186.
10. Ruth Bell Graham, *Footprints of a Pilgrim: The Life and Loves of Ruth Bell Graham* (Nashville: Word Publishing, 2001), 152.
11. Billy Graham, *Just as I Am,* 587.
12. Donald Morison, ed., *Mikhail Gorbachev: An Intimate Biography* (New York: Time Incorporated, 1988), 203–4.
13. Billy Graham, *Just as I Am,* 593.
14. Pollock, *The Billy Graham Story,* 298–99.
15. Jon Meacham, "The Prayer Breakfast Presidency," *The Washington Post,* Sunday, 16 April 2006; B01. Available online at http://www.washingtonpost.com/wp-dyn/content/article/2006/04/14/

AR2006041401908.html (cited June 2006).

16. President Clinton, at a Washington dinner on 2 May 1996, after Ruth and Billy Graham received the Congressional Gold Medal. Larry Jordan, "A Conversation with Billy Graham," *Midwest Today,* January 1997. Available online at www.midtod .com/9612/billygraham.phtml (cited June 2006).

17. Bill Clinton, *My Life,* (New York: Alfred A. Knopf, 2004), 39.

18. Ibid.

19. Billy Graham, *Just as I Am,* 651–52.

20. Ibid., 653.

21. Billy Graham interview, *U.S. News & World Report,* 3 May 1993, 6, cited in "Billy Graham Soils His Evangelist's Robe by Exchanging Loving Compliments with Bill Clinton," The Cutting Edge Web site. Available online at http://www.cutting edge.org/news/n2050.cfm (cited June 2006). Also "Billy Graham: General Teachings/Activities," Biblical Discernment Ministries Web site. Available online at http://www.rapidnet.com/~jbeard/bdm/ exposes/graham/general.htm (cited June 2006).

22. Billy Graham, *Just as I Am,* 654.

23. Ibid, 656.

24. Ibid.

25. Billy Graham, interview on *The Today Show,* NBC, 5 March 1998. Cited by Rev. Robert H. Tucker, "Online Sermons: The Scarlet Letter," 30 August 1998. Available online at http://www.bobandmaggi.com/sermon19980830.html (cited June 2006).

26. "Politically Incorrect with Bill Maher," 5 March 1998. Available online at: http://user.mc.net/manos424/python/eric_pi.htm (cited June 2006).

27. Joseph Farah, "The Dumbing Down of Christianity," WorldNetDaily exclusive commentary, 11 March 1998. Available online at www.wnd.com/news/article.asp?ARTICLE_ID=14443 (cited June 2006).

28. Monique El-Faizy and Tracy Connor, "Bill, Hil, Join Hands at Graham Crusade," *New York Daily News,* 26 June 2005. Available online at http://www.nydailynews.com/news/local/story/322548p-275769c.html (cited June 2006).

29. Ken Garfield, "Graham Didn't Intend to Endorse Clinton," *Charlotte Observer,* 1 July 2005. Available online at http://www.charlotte.com/mld/observer/news/local/12030058.htm (cited February 2006).

30. "The First Thanksgiving," *A Puritan's Mind.* Available online at http://

www.apuritansmind.com/ChristianWalk/
FirstThanksgiving.htm (cited June 2006).

31. For a detailed account of this process, see David Aikman, *A Man of Faith: The Spiritual Journey of George W. Bush* (Nashville: W Publishing Group, 2004), 69–79.

32. Barbara Bush, telephone conversation with the author, November 2003.

33. Aikman, *A Man of Faith,* 75.

34. George W. Bush, *A Charge to Keep,* (New York: William Morrow and Company, 1999), 136.

35. Ibid.

36. Aikman, *A Man of Faith,* 77.

37. "The Jesus Factor," PBS "Frontline" series, 2004, WGBH Educational Foundation. Available online at http://www.pbs.org/wgbh/pages/frontline/shows/jesus/etc/script.html (cited July 2007).

38. Jon Meacham, "Billy Graham's New Thinking on Politics, the Bible," *Newsweek* magazine, 14 August 2006. Available online at http://www.msnbc.msn.com/id/14204483/ (cited May 2007).

Chapter Eleven

1. See especially Way of Life Literature's Fundamental Baptist Information Service, http://www.wayoflife.org/ (cited May

2006) and *Bible Bulletin Board,* www
.biblebb.com (cited June 2006).

2. "Why I Can't Play God Anymore," *Mc-Call's* magazine, January 1978. Cited in
"Filling the Blanks with Fuller: The Original Five," 21 January 2000. Available online at http://www.seekgod.ca/fuller1.htm
(cited June 2006).

3. Ruth Graham, conversation with the author, Montreat, North Carolina, February 1991.

4. Billy Graham, interview with Richard N. Ostling, "Of Angels, Devils and Messages from God," *Time* magazine, *15* November 1993, 74.

5. Billy Graham, interview with Robert H. Schuller, *Hour of Power,* 31 May 1997; partial transcript cited in "Billy Graham, American Television and Audience Evangelist" entry on the Web site "On Doctrine, Discerning Truth and Error." Available online at http://www.ondoctrine.com/10grahab.htm (cited June 2006).

6. Jon Meacham, "Billy Graham's New Thinking on Politics, the Bible," *Newsweek* magazine, 14 August 2006. Available online at http://www.msnbc.msn.com/id/14204483/ (cited May 2007).

7. Billy Graham, interview with David Frost, "Billy Graham Talking with David

Frost," David Paradine Television, WETA-TV, Washington, DC, PBS video, 1993.

8. Billy Graham, interview on ABC's *Good Morning America,* 5 September 1991. "Billy Graham, General Teachings/Activities" entry of Web site "Bible Discernment Ministries." Available online at www.rapidnet.com/~jbeard/bdm/exposes/graham/general.htm (cited June 2006).

9. Billy Graham, "Give Up Sin, Give Life to Jesus," *Chattanooga Times Free Press,* 26 November 2003.

10. "Billy Graham Retracts Statement on AIDS as God's Judgment," United Press International, 9 October 1993.

11. "Billy Graham Does an 'About Face'," *The Baptist Pillar* Available online at http://www.baptistpillar.com/bd0342.htm (cited June 2006).

12. Larry Jordan, "A Conversation with Billy Graham," *Midwest Today,* January 1997. Available online at http://www.midtod.com/9612/billygraham.phtml (cited June 2006).

13. Meacham, "Billy Graham's New Thinking."

14. Jordan, "A Conversation with Billy Graham."

15. "How Firm a Foundation," variously attributed to John Keene, Kirkham and

John Keeth, in the hymn collection by John Rippon (1787).

16. Full transcript available on American Rhetoric Web site's "Reverend Billy Graham — Oklahoma Bombing Prayer Service Address" at www.americanrhetoric .com/speeches/billygrahamoklahomabomb ingspeech.htm (cited June 2006).

17. Pollock, *The Billy Graham Story,* 308

18. "Oklahoma City Marks Bombing Anniversary," *CNN Live Today,* 19 April 2005. Available online at http://transcripts.cnn .com/TRANSCRIPTS/0504/19/lt.01.html (cited June 2006).

19. Full transcript available on American Rhetoric Web site's "Billy Graham — Address at the Episcopal National Cathedral." Available online at http:// www.americanrhetoric.com/speeches/ bgrahammemorialgo.htm (cited June 2006).

20. "The Remarkable Life of Billy Graham Documented on Video," news release on Gaither.com Web site, 12 March 2006. Available online at http://www.gaither .com/news/news.php?uid=1112 (cited June 2006).

21. "Billy Graham Returns with Big Easy Sermon," 13 March 2006, Associated Press. Available online at http://

www.usatoday.com/news/nation/2006-03-12-graham-service_x.htm (cited June 2006).

Chapter Twelve

1. Ruth Bell Graham, *Footprints of a Pilgrim,* 29.
2. Ibid., 132.
3. Ibid., 32.
4. Ibid., 29.
5. Ibid., 133.
6. Reported by Associated Press correspondent Charlene L. Fu, who covered the visit of the Grahams to China in 1988.
7. Ruth Graham, *A Legacy of Love: Things I Learned from My Mother* (Grand Rapids: Zondervan, 2005), 42.
8. Ruth Bell Graham, *Footprints,* 34.
9. Ibid., 45.
10. Ibid., 59.
11. Ibid., 58.
12. Ibid., 54.
13. Ibid., 58.
14. Ibid., 67.
15. Ibid., 66.
16. Jordan, "A Conversation with Billy Graham."
17. "Ruth Bell Graham" biography for TV program "Ruth and Billy Graham: What Grace Provides," on UNC-TV Online.

Available online at www.unctv.org/ruthandbillygraham/family/ruthbellg.html (cited June 2006).

18. Ruth Bell Graham, *Footprints,* 79.

19. Billy Graham Evangelistic Association, *Billy Graham, God's Ambassador,* 232.

20. Ruth Graham, *A Legacy of Faith,* 20.

21. Patricia Cornwell, *Ruth: A Portrait of Ruth Bell Graham* (New York: Doubleday, 1997), 121.

22. Ibid., 167.

23. Martin, *A Prophet with Honor,* 92.

24. Billy Graham, interview on CNN's talk show *Larry King Live,* "Interview with Billy Graham," aired 16 June 2005. Available online at http://transcripts.cnn.com/TRANSCRIPTS/0506/16/lkl.01.html (cited June 2006).

25. "Billy and Ruth Share a Lifetime of Love," Nanci Hellmich, *USA Today,* 12 December 2001. Available online at http://www.usatoday.com/life/books/2001-12-10-graham-love.htm (cited June 2006).

26. Martin, *A Prophet with Honor,* 127.

27. Ruth Bell Graham, *Footprints,* 67.

28. Martin, *A Prophet with Honor,* 102.

29. Ibid., 127.

30. Ibid., 598.

31. Jordan, "A Conversation with Billy Graham."

32. Martin, *A Prophet with Honor,* 243.

33. Ruth Graham, *A Legacy of Love,* 86.

34. Martin, *A Prophet with Honor,* 153.

35. Ibid., 599.

36. Ibid., 17.

37. Ibid., 33–34.

38. Anne Graham Lotz, interview on CNN talk show *Larry King Live,* "Is Billy Graham Passing the Torch?" 21 December 2000. Available online at http://transcripts.cnn.com/TRANSCRIPTS/0012/21/lkl.00.html (cited June 2006).

39. Franklin Graham, *Rebel with a Cause* (Nashville: Thomas Nelson, 1995), 41.

40. Ibid., 99.

41. Ruth Graham, *A Legacy of Faith,* 55.

42. Ruth Graham's Web site describes her as "a conference speaker and Bible teacher known for her honesty and authenticity." She is the author of *In Every Pew Sits a Broken Heart* and two books about her parents, *A Legacy of Love: Things I Learned from My Mother* and *A Legacy of Faith: Things I Learned from My Father.* She is coauthor with Dr. Sara Dormon of *I'm Pregnant . . . Now What? A Resource of Choices for Unplanned Pregnancies* and coauthor of the forthcoming *So You Want to Adopt . . . Now What?* Ruth founded the

ministry Ruth Graham & Friends in 2004 to bring her trademark message of hope and healing to women around the country. The mission of the ministry's events is to encourage and equip women in a meaningful and growing relationship with a real God for real life. This is done through in-depth study of Scripture, prayer, and ministering to one another with love, compassion, and honesty. See http://www.ruthgrahamandfriends.com and http://www.ruthgrahamministries.com (cited June 2006).

43. Tony Carnes, "Ministries: Ned Graham's Woes Shakes East Gates," *Christianity Today,* 6 December 1999. Available online at http://www.ctlibrary.com/ct/1999/december6/9te026.html (cited June 2006).

44. Laura Sessions Stepp, "A Family at Cross-Purposes; Billy Graham's Sons Argue over a Final Resting Place," *Washington Post,* 13 December 2006, page A01.

45. Meacham, "Billy Graham's New Thinking."

46. Torrey Johnson, interview by Rober Shuster for the Billy Graham Center Archives of Wheaton College, 13 February 1984, Collection 285-Torrey Johnson, T4 Transcript. Available online at http://

www.wheaton.edu/bgc/archives/trans/ 285t04.htm (cited June 2006).

47. Billy Graham, *Larry King Live,* "Interview with Billy Graham," 16 June 2005.

48. Garth M. Rosell, "Grace Under Fire," *Christianity Today,* 13 November 1995, 30–34.

49. Billy Graham, *Larry King Live,* "Interview with Reverend Billy Graham," 25 December 2005. Available online at http:// transcripts.cnn.com/TRANSCRIPTS/ 0512/25/lkl.11.html (cited June 2006).

50. Lynn Grossman, "Billy Graham's Son Takes the Pulpit, His Own Way," *USA Today,* 7 March 2006. Available online at http://www.usatoday.com/news/nation/ 2006-03-07-franklin-graham-cover_x.htm (cited June 2006).

51. Billy Graham, *The Journey: Living by Faith in an Uncertain World* (Nashville: Word Publishing, 2006).

52. Ruth Bell Graham, *Footprints,* 53.

53. Billy Graham Evangelistic Association, *Billy Graham, God's Ambassador,* 22.

54. Bill Bright, in conversation with the author, 17 April 2001.

55. Billy Graham, in conversation with the author, Los Angeles, 13 November 1999.

INDEX

crusades (*continued*)
>186, 195–96, 203–4, 207–9, 211, 219–28, 230–33, 260–61, 278–85, 291, 296, 302, 313, 316, 359–60, 364, 380, 387, 416, 437–38, 443, 452–53, 458, 461, 468. *See also individual crusade locations*

Cuba, 173, 285
Cushing, Richard James (cardinal), 196
Czechoslovakia, 242, 269–70
Dallas Theological Seminary, 120
Darby, J. N., 119–20. *See also* dispensationalism; Plymouth Brethren
Darrow, Clarence, 36
Decision magazine, 109–10. *See also* Wirt, Sherwood Eliot
Democracy in America (Toqueville), 134–35
democracy, 30–32, 276
Deng Xiaoping, 251, 256, 273
Desert Storm/Gulf War, 25, 374, 397
Detroit (MI), 224
Dexter Avenue Baptist Church, 225
Dienert, Ted, 125–26, 450
dispensationalism, 103–4, 118–21, 193–94, 196–98: doctrines of, 54–55
Dobrynin, Anatoly, 255–56, 377
Dulles, John Foster, 138, 161–65
East Gates International (also East Gates Ministries International), 448, 451
East Germany, 156, 269, 276–77

Graham, Billy, Jr. (*continued*)

Northwestern Schools, 101, 117, 196–97, 440–41; press/public faux pas of, 159–60, 290–91, 385–87; relationship with/marriage to Ruth, 78–82, 122, 428–29, 433, 436–43; relationship with U.S. presidents, 287–398 (*see also individual presidents*); role as consoler, 399–427; role in collapse of Communism, 276–79; and Roman Catholics, 19, 117–18, 189, 194–95, 206–7, 218, 239, 269, 306, 400–402, 457; and *Songs in the Night,* 83–85; stance on race relations, 196–98, 227–29; Toronto meeting, 122–23; Washington DC meeting, 129–30; and Youth for Christ, 99–102, 111, 127–28, 137–39

Graham, Bunny. *See* Graham, Ruth, Jr.

Graham, Catherine, 46, 51

Graham, Crook, 43

Graham, Frank, 32, 43–47, 53–57, 60, 66: conversion of, 45, 54–57

Graham, Franklin, 13, 132, 138, 395: as CEO of BGEA, 389, 424–26, 447; problems in schooling, 453–55, 449–50

Graham, Gigi, 132, 432, 443, 447, 451

Graham, Jean (Ford). *See* Ford, Jean

Graham, Melvin, 46, 48–49, 71, 465–66

Graham, Morrow Coffey, 32, 43–46, 53–56, 58–59, 64–66, 330–31

Graham, Nelson (Ned), 132, 443, 447, 451, 455

Graham, Ruth Bell (Ruth McCue Bell), 102–3, 122, 132, 138, 141–42, 185–86, 211, 237, 251, 280, 309–10, 315, 353, 358–59, 368, 402, 455, 465, 471–72: on her friendship with the Bush family, 375–76; on her meeting Billy Graham, 77–81; on her return visit to China, 272–75; and Queen Elizabeth, 157–58; supporting her husband, 428–52; on teasing Billy for his theatrics, 115; on the Watergate scandal, 342; and the White House, 364–66, 382–84

Graham, Ruth, Jr. (also Ruth Jr. or "Bunny"), 132, 438, 443, 446

Graham, Virginia ("Gigi"). *See* Graham, Gigi.

Graham-Lotz, Anne, 277, 443, 447, 451–52

Great Awakening, 15, 122–23

Greenville (SC) crusade, 123, 129, 216–17, 219–22

Guangzhou, China, 275–76

Gustafson, Roy, 103

Haig, Alexander, 352

National Council of Churches (*continued*)
    248. *See also* Templeton, Charles
Nehru, Jawaharlal, 160–61, 164–65
neo-evangelicalism (also New
    Evangelicalism), 14–15, 136–37,
    158–59, 191–92, 211–13, 399–400,
    402–3
New Orleans (LA), 425–27
Newsweek, 13–14, 111–12, 348–49, 404–5,
    455–56, 465–66
New York (NY) crusade, 21–22, 41–42,
    104, 114, 152–53, 192, 195, 219, 295,
    301–2, 304, 332, 370–71: and
    Flushing Meadow, 387–88; "high
    water mark" of Graham's crusades,
    203–15; and Martin Luther King Jr.,
    226–32; and the World Trade Center,
    412–13, 420
New York Herald Tribune, 210
New York Times, 287–88, 297–98, 310,
    348–51, 355
New Zealand crusade, 136, 157, 166,
    174–76
Niebuhr, Reinhold, 205–7, 225
Nineteenth Amendment, 40
Nixon, Richard M., 175, 209, 251–52,
    299–300, 313, 319, 364, 376, 463–64;
    and Eisenhower, 302–3; on Graham's
    response to media about being used,

Billy Graham, 357–69, 396–97; *imprimatur,* 252
Red Scare, 34
Religious Right, 13, 27, 129
Restless Ones, The (BGEA film), 357
Rice, John R., 202–3
Richardson, Sid, 131, 292–93
Romania, 242, 251–52, 259–60, 269–72, 277, 285, 354
Roy, J. Stapleton, 281
Russian Christians, 264
Russian Orthodox Church, 259–61, 268–69, 285
SS *United States,* 141–42
SALT 2 agreement, 248
Samaritan's Purse, 447
San Francisco (CA) crusade, 215–16, 355
Schlosskirche, 269
Schuller, Rev. Robert H., 403–4
Schumer, Charles, 387
Scofield Reference Bible, The, 119–20
Scopes Trial, 36–38, 135
Scripture, 45–46, 53, 172, 212–14, 295–96, 363, 368–69, 403, 410–11, 442–43: inerrancy of, 34–35, 191, 197, 400, 465; key doctrines, 34–35, 92, 119–21, 158–59, 192–93, 400–401
segregation in the U.S. South, 21–22, 169–70, 178–79, 219–29, 231–33, 260, 301–2, 380, 387